MASTERPIECES OF CLASSIC GREEK DRAMA

Recent Titles in
Greenwood Introduces Literary Masterpieces

Masterpieces of French Literature
Marilyn S. Severson

Masterpieces of Modern British and Irish Drama
Sanford Sternlicht

Masterpieces of 20th-Century American Drama
Susan C. W. Abbotson

MASTERPIECES OF CLASSIC GREEK DRAMA

Helaine L. Smith

Greenwood Introduces Literary Masterpieces

GREENWOOD PRESS
Westport, Connecticut • London

Library of Congress Cataloging-in-Publication Data

Smith, Helaine.
   Masterpieces of classic Greek drama / Helaine Smith.
      p. cm. — (Greenwood introduces literary masterpieces, ISSN 1545–6285)
   Includes bibliographical references (p.) and index.
   ISBN 0–313–33268–1 (alk. paper)
   1. Greek drama—History and criticism—Handbooks, manuals, etc. I. Title. II. Series.
PA3131.S59 2006
882'.0109—dc22   2005019210

British Library Cataloguing in Publication Data is available.

Library of Congress Catalog Card Number: 2005019210
ISBN: 0–313–33268–1
ISSN: 1545–6285

First published in 2006

Greenwood Press, 88 Post Road West, Westport, CT 06881
An imprint of Greenwood Publishing Group, Inc.
www.greenwood.com

Printed in the United States of America

To Hiram, Lucille, and Stuart, with love

Contents

Preface

This text is an introductory guide to the literary study of Greek drama. It includes both tragedy and comedy and is intended for use by high school and undergraduate English students and their teachers. No knowledge of Greek is necessary, and all essential background information—historical, cultural, and religious—is provided. The 10 plays discussed are the plays most frequently studied at those levels: the *Agamemnon*, *Choephoroi*, and *Eumenides* (the *Oresteia*) of Aeschylus, the *Antigone*, *Oedipus Rex*, and *Oedipus at Colonus* of Sophocles, the *Medea* and *Bacchae* of Euripides, and the *Birds* and *Lysistrata* of Aristophanes.

The approach of this text is literary rather than thematic. Where standard Aristotelian terminology is helpful, it is included, but discussions are not shaped with such terms in mind. The great Greek playwrights were profoundly interested in how one should live, in the power of emotion, in the nature of the gods, and in the limitations of human understanding. This text assumes that the best way to appreciate these plays is to regard all that is in them—their images, their contrasts, their use of myth, the sequence of scenes—as intentional artistry. It further assumes that sometimes the playwright's focus is thematic and sometimes purely human and that each play, when studied closely, reveals its essential nature. Comedy is included in this volume because the spirit of Athens is in some measure grasped by knowing that alongside tragic performance, and in times of war and dire political circumstance, uproarious comedies were enjoyed along with the most searing tragedies. Aristophanes is not only a bawdy and witty comic genius but also a playwright who offers us a window into the life—religious, political, and domestic—of fifth-century Athenians. From such reading we come as close as we can to that distant reality and find it vibrantly before us.

When speeches, odes, or scenes are analyzed, they are referred to but not reprinted. Individual chapters include the following, about which a word needs to be said:

- *"The Use of Myth"*: These sections, by indicating what the received myth was, clarify the dramatist's own invention and emphasis. Attention is also drawn to myth to distinguish it from stage action—from what the playwright sets before us in the hour or so of performance—for that dramatic action is the source of the play's meaning. The *Oedipus Rex* is, for example, a play about discovery.
- *"Historical Context"*: Political, social, and religious background with direct relevance to individual plays appears in these sections. The Peloponnesian War, for example, receives particular attention in the Aristophanes chapters, rituals surrounding hero cults are discussed in the *Choephoroi* and *Oedipus at Colonus* chapters, Dionysiac practice in the *Bacchae* chapter, the status of women and foreigners in the *Medea* chapter, the Athenian judicial system in the *Eumenides* chapter, and so on.
- *"Synopses"*: There appear in each chapter a single-sentence summary of the plot, a list of scenes, and a scene-by-scene synopsis of the action. In the chapters on comedy there is, with each synopsis, a discussion of comic techniques.
- *"Passage and Scene Analysis"*: Speeches and odes of varying length and type are discussed in detail in relation to plot, character, and theme, and attention is paid to nuances of language and imagery. Minor and major characters are analyzed closely, and individual scenes that are central to plot construction or that represent emotional climaxes of the action are examined: arguments are made, for example, for the dramatic necessity of Polyneices' scene in the *Colonus*, of Cassandra's scene in the *Agamemnon*, and so on. Attention is given also to the remarkably "modern" techniques of these playwrights—the dream-work of the *Bacchae* and the fusing of audience and characters in the conclusion of the *Colonus*.
- *"Stagecraft"*: These sections draw attention to the great importance of what is seen on stage, and examine the range of theatrical resources available to these playwrights and the skill with which they were deployed. Dramatic variations in type-scenes like the dirge and messenger scenes, offstage speech, and theatrical devices, like the revolving

platform and the crane, as they serve the particular thematic needs of different plays, are discussed. Dramatized metaphors are also looked at.

- *Translations, Line Numbers, and Transliterated Words*: All Greek plays are written in verse lines that are numbered. Translations vary in how they deal with line numbers: free translations omit line numbers; exact translations retain them. It has been my experience in studying the texts for this volume that the more strict translations are the more illuminating. Where essential to the discussion, Greek words and phrases are transliterated and explained; if necessary, lines numbers are given in parentheses. Occasionally, lines in the texts are not continuous and the "Scene Divisions" portions of chapters will necessarily reflect such discontinuity.

It is hoped that this text, when coupled with careful study of the plays themselves, will help the reader to see how splendid these works are. These plays are the standard against which all subsequent Western drama has been measured. The well-made plays of Ibsen and the radical innovations of Beckett are felt as such because of the classical model that stands behind them.

I am indebted to the many fine scholars whose work I have read and cited in these pages; their perceptions directed and deepened mine. Special tribute must be paid, however, to H.D.F. Kitto and to E.R. Dodds. Not only does the clarity of their prose stand as an enduring model, but, repeatedly, they show their readers the right questions to ask, and there is no greater gift than that.

Introduction

The first reference in Western literature to a playing stage and a chorus of dancers is in Book 18 of *The Iliad*, where Homer describes the great shield of Achilles that Hephaistos fashions. Drama, as we know it, is a much later Athenian invention, but it derives from the Chorus, a group of perhaps 50 men who sang and danced in unison in festive and ritual retellings of myths of the gods. To this day, at the palace of Knossos in Crete, there stands an ancient rectangular dancing floor, perhaps the first stage. Indeed, the word *orchestra*, the circular performing area of Greek theatres, comes from the verb *orcheomai*, to dance in a row, and from *orchestes*, dancer.

THE ORIGINS OF THE DRAMA

It is generally thought that worship of the god Dionysus included hymns sung by a Chorus of priests; that eventually the Chorus divided into two parts, one answering the other in antiphonal response; that later one priest, with dramatic inflection and gesture, narrated portions of the stories of the god; and that a second speaker was eventually added so that the history of the god might be shown, not simply narrated. Thus, drama was born.

Because Greek tragedy presents the intersection of god and man and asserts the limitation of human understanding and endeavor, a sacred origin for drama seems likely. The presence of an altar in the orchestra ground, the front-row seat in the amphitheatre for the priest of Dionysus, the absence of female performers, the use of the mask, and the convention that forbids the show of violence onstage also point to hieratic origins.

An Athenian named Thespis is said to have been the one to add an "answerer" to the Chorus in 534 B.C. In honor of this imputed innovation, he is called "the father of the drama."

THE DRAMA FESTIVALS

Twice a year, in late January at the Lenaia and in late March at the Dionysia, the activity in Athens came to a halt and all citizens, numbering 15,000 to 20,000, repaired to the Theatre of Dionysus for the three days of drama festival. The holidays were civic and religious, honoring the gods, celebrating military and civic achievement, and presenting plays of unparalled quality.

The Competition and Judging

The selection and judging process showed popular democracy in action:[1] playwrights submitted either synopses or scripts six or seven months before the date of performance. Citizens selected by lot then decided which of those playwrights would be allowed to participate in that year's competition. Each tragic playwright was required to present four plays: three tragedies and a satyr-play. The only extant example of the satyr-play is the *Cyclops* of Euripides, dated perhaps 425 B.C. It is assumed, from the *Cyclops*, from fragments, and from scholarly commentary, that the satyr-plays spoofed the tragic material of the playwright's preceding three plays. Each comic playwright presented one comedy. The "City" or "Great" Dionysia lasted three days, with a different tetralogy and comedy presented daily. Occasionally there were revivals of particularly honored works, but then, too, for a single performance. Actors were assigned to playwrights by lot and the rehearsal period was long. A wealthy citizen was designated to underwrite rehearsal and production costs. At performance, 10 judges were chosen, again by lot, from lists submitted by each of the 10 divisions of the city; 10 votes were cast and 5 of the 10 were then drawn at random, and a verdict announced. The great skill and power of the Chorus was recognized by the fact that "when the prize was awarded, it was the chorus-trainer, not the author, whose name was cited."[2] As the tragedies and comedies in this volume reveal, the functions to which dramatists put their Choruses were enormously varied and central to the dramas.

THE PHYSICAL ASPECTS OF THE GREEK THEATRE

The Physical Structures

The Greek theatres were out-of-door amphitheatres set into hillsides and built to accommodate huge numbers of people at one time. Acoustically, they are miraculous: one can, in the last row of the great theatre at Epidaurus, hear someone whisper on the stage below. The stage has two parts: an *orchestra*, which is a circular playing area with a diameter of about 600 feet used primarily by the Chorus, but sometimes by actors, in the center of which is a raised altar to Dionysus; a platform, called a *proskenion* ("proscenium") about 9 feet deep and 20 feet long, raised above the orchestra by a few steps and backed by the building known as the *skene* ("tent"). Central double doors of the *skene* opened onto the platform; the doors generally represented a palace or some other relevant interior space; through these doors actors entered and exited. There may have been lateral doors as well. Inside, the *skene* functioned as a changing room for the actors and as a storage place for stage machinery such as the *mechane* ("crane") and the *ekkyklema*, a revolving platform on which a group of actors could be wheeled out of the central doors to represent an interior scene. Although some sort of "tent" must have existed for costume and mask changes and for other basic theatrical purposes from very early in theatre history, the *skene* as dramatic setting (palace, temple, cave, copse) perhaps began with the production in 458 B.C. of the *Oresteia*.[3] On either side of the *skene* is a passageway originally called *eisodos*, and later *parodos*, by which the Chorus entered and departed.

Masks

A mask was worn by every performer and was probably constructed of linen. All members of the Chorus wore identical masks. With the use of masks, the two, and eventually three, actors assigned to each playwright were able to come onstage as different characters in different scenes and, as all performers were men, to play women's roles. Masks emphasized significant facial features—the cryptic smile of Dionysus, for example, in the *Bacchae*, the suffering look of Oedipus in the *Oedipus at Colonus*, the smiles of Medea's children, and so on, and the slight distance between the mask contours and the mouth may have provided a kind of "megaphone effect" in the vast open theatre. Masks also meant that emotional nuance could be conveyed only through the playwrights' words and stagecraft and through movement and voice.

In emotional terms, masked drama negotiates at the boundary of the familiar and the strange, for masks create uncanny distance. Masked figures suffer a loss of identity; in place of that identity they come to represent humanity in the paradigmatic terms that these great dramas require. The audience, likewise, is forced, within the safety of the theatre, to leave what is familiar and to confront the unreachableness the mask represents. The mask, therefore, also invests these dramas with a religious sensibility, for it promises access to another realm of being.

Movement and Music

All performers were trained singers and dancers. Choral lyrics were choreographed and sung to musical accompaniment that was both melodic and rhythmically complex. The division of odes into strophe and antistrophe corresponds to the assignment of alternating stanzas to one and then the other half of the Chorus, who sang and danced each strophe in unison. Dance movements included row formations with interweaving movements, double dances "with two half-choruses facing and matching one another," acrobatic leaps, splits, processionals, and dances of victory, defeat and madness.[4]

DRAMA'S BASIS IN MYTH

Whereas comedy was absolutely topical and full of fantastic invention of plot and character, tragedy drew for its subject matter on the already-set myths and legends of gods and heroes, figures immediately identifiable to the audience. The use of contemporary material was rare, and, as the poor reception that Aeschylus' the *Persians* received suggests, considered not proper.

That the broad outlines of the stories dramatized by the playwrights were already known presented the dramatist with opportunities for subtle ironic effect, suspense, and complex reversals of expectation. An audience already cognizant of the legend on which a play was based was a discriminating audience able to focus on nuances of action and meaning. We expect authors in our day to make up stories; the tragic playwrights of ancient Greece, like the epic poets before them, proved their mettle by how they used the already-shared stock of myth. In fact, as Homer and Hesiod's invocations to the Muse demonstrate, epic poets believed or articulated the belief that nothing was invention, but that they simply "recorded" what the Muse breathed into them.

REALITY AND RELIGION IN GREEK DRAMA

Greek dramas are about death, about kinship in all its compelling and sorrowing complexity, about loss, about young girls who never marry and never receive the portion of life allotted to them, about the limits of what one knows set against what one thinks one knows, about pride and evil and error, and about truth. They are full of powerful ritual and, although not naturalistic, are profoundly realistic in that they address life's deepest realities. Greek drama is about coming to know what lies beneath the surface of things, and the image of Cassandra, the garments of the god cast aside, going clear-eyed to what she cannot avoid, is an emblem of this drama.

Religion is part of the very fabric of Greek theatre. Greek tragedy is religious not because gods appear onstage, but because they are understood to stand behind all things. The *Medea*, where no god appears, is as religious as the *Oedipus at Colonus*, in which Oedipus experiences a divine apotheosis. When Medea speaks in lament for the central moments that mark a life and that she will not have, her grief is predicated on a sense of pattern and order, a cosmic scheme in which humans participate. In these plays humans do not lack free will, but they and the gods together shape human destiny. The plays in this volume, although they do not cohere around any single theme, nevertheless reveal how tightly Greek drama is tied to ritual stages of life and how fully two spheres—the divine and the human—are joined.

These plays are made realistic not only by subject matter but also by dramatic technique. In many ways audience and characters are linked. The lament of Ismene and Antigone in the *Colonus* runs roughly parallel to a real-time lament and thus makes the audience co-participant; ritual *catharsis* is experienced first-hand by the audience. The suddenness of Orestes' visions at the end of the *Choephoroi* lets the audience feel the terror that besets him. The offstage cries of Medea at the beginning of the *Medea* create the impression for the audience of something accidentally overheard, which in turn produces the illusion that the character has a "real" inner life and is therefore "real." In subtle and varied ways that modern theatre is still discovering, these dramatists dissolve the "fourth wall."

THE DIVISIONS OF THE DRAMA

Greek tragedy and to a lesser extent Greek comedy are divided into episodes separated by Choral songs.

Names of Structural Divisions[5]

- Prologue: whatever dialogue precedes the entry of the Chorus. (This may be a single speech of an actor or dialogue between actors.)
- *Parodos*: the entry of the Chorus, in choral song.
- Episode: a scene of spoken dialogue.
- Choral Song: any song of the Chorus after its entrance. Episode and choral song, also called *stasimon*, alternate throughout the play.
- *Exodos*: the concluding dialogue of the play, followed by the departure of the Chorus.

Specific Types of Scenes and Songs

- *Angelia:* a messenger-speech describing at length what has happened offstage.
- *Ephymnia:* refrains between choral stanzas.
- *Epirrhema:* alternation of choral song with iambic speech from an actor.
- *Kommos:* a shared lament between Chorus and actor(s).
- *Parabasis:* in comedy, direct address by the Chorus to the audience about matters possibly, but not necessarily, related to the play.
- *Paean:* a song of praise to a god.
- Stichomythia: rapidly alternating lines of dialogue, usually in scenes of argument or interrogation.

Additional Theatrical Terms

- *Choragos:* the wealthy citizen who underwrites the cost of training the Chorus assigned a particular playwright.
- *Koryphaios:* the Chorus leader, who both sings and engages in dialogue.
- *Protagonistes:* the lead actor in a drama.
- *Deuteragonistes:* the second actor in a drama.
- *Tritagonistes:* the third actor in a drama.
- Scholia: the earliest critical commentaries on these plays, usually in the form of marginal notes in Greek on play scripts.
- Strophe, Antistrophe, and Epode: the usual pattern of a choral ode, in which the meter and length of the first stanza (the "strophe"), sung by half the Chorus, is mirrored in the second stanza (the "antistrophe"), sung by the other half of the Chorus, followed by a shared and metrically different final stanza (the "epode").
- Trilogy: the three-play unit in which tragedies were originally composed.
- Satyr-Play: the fourth play that a tragic playwright was expected to present; it parodied aspects of the trilogy and was performed at the trilogy's conclusion.
- Tetralogy: the name given to the four-play group of trilogy and satyr-play.

ARISTOTLE'S POETICS

The *Poetics* is the earliest extant work of dramatic analysis in Western culture. Aristotle lived and wrote the *Poetics* around 335 B.C., a half-century or more after the great playwrights of classical Greece—Aeschylus, Sophocles, Euripides, and Aristophanes—had died. In the *Poetics* he attempted to define what tragic structure and the tragic effect consisted of. He seems also to have written a second book of the *Poetics* discussing comedy, but that has not survived. Aristotle introduced into our critical vocabulary terms that, properly deployed, help us define the structures of individual plays. The tragedy he most admired was Sophocles' *Oedipus Rex*, and it is important to remember that many great tragedies are constructed differently and are no less great for being differently designed.

A tragedy is a play, he says, that presents the fall from good fortune to bad of a good, indeed, a great man who errs out of ignorance or misunderstanding. This fall or "reversal of fortune" is called, in Greek, *peripeteia*. The "error" made as a result of ignorance or flawed understanding is called *hamartia*. What makes the figure "tragic," though, is not simply these two things, but the person's recognition of whatever he or she did not understand before. That "recognition" is called *anagnorisis*. When we watch such a figure, we experience a release of the emotions of pity ("alas for man") and terror ("this could be me"). That "release" or purgation is called *catharsis*. Aristotle says that tragic effects are heightened by compression, and that therefore tragedy, unlike epic, requires a single event occurring within a brief and continuous period of time. The pressure of the plot is heightened if everything within the plot helps to bring about the *anagnorisis* and the *peripeteia* and if both occur simultaneously. He says, further, that the Chorus should be treated as one of the actors in that it should participate in the action. He says that to write a tragic plot is more difficult than to create a tragic character.

The term *hubris* is often conflated with *hamartia*. They are not the same: *hubris* is a particular category of *hamartia* and not itself a criterion of tragedy. It is used to refer to two forms of impiety: impiety in which the prideful think themselves equal to the gods, or in which they act with violence.

ATHENIAN HISTORY AND THE SPIRIT OF ATHENS

Political Background

Beginning in the sixth century, arts and politics began to flourish in Athens as nowhere else in Greece. In the fifth century, Athens, in league with Sparta and other city-states, repelled two Persian invasions, in 490 and in 480 B.C. Although Athens was burned, its people were saved by an expedient retreat to Salamis. Its warships destroyed the Persian fleet in 480 B.C., and its soldiers defeated the Persian land force the next year (479 B.C.) at Plataea. Athens had to be rebuilt, but as a consequence of its leadership in the war, she rose to a position of dominance in the Greek world. In 477 B.C., the Delian League, with its treasury on the holy island of Delos, was established to stand against the Persian threat. In 454 B.C., as a sign of Athenian ascendancy in the League, the treasury was moved to Athens and funds from it were disbursed to rebuild the temples of the Acropolis. Its Former "allies" gradually became subject states, and its relations with Sparta and the Peloponnesus grew openly confrontational. Meanwhile, Athens exacted regular tribute payments from her former allies and asserted judicial control over them, insisting that local cases be tried in Athenian courts. Sparta, fearing Athenian hegemony and eager to assume such a position itself, came to open conflict with Athens in 431 B.C., and the great conflict known as the Peloponnesian War (431–404 B.C.) began. Throughout the early years of the war, Athenian expansion continued. In 421 B.C., Nicias concluded a short-lived peace with Sparta, called the "Peace of Nicias." In 415 B.C., to punish the island of Melos for refusing to join the Athenian alliance, Athens retaliated with what was known as the "Melian starvation," an expedition to Melos that, after ringing the island and starving its population, put all its men to death and enslaved all its women and children. The Sicilian expedition of 413 B.C. ended with the decimation of the Athenian fleet, a disaster from which Athens never recovered. In 404 B.C., a date later than the composition of any of the plays in this volume, the Athenian fleet was destroyed at Aegospotami at the mouth of the Hellespont. By that year, all three great dramatists of ancient Athens, Aeschylus, Sophocles, and Euripides, were dead; Aristophanes lived on for 20 years, until 385 B.C., but the age of classical drama, unmatched in its productivity and genius, had ended, along with the end of Athens as a great power. What is remarkable is that throughout this period of political unrest and foreign war, including a disastrous siege of Athens by Sparta in 430–429 B.C. and plague within the city, some of the greatest art and drama of all time was created and lauded by an indomitable population. Athens truly was, in the words of Pericles, "the school of Hellas."

IMPORTANT DATES

Many of the following dates are approximations.

Playwrights and Others:

Aeschylus	525–456 B.C.
Pericles	496–429 B.C.
Sophocles	495–406 B.C.
Euripides	485–406 B.C.
Socrates	470–399 B.C.

Thucydides	460–400 B.C.
Aristophanes	450–385 B.C.
Plato	429–347 B.C.
Aristotle	384–322 B.C.

The Plays in this Volume:

The *Oresteia*:	458 B.C.
The *Agamemnon*	
The *Choephoroi*	
The *Eumenides*	
The *Antigone*	442 B.C.
The *Medea*	431 B.C.
The *Oedipus Rex*	426 B.C.
The *Birds*	414 B.C.
The *Lysistrata*	411 B.C.
The *Oedipus at Colonus*	written 406 B.C., performed 401 B.C.
The *Bacchae*	written 406 B.C., performed 405 B.C.

Wars:

| The Persian Wars | 490–480 B.C. |
| The Peloponnesian War | 431–404 B.C. |

NOTES

1. K.J. Dover, *Aristophanic Comedy* (Berkeley: University of California Press, 1972), pp. 15–16.

2. David Barrett, "Aristophanes, Comedian and Poet," in *Aristophanes*, ed. David Barrett and Alan H. Sommerstein (New York: Penguin Books, 1985), p. 24.

3. Oliver Taplin, *The Stagecraft of Aeschylus: The Dramatic Use of Exits and Entrances in Greek Tragedy* (Oxford: Clarendon Press, 1977), pp. 452–459.

4. John Ferguson, *A Companion to Greek Tragedy* (Austin: University of Texas Press, 1973), pp. 12–25.

5. Jeffrey Rusten, *Sophocles Oidipous Tyrannos: Preface, Introduction, Greek Text* (Philadelphia: Bryn Mawr Greek Commentaries, 1990), pp. 1–2.

1

Aeschylus
The *Agamemnon*
(458 B.C.)

AESCHYLUS' LIFE AND REPUTATION

Aeschylus' date of birth is usually given as 525–524 B.C.; he died in the middle of the next century, in 456 or 455 B.C., two years after the *Oresteia* was performed. Lattimore[1] estimates a later date of birth—around 512 B.C.—pointing out that it was the habit of ancient biographers short on facts to take the first signal achievement of their subject's life, assume the person needed to have been at least 40 at the time, and then calculate back 40 years to a presumed date of birth. In 484 B.C. Aeschylus is recorded as winning his first "first prize" in the dramatic competition; 40 years earlier is 524 B.C.

His epitaph states that he fought in the Persian Wars, that his father's name was Euphorion, and that he died in Sicily. No mention is made of his glory as a dramatist, and his epitaph, if self-composed, suggests the supreme value he placed on his service to the state:

Under this monument lies Aeschylus the Athenian,
Euphorion's son, who died in the wheatlands of Gela. The grove
of Marathon with its glories can speak of his valor in battle.
The long-haired Persian remembers and can speak of it too.[2]

Two of Aeschylus' sons also became tragic dramatists and Philocles, the son of Aeschylus' sister, later won first prize against Sophocles' *Oedipus Rex*.[3] Aeschylus comes in for a great deal of ribbing in Aristophanes' the *Frogs* (405 B.C.) in which he and Euripides are paired in a dramatic competition in Hades, which he wins. The honors accorded him in the *Frogs* reflect the honors accorded him in Athens where, by special allowance, his plays were revived for performance.

CHARACTERISTICS OF AESCHYLUS' STYLE

The theory that the Chorus originally played the central role in tragedy is borne out by the *Oresteia*, in the length and complexity of the odes of the *Agamemnon* and in the dramatic use of the Chorus of Libation Bearers and Furies.

Aeschylus wrote trilogies, a form particularly suited to recurring motifs, interlocking images, and movement through time. The three-play sequence of the trilogy combines the tragic sweep of the whole with the tragic compression of each individual play and is thus able to show that the past impinges on the present and that actions have counteractions in humanity's slow progress from savagery to civilization.

Aeschylus' writing is rich in imagery, and part of Aeschylus' genius is the turning of images first presented as metaphors into onstage action. In addition, "kindred imagery … establishes the causal connection between [events]."[4] Through deliberate ambiguities, in which context is temporarily withheld and in which one event is conflated with another, Aeschylus emphasizes morally similar situations.

A LIST OF AESCHYLUS' PLAYS

Aeschylus wrote more than 70 plays, 7 of which survive. The *Oresteia* (the "Tale of Orestes") is the only extant trilogy in all of Greek drama, and in it Aeschylus achieves a perfect balance of speech and choral song. Prizes in the following list are for the entire tetralogy of which the extant plays were a part.

The *Persians*	472 B.C.	1st Prize
The *Seven Against Thebes*	467 B.C.	1st Prize
The *Suppliant Maidens*	463 B.C.	1st Prize
The *Oresteia*	458 B.C.	1st Prize

[*Agamemnon, Choephoroi, Eumenides*, followed by the lost satyr-play, *Proteus*]

The *Prometheus Bound*	date uncertain

SUMMARY OF THE *AGAMEMNON*

The *Agamemnon* is the story of Agamemnon's victorious return to Argos with Cassandra after 10 years of fighting at Troy and their murder by his wife Clytaemestra and her lover Aigisthus.

AESCHYLUS' USE OF MYTH IN THE *AGAMEMNON*

Mythic Background

The brothers Thyestes and Atreus vied for the throne of Argos and for Atreus' wife, Aerope. Thyestes seduced her and, in revenge, Atreus slaughtered Thyestes' young sons and served them to their unsuspecting father in a stew. Thyestes' third child, Aigisthus, was saved, lived to manhood, and became the lover of Clytaemestra, repeating his father's crime of adultery. Atreus' sons, Agamemnon and Menelaus, married Clytaemestra and Helen, respectively, daughters of King Tyndareus of Sparta. While a guest in Menelaus' house, Paris, prince of Troy, stole Helen and carried her off to Troy. Agamemnon, as commander-in-chief, assembled a great army of Greeks to recover Helen. Cassandra, sister to Paris and daughter of King Priam, was beloved of Apollo, received from him the gift of prophecy, declined his bed, and was punished by being brought to Argos to die. Despite her rejection of Apollo, she remained consecrated to him as bride; Agamemnon's taking of her as booty was an act of *hubris*. Clytaemestra is sometimes called "Clytemnestra." Paean, Loxias, and Phoebus are names for Apollo. Scamander and Simois are rivers near Troy, another name for which is Ilium. Paris is also called "Alexander."

Homer's Emphasis and Aeschylus' Art

The *Odyssey* tells the story of Aigisthus' seduction of Clytaemestra and his killing of Agamemnon. Homer makes no reference to Iphigenia or to Clytaemestra's grief at her death; Clytaemestra's motive for murder, as presented by Homer, is lust unmixed with resentment or sorrow. In the Homeric tradition that Aeschylus inherited, Aigisthus, not Clytaemestra, kills Agamemnon and does so when Agamemnon is feasting with his comrades at Aigisthus' banquet table (11:409–430). The system of beacon flares and Clytaemestra's magisterial fire speech are absent from Homer and must be understood as Aeschylus' invention. There is a Watchman in the mythic tradition, but he is suborned by Aigisthus, not a loyal servant eager for his lord's return from Troy (4:524–537). The tradition in which Agamemnon brings Cassandra home as a prize was already established in Homer's day, but the great scene of prophetic vision is Aeschylus' own. Her vision, Aeschylus' use of the Watchman to set the mood of foreboding at the beginning of the play, the complexity of motive Aeschylus ascribes to Clytaemestra, the manner of Agamemnon's death, and the reverberating images of net and urn and of many other things are attributable to the artistry of the playwright, working within a body of shared myth. Aeschylus' purposes and themes are, of course, radically different from Homer's; that the same story can, in the hands of different poets, be used in such different ways is itself a sign of the dynamic nature of Greek literary creation.

THE PLOT OF THE *AGAMEMNON*

General Comments

The plot of the *Agamemnon* is simplicity itself: a man returns home and is murdered. Nothing goes wrong. There are no impediments and no complications. The *peripeteia* of the *Agamemnon* is doubled: in a reversal of fortune, grim death comes to the victorious Agamemnon and to Cassandra, a rise in fortune to royal power comes to Clytaemestra and Aigisthus. Of the four figures, only Cassandra experiences *anagnorisis* and hers is probably the most stunning and extended such moment in all of Greek drama.

Secondary figures in the works of Sophocles and Euripides are brought on to "complicate" the action, by which is meant that after they appear, something is different. In the *Agamemnon*, the Watchman and the Herald are simply part of an action already conceived and underway, and thus they emphasize the inexorability of that larger action, as no single individual alters it.

Setting

The setting is outside the palace of Agamemnon in Argos on the day of Agamemnon's return from Troy. The time is the heroic age, specifically about three weeks after the end of the Trojan War.

Dramatis Personae

Watchman	of the palace of Argos
Chorus of Argive Elders	
Clytaemestra	queen of Argos, wife to Agamemnon
Herald	
Agamemnon	king of Argos, commander-in-chief

		of the Trojan expedition
Cassandra		princess of Troy, Agamemnon's war prize
Aigisthus		Clytaemestra's lover

Scene Divisions

Prologue:	1–39	[Watchman]
Parodos:	40–257	[Chorus]
Episode One:	258–354	[Chorus, Clytaemestra]
First Ode:	355–502	[Chorus]
Episode Two:	503–680	[Chorus, Herald, Clytaemestra]
Second Ode:	681–781	[Chorus]
Episode Three:	782–974	[Chorus, Agamemnon, Cassandra, Clytaemestra]
Third Ode:	975–1034	[Chorus, Cassandra]
Episode Four:	1035–1330	[Chorus, Clytaemestra, Cassandra]
Fourth Ode:	1331–1371	[Chorus, Agamemnon *offstage*]
Exodos:	1372–1673	[Chorus, Clytaemestra, Aigisthus]

Synopsis

| Prologue: | 1–39 | [Watchman] |

It is predawn. A Watchman on the roof of the palace complains that for a weary year he has waited for a beacon that will signal the fall of Troy and the homecoming of King Agamemnon. He says that the royal house is not ordered for the best, as it once was, but he does not specify what is wrong. Suddenly a signal-fire appears. He calls out to awaken the queen, expresses the hope that he may clasp the king's hand in his own, and exits.

| *Parodos:* | 40–257 | [Chorus] |

The Chorus enter in response to the Watchman's shout. They ask why the altars of the city are ablaze with incense and recall the army's setting forth to Troy. They pray to Zeus that all may be well, but they speak with foreboding.

| Episode One: | 258–354 | [Chorus, Clytaemestra] |

Clytaemestra appears and announces the fall of Troy. Her proof to the Chorus is the beacon flares lit on successive mountaintops from Troy to "this Argolid palace." She expresses the hope that the Greek army is not violating the altars of the gods, and she reenters the palace as the Chorus say that they will offer a prayer in thanksgiving.

First Ode: 355–502   [Chorus]

The Chorus compliment Clytaemestra for speaking "like a prudent man," condemn Paris, and speak of the sorrow that Helen brought to both the house of Menelaus and the house of Priam. Ares is likened to a banker who exchanges flesh for dust. They pray that they chart a more moderate course, attaining no great wealth and not plundering cities.

Episode Two: 503–680   [Chorus, Herald, Clytaemestra]

A Herald announces the imminent return of Agamemnon. The Chorus feel both joy and foreboding. The Herald speaks of his suffering as a soldier and of his joy at returning home. Clytaemestra gives him a message for Agamemnon in which she asserts her fidelity.

Second Ode: 681–781   [Chorus]

The Chorus describe Helen's sea voyage to Troy and liken her to a lion cub, brought into a house where it does not belong and where it wreaks havoc. Righteousness, they say, guides all things to their proper ends.

Episode Three: 782–974   [Agamemnon, Cassandra,
                                      Clytaemestra, Chorus]

Agamemnon and Cassandra enter in a chariot and are welcomed by the Chorus who warn that not all mortals are sincere. Clytaemestra appears and insists that Agamemnon enter their house by walking on a cloth of rich purple that her handmaids have spread on the ground. He regards her suggestion as *hubristic*, but he complies. She follows him offstage, crying out to Zeus in exultant prayer.

Third Ode: 975–1034   [Chorus, Cassandra]

The Chorus try to reason away their fear, but cannot.

Episode Four: 1035–1330   [Chorus, Clytaemestra, Cassandra]

Clytaemestra reappears and orders Cassandra inside. Cassandra ignores her and Clytaemestra exits. Cassandra addresses herself to the god Apollo in cries of woe. The Chorus speak gently, telling her that Apollo is not a god associated with lamentation. Suddenly she understands her destiny to be a pun on the name of the god, for *apollon* means "destroyer." She sees a floor swimming in blood and hears the wailing of babies, crying because their flesh has been eaten by their father. The weight of prophecy suddenly lifts but then returns in greater force. Cassandra feels Apollo stripping her prophetic robes from her. She enters the palace, knowing that she goes to her death.

Fourth Ode: 1331–1371   [Chorus, Agamemnon *offstage*]

The Chorus note that no one, high or low, is immune from dark destiny. Agamemnon's voice is heard from offstage: "Ay me! I am smitten deep with a mortal blow." The Chorus debate what they should do and anticipate tyranny once their lord is dead.

Exodos: 1372–1673   [Chorus, Clytaemestra, Aigisthus]

The bodies of Cassandra and Agamemnon are displayed by an exultant Clytaemestra. The Chorus are appalled. Aigisthus appears, accompanied by his armed guard, and threatens them with jail and torture. Clytaemestra urges him to be calm, as power is theirs. The play ends.

THE CHORAL ODES

The *Parodos*: 40–257

The *parodos* of the *Agamemnon* is exquisitely and complexly constructed to move back and forth in time, to create a sense of foreboding, and to put the action that will follow into an historical frame. Movement in time begins when the Chorus recall the omen (an omen being a thing that looks to the future) of eagles that appeared 10 years before to the departing kings, Agamemnon and Menelaus. The Chorus then interrupt their narrative to pose a question about the city altars, and their question reminds us of present time. Their question is not answered until Clytaemestra speaks 200 lines later, but it reminds us that we are anticipating Agamemnon and the fleet's return. The Chorus return to their story and speak of the prophecy by Calchas of what was then the future but is now the past. Their narrative of his prophecy is punctuated by three identical refrains, "Sing woe, sing woe, but may the good prevail," that at first are their present-moment response, then Calchas' cry of years past, and finally, the two conflated and only belatedly contextualized as his cry rather than theirs. They pray to Zeus and, as they begin their prayer, they speak of the deep past, of earlier generations of gods, of Uranus and Cronos. Within their narrative of the death of Iphigenia is also a narrative of the deeper past, of her singing to her father's dinner guests when a little girl.

Linked to the temporal movements of the *parodos* are Cassandra's visions later in the play, which go further into the past, into the present, and into the far future than the Chorus can imagine. The majestic beacon speech of Clytaemestra's also continues the trope of time, for the swiftness of the message sent by the flares cancels time as, Lattimore argues, she would wish to do in revenging her child's death.[5] These complex temporal movements brilliantly emphasize Aeschylus' perception that past, present, and future are inextricably linked, and that actions have endless, unforeseen consequences.

The *parodos* has not only temporal sweep but also spatial sweep, from Argos to Aulis to Troy. Thus, the death of Agamemnon that is the climax of this play is, placed in a context that gives it enormous weight and that creates an overwhelming sense of foreboding.

The *parodos* also sounds a critical theme of the trilogy when it presents the sacrifice at Aulis in terms of moral choice. Through anaphora, Aeschylus emphasizes the double option the king perceives when Agamemnon says, "'Hard [*bareia*] is my fate to refuse obedience,'" and "'Hard [*bareia*], too, if I must slay my child'" (206–208). The struggle implied by such parallelism quickly disappears, and the Chorus note that "he hardened his heart" (223). To emphasize the magnitude of Agamemnon's abandonment of paternity, Aeschylus thereafter ironically substitutes the word "father" for "king" and for "Agamemnon" (227, 230, 244, 245).

The *parodos* also introduces an image of Iphigenia, her saffron robes falling from her, the horse's bit in her mouth, that will be echoed in the Cassandra scene later in this play but that will not find its resolution until the final moment of the *Eumenides*, when joyous little girls in saffron robes march in triumphant procession, marking the end of vengeance and blood feuds. For all these reasons, the *parodos* is a choral ode of tremendous power and dramatic importance.

The Second Ode: 681–781

Both the *parodos* and the first ode speak of Agamemnon. The second ode does not focus on Agamemnon at all, but on Helen, so that Agamemnon's appearance, at its conclusion, is all the more striking for being unexpected. The second ode begins by punning on the name "Helen," and the puns are bitter. The simple past tense form of the verb "to kill" is *helein*, and Helen is called *Hele-nas* ("killer of ships"), *Hel-andros* ("killer of men"), and *Hele-ptolis* ("killer of a city," 689). The Chorus describe the armies of Greece as tracking the ship that takes Helen to Troy, and in their metaphor she is the "quarry," the soldiers are "huntsmen," and the impress of oars on the waves is the "track" that vanishes instantly. Ironically, the prey is fatal and the hunters, not the quarry, "end in blood." The marriage song sung for her by the bridegroom's kin turns into a song of mourning as Troy grieves for the "slaughter of her sons." The ode continues to conflate loveliness and danger, and ends with the monitory fable of the lion cub, a warning that one should know what one has within one's house, ironically sounded as Agamemnon enters. In much the same way that the *parodos* expands the historical canvass, so the choral references to Helen make her and those she touches fully a part of this tragedy.

AGAMEMNON

When Aeschylus at last brings Agamemnon onstage in the third episode of the play, Agamemnon's speech reveals what a man who can choose to kill his own child is like and how such a choice can affect a man. That Agamemnon does not speak of his joy at his return, as the Herald so pointedly does in the preceding scene, reveals an emotional coldness in Agamemnon, a trait borne out by the rest of what he says and does in this scene.

Three times in his opening speech Agamemnon boasts that Troy still burns and that the Greeks have been fierce as lions in their assault. His animal imagery echoes the language he used after his moral choice at Aulis, ordering that a horse's bit be placed in his daughter's mouth to silence any cry against his house, and that she be lifted above the altar like a kid of a goat. Agamemnon's sensibility is dulled by willed blindness and pride. He can speak blithely of making a sacrifice to mark his homecoming or say that he and Odysseus were "yoke-fellows" (842) without hearing in his mind the parallel sacrifice of his child or remembering his putting on "the yoke of necessity" (217).

Agamemnon speaks of the gods who have "helped" him to his safe return "and to the justice I exacted from Priam's town" (810–813). If he does not see himself as the instrument of Zeus but instead sees Zeus as his assistant, as the word "helped" suggests, then the impiety and *hubris* of what he has done to Iphigenia and to Priam's town are beyond measure. When Agamemnon chooses to tread on the carpet, he does so knowing that what he does is impious. As earlier, he puts aside his qualms. We know the carpet choice to be wrong because of the exultation it produces in Clytaemestra. It is, for her as for him, a reenactment of his actual choice at Aulis.

CLYTAEMESTRA

Her Essential Duality

Clytaemestra appears in every episode of the play, pretends to subscribe to the shared values of her society, and then, the murder accomplished, boastfully and defiantly asserts that she is a law unto herself. Unlike her husband, whose conscience is weak, Clytaemestra finds her strength in the absence of conscience. At the heart of the trilogy is the concept of moral choice. Clytaemestra, alone of all the characters in the trilogy, operates outside the realm of choice. Nothing intervenes between impulse and act, neither doubt nor qualm. In this, as in her deeds, she is a moral primitive.

Cassandra likens Clytaemestra to the *amphisbaina*, the fabled snake who moves backward and forward and whose ends are each both head and tail, for Clytaemestra is unnatural and duplicitous. Where one expects a retreating back, there is an attacking front; where one expects female acquiescence, there is a deadly male who seeks "victory" and whose cry at her husband's homecoming is a battle cry. The Watchman describes her as "a woman with a man's will" (10–11), and indeed the verb *krateo* ("to rule, to conquer, to get the upper hand") recurs throughout the text in reference to Clytaemestra. In the prologue, the Watchman speaks of Clytaemestra's "rule" and in her final lines she says to Aigisthus that they together will set the house in order and "rule" it. Her mannishness is suggested also in the images of her lover: he is feminized as the voluptuary who rests in bed inside the palace while others go to war, and he is called the "wolf" who couches with the more powerful "lioness" (1258–1259).

Her Various Motives

Clytaemestra's determination to destroy Agamemnon initially seems to derive solely from anguish at the loss of Iphigenia. The very timing of her entry emphasizes her connection to her dead child, for she comes onstage to announce the fall of Troy just after the Chorus have concluded their description of the death of Iphigenia. Later Clytaemestra is shown to be driven also by lust, an idea she introduces in a series of denials. She instructs the Herald to tell Agamemnon that she "has not broken seal" (609–612) of the house's wealth, nor of her own body. "Of pleasure with other men I know no more than how to dip hot metal," a comparison that can be confirmatory or nonconfirmatory, depending on whether dipping metal is understood to mean "into a blacksmith's furnace in order to shape and temper a sword" or "into a body to bring the sword into contact with hot blood." Her public declaration of chastity is indecorous, and, after murdering her husband, she flaunts her adulterous liaison with Aigisthus and reveals herself as motivated by sexual jealousy as well, for she anticipates that the "relish" (1477) of their bed will be enhanced by sexual jokes about the now-dead Cassandra. In such a context, Clytaemestra's method of killing Agamemnon, naked and bathing, is itself lust distorted into murder, as is the pleasure she feels in stabbing him and experiencing his blood spurt onto her, like rain on a fertile field.

Such motives, gradually revealed, compromise Clytaemestra's claim to be acting out of revenge for Iphigenia's death. In fact, the images that surround Cassandra—Clytaemestra's references to Cassandra's needing to feel the horse's "bit," the robes of the god dropping from Cassandra—make Cassandra an analogue, as she goes to her death, of Iphigenia and put Clytaemestra's deeds in the same moral category as Agamemnon's killing of their child.

Her Ambiguous Language

Clytaemestra's language is rich in double meanings. When, contemplating the fall of Troy, Clytaemestra lists deeds of sacrilege that she hopes the army will avoid, and when, shortly thereafter, the Herald enters and announces, "Demolished are the altars and the shrines of [Troy's] gods" (527), there is produced, along with fear of the gods' wrath, fear of Clytaemestra's incantatory power. Her speech concludes in ominous ambiguity: "But even if, void of such offence towards the gods, our host should reach home, the grievous suffering of the dead might still prove wakeful" (345–347). By "the dead" she presumably means the Trojan dead, but Iphigenia is also dead, and Clytaemestra is also wakeful, the "watchdog," as she asserts, "of his house" (607). Thus, her solicitude for the soldiers is also understood as a veiled threat against her lord Agamemnon.

Her dialogue with Agamemnon is replete with ambiguity. Describing her fears for his safety, she says, "And as for wounds, had this my lord received so many as rumor kept pouring into the house, no net had been pierced so full of holes as he" (866–868). Her graphic emphasis on ill report suggests a concealed wish, and her simile's explicit reference to a "net" hints at what she will do. She says that "for this cause," which not until the middle of the *Choephoroi* is revealed to be a desire to live openly with Aigisthus, Agamemnon "will not see standing here beside her their child, the love pledge between them, as he should, Orestes." The Greek word for "child" (*pais*, 877) is gender neutral, and the pronoun in Greek is part of the verb formation; thus, not until her second appositive does Clytaemestra make it clear that she means "Orestes" (879), having let the possibility that she is speaking of Iphigenia hang in the air.

She urges Agamemnon to tread on the purple fabric, saying "With purple strewn let his path be, that Justice may usher him to a home he ne'er hoped to see." He understands something like, "with honors let him enter his palace"; we hear "trampling upon blood, let him go down to the house of Hades." When he treads on the carpet, Clytaemestra speaks of the boundless sea with its "plenteous purple," of which their house has ample store. If the "purple" is also blood, her words speak both of the precious blood of her child and of her current intentions, not of the dyed rug. As he enters the house, her ambiguous images turn from the purple of the sea's dye to the purple of the grape. She says that her lord Agamemnon is warmth in wintertime and that "when Zeus makes wine [in summer] from the unripe grape, then forthwith there is coolness in the house when its rightful lord ranges through its halls" (968–972). She appears to be saying that the influence of the rightful lord on his house is strong and positive: he brings what is needed, as gods do: warmth in winter and coolness in summer. The verb, "makes from unripe grapes," suggests, however, her virgin daughter, for a virgin is "unripe," and blood has been pressed from her body. The reference to "coolness" is easily turned into a reference to the death that will shortly occur within the house. "Unripe" is also translated as "bitter." Is it Clytaemestra's meaning that, from the "bitter" sorrow of Iphigenia's death, Zeus will send a "sweet" revenge, a new death in the house? When Clytaemestra displays the bodies, she says that Agamemnon has now "drained to the dregs" (1398) the mixing-bowl he has left for his house.

The murder accomplished, her metaphors continue, but, as when she compares Agamemnon's blood to rain upon the field, they are made unambiguous and not tension-filled but grotesque.

Sympathy for Clytaemestra

So that the audience may recognize the appeal of vengeance before rejecting it, Aeschylus, in confident artistry, first creates sympathy for Clytaemestra and then eliminates it. Clytaemestra's language in the beacon speech, for example, is beautiful: her metaphors animate the mountain tops and islands, her description is suffused with light and speed, and all nature and the god Hephaestus seem at her command. Her nature throughout the play is likewise energized and passionate. She is a figure of awe to those around her, and she persuades the commander of the fleet, the victor of Troy, against his better judgment, to do as she wishes.

Aeschylus builds sympathy for Clytaemestra through other devices as well. The description of Iphigenia's death at the end of the *parodos* fills us with sadness. Immediately thereafter Aeschylus brings Clytaemestra on stage and some of the sympathy that has been aroused attaches to her. The next ode develops the theme of war and its human cost in searing images such as that of Ares as "banker" who weighs human flesh in his scales and in exchange "sends home ashes in an urn" (438–455), and that of families who praise their dead "through their tears," saying the little they can to comfort themselves—"how this man knew well the craft of battle, how another went down splendid in the slaughter," and how "young men in their beauty" by the walls of Ilium "keep graves deep in the alien soil they hated and conquered." Clytaemestra herself, in her announcement of the fall of Troy, has expressed reservations about conquest and an understanding of human hardship, and so we associate her with the searing emotions of this subsequent ode. When the ode introduces the idea of "grief charged with resentment" that "spreads stealthily against the sons of Atreus," Aeschylus again aligns Clytaemestra in her grievances with the people, and thus sympathy for her cause remains in play.

The Cassandra scene is the moral pivot of the play, and through it Aeschylus sharply turns the audience from Clytaemestra who, for the first time in the play, is unable to persuade a character or control the action. Any impression that Clytaemestra feels compassion for the vanquished is now undermined, for she says that Cassandra needs to accommodate herself to servitude, just as a mare needs a cutting bit in its mouth to be tamed. Clytaemestra's murder of Cassandra, the character to whom Aeschylus assigns the longest scene of the play and in which he shows Cassandra in every sense noble, creates revulsion for Clytaemestra. Aigisthus is only now alluded to and the motive of a mother's grief becomes a compound of lust and jealousy. Clytaemestra's admired subtlety is now viewed as pure hypocrisy, and the sense of having been tricked by her heightens audience revulsion.

Romantic critics who admire her as "gloriously culpable," "touching" or as the unjustly maligned emblem of heroic opposition to feminine oppression respond to Aeschylus' making her a compelling and charismatic presence, full of passionate energy, but ignore the ultimate purpose for which Aeschylus crafts this figure. He has no aesthetic of evil and presents Clytaemestra as progressively more vile throughout the trilogy, until in the *Eumenides* she is physically what she is morally, a shrieking and rotting corpse, hate-filled. Her maternal function, whatever it may be imagined once to have been, is presented in the *Choephoroi* as entirely dysfunctional: she has exiled her son, stolen his inheritance, locked up her daughter Electra, whom she has kept unbetrothed and undowried, and calls for an axe with which to strike Orestes down. In her last speech, she calls her son a "snake" whom she has reared. Her rule of the city is wasteful and tyrannical. Retrospectively, her laying down of the purple fabric seems a misuse of the wealth of the house, just as walking on it is a sign of Agamemnon's *hubris*. The energy that she releases is deadly to all around her, and it is away from such unbridled violence that the trilogy moves in its progress from barbarism to civilization.

CASSANDRA

Cassandra and Iphigenia

Both Cassandra and Iphigenia die far from home, slaughtered like animals and unwept for. From both, robes fall or are stripped; one is actually "bitted" in the mouth and the other is spoken of as needing to be. Both are virgin sacrifices to the gods, Iphigenia to Artemis, Cassandra, despite her violation by Agamemnon, to Apollo whose bride she still is. The last thing heard of each is a reference to song: "for oft had she sung where men were met at her father's hospitable board" (243–247) and "she who, like a swan, hath sung her last lament in death" (1443–1446). Such duplication invests both characters with a double weight of lyrical sorrow and the play with the sense that all events are intertwined, and that vengeance is always corrupt.

Cassandra's Visions

The prophetic powers that Aeschylus imagines for Cassandra are unlike the prophetic powers of Calchas. Calchas interprets external signs that are visible to all; she has visions. Aeschylus has imagined what it might be like to be compelled by inner vision, to possess a mind that apprehends rather than a mind that deduces. Cassandra sees pictures that gradually come into clearer focus and that then shift to other pictures; these pictures are accompanied by sound and smell. She does not see identifiable people and she does not speak cryptically; she reports exactly what she sees: a floor running in blood, a cow goring a bull, little children with their chewed entrails in their hands, a wolf couching with a lioness, a fawning dog with its ears laid back in welcome. What is terrifying to her in this is the lack of context. What are these things?

Without context she cannot predict what will come at her next, and thus her visions are particularly horrifying. Concentration on the image is absolute. She can, in a single moment, see what happened in the palace 40 or 50 years earlier, as well as what will happen there in the next moment. She can hear old cries—they have not stopped—and smell old smells, and she can hear and smell the horrors that await her. It is a remarkable portrait.

Cassandra and Aristotle

Aeschylus has created a scene in which *anagnorisis* ("recognition") and *peripeteia* ("reversal of fortune") occur simultaneously. The entire visionary experience might be called a radical *anagnorisis*. Cassandra's recognition of her own doom and of the evil the house exudes is extended and agonizing. That Cassandra's reversal of fortune does not come about because of anything she has done, any error of judgment or understanding ("*hamartia*"), but simply because of the fortunes of war and the will of the gods, makes her endurance heroic and enhances our sympathy for her.

Agamemnon goes to his doom without understanding that it is coming or that he has, in large measure, brought it about. Agamemnon's entry into the palace is ritualized by his treading on the purple carpet; Cassandra's is marked by her apprehending the odor of death. The attention drawn to both these exit moments allows us to compare them so that, from that contrast, Cassandra may emerge as a tragic hero.[6] Cassandra realizes that it is Apollo who has brought her here to die and who is stripping her robes from her, and that *anagnorisis* removes her forever from Clytaemestra's tawdry machinations. Although Clytaemestra remains convinced that her own right hand was "a workman true" (1406) and struck Cassandra down, Cassandra knows her destroyer ("*apollon*") to be *Apollon* the god. She goes to her death at the moment she selects, with a mind clear, quieted and fully rational, just as a great hero faces battle. The calm and readiness that come to Cassandra come also to the audience and make this scene one not only of *anagnorisis* and *peripeteia*, but also of *catharsis*.

IMAGERY

Of Law Courts and Voting Urns

From the opening moments of the *Agamemnon*, in anticipation of the trilogy's conclusion in which the Court of the Areopagus is established, language is legalistic. When the Chorus call Menelaus "Priam's mighty adversary" (40–41), the word used for adversary is *antidikos* ("plaintiff in a lawsuit"). Agamemnon says of the Trojans that "Hearkening to no pleadings by word of mouth, without dissentient voice, they cast into the urn of blood their ballots for the murderous destroying of Ilium; but to the urn of acquittal, that no hand filled" (813–817). In other words, the Trojans, by condoning the theft of a wife, were both defendant and their own jury, and "voted" to be destroyed; according to his self-absolving metaphor, Agamemnon simply executed the sentence they themselves had decided on. To describe the voting urn as an "urn of blood" (815) suggests not just the bloodiness of war but a perversion of the idea of law and justice, which design civil procedures as substitutes for the practice of bloody revenge. The word "urn" (*teuchos*) means both "urn" and "bathing tub," any open vessel that holds something. Agamemnon's legal joke at the Trojan's expense turns out to be a terrifying joke about what lies in his own future, a tub of blood. The Chorus sing of Ares sending home "urns and ashes" (435), using the word *teuchos*, and anticipating the bathing "urn" of Agamemnon's death. And, of course, the legal references in the *Agamemnon* themselves prefigure the stage action in the third play of casting votes into urns.

Of Sleep

The idea of some task or danger interfering with sleep, whether the sleep of the Watchman or the sleep of the soldiers at Troy (334–337), is emphasized so that the importance of the tribunal established in the *Eumenides* is appreciated. Athene calls the Court of the Areopagus "a guardian of the land, vigilant in defense of them that sleep." The Areopagus, a wakeful guard, is a "significant contrast ... with the sleepless watchman of the Agamemnon ... whose loyal performance of his task serves only to alert the king's murderers: the Areopagus' 'sleeplessness' will prevent wrongdoing."[7]

For an innocent figure like the Watchman, dreams are equated with restful sleep and are to be desired: he says that whenever he makes his bed on the roof of the palace, he is "unvisited by dreams"(12–15), for instead of sleep "fear stands ever by my side." For Menelaus, however, dreams are avenues of longing and sorrow: Helen having fled, Menelaus dreams her back night after night. Menelaus' dream, prompted by love and loss, is echoed in the dreams of those who lament in their houses the death of men sent forth to Troy in his cause. His sorrowful dreams have caused theirs. Nonetheless, Menelaus' dreams are themselves emblems of love and, as such, stand in mute contrast to Clytaemestra's pretense of troubled dreams, nightmares of endless disasters falling on her lord, agitation so great that the "faint whirring of the buzzing gnat" would awaken her (891–894). Indeed, she may not be lying, for if dreams are not only portents but wishes, as Menelaus' dreams are, then what Clytaemestra describes are welcome nightmares, answered by the gods in the terrifying nightmare finally sent her in the *Choephoroi*.

Of the Lion in the House

The rich complexity of Aeschylean imagery is perhaps best seen in the image of "the lion in the house." In the second ode the Chorus tell a fable of a lion's whelp, reared in a house, at first gentle, "kindly to children, and a delight to the old." It was "held in arms like a nursling child," and fawned "under compulsion of its belly's need." When it came to full growth, however, it showed that it had the feral nature of its parents, for it slaughtered the flocks and defiled the house. The immediate application of the fable is to Helen, who at first seemed lovely, a "delicate ornament" brought to Troy, but who then caused the ruin of Priam's house. But the image has larger applicability. The lion was "a priest of ruin, by ordinance of God" (735). In its bloodiness it was a divine minister or scourge. Thus, the lion is not only Helen, punishing the Trojans, but any active and deliberate avenger: it is even Clytaemestra, a danger "in the house" unrecognized by Agamemnon. It is also Agamemnon. Zeus has sent Agamemnon to punish Troy, and Agamemnon brags of himself and the Achaeans as fierce cubs in the belly of the wooden horse, and of the army as "the ravening lion" (826–827) who swarmed above the towers of Troy to glut its hunger by lapping at the blood of kings. A lion in the house cannot be countenanced; it must be destroyed. The question of the third play is what shall happen to Orestes who, as he goes to kill Clytaemestra and Aigisthus in the *Choephoroi*, calls himself a lion in the house and has indeed been nursed there as an infant.

THE THEME OF KINGSHIP

The importance to a people of their sceptered king is emphasized from the beginning of this play in which a sceptered king is killed. The Watchman, looking at the movement of the stars, thinks of them as "rulers" that are "radiant" and thinks of the constellations that they form as an "assembly" or "meeting." The association of kingship with order in the universe is immediately made. The presence of the sceptered king is also associated with the well-being of his people: with Agamemnon safely returned, the Watchman can sleep at night and will no longer have to lie on the palace roof on crooked arm, "after the manner of a dog."

The confrontation between Aigisthus and the Chorus at the end of the play makes it clear why the people of Argos honor a true king over a usurper, whatever their reservations about the deeds of the royal house. This new ruler is a coward, a despoiler of the marriage bed, a snob and a seeker after power and wealth not rightly his. Whereas Clytaemestra used an image of rowers' benches on board ship to degrade Cassandra, Aigisthus uses the same image to put the Chorus in their place: they are merely rowers of the lower deck who dare to instruct the ship's master. He threatens to "yoke" the citizens of the Chorus with a heavy collar, and the use of the word, so clearly associated with Agamemnon's subduing of Troy, now in an autocratic rather than a glorious context and applied to citizens rather than to enemies, suggests the radical debasement of Argos that Agamemnon's death has brought. Aigisthus will injure the *polis* directly rather than indirectly through deaths in war. He will imprison whoever defies him so that they know only "loathsome hunger, bonds and darkness." Thus, the vengeance of Clytaemestra is shown to be wrong in practical, as well as in moral terms, and the killing of a sceptered king is shown never to be only a private act with private consequences.

ASPECTS OF STAGECRAFT

The Spreading of the Carpet

The carpet scene contains perhaps the most famous stage effect in all of Greek tragedy. A long swath of fabric, actually not a "carpet" at all, is unrolled from chariot to palace door, and Agamemnon is invited to tread on it (905–962). It is fabric of precious dye, as might bedeck the shrine of a god. It seems the color of both blood and majesty. Insofar as it, when spread, runs from the chariot to the entranceway, it represents, at least in Clytaemestra's mind, the spilled blood of their child, and the blood guilt that Agamemnon has brought to the house.

The next time in the trilogy that a swath of the same color appears on stage is in the procession of the Furies at the end of the *Eumenides*, each draped in scarlet vestments and forming a long line as they walk single file in the procession of Athene. And the movement of that procession is not toward the central doors of the *skene*, but away from the doors, away from "the house," out of the theatre, a visual resolution to the direction in which the carpet is spread, and a sign that the blood guilt of the house has been removed.

The Use of the *Ekkyklema*

The *ekkyklema* is rotated out, perhaps in its first stage use, to display the dead bodies of Agamemnon and Cassandra at line 1371 and remains in use until the play's conclusion at line 1673. The sight of Agamemnon, naked and entangled in a net, covered in blood and kept so long on view, is deliberately "grotesque." There is nothing Clytaemestra or Aigisthus can say in self-justification that is not undercut by the audience's sight of the shamed bodies.

The Adaptation of the *Kommos*

In the *Agamemnon*, Aeschylus assigns to the Chorus and Clytaemestra a dramatically brilliant variant (1448–1576) of the traditional shared dirge. The Chorus grieve for the death of their king in strophes and antistrophes, followed by *ephymnia,* while she responds, not with answering grief as in a traditional *kommos,* but with exultation. Gradually, the emotions of the lament overpower the rage Clytaemestra feels, and she mourns, not for Agamemnon, but for "my sweet flower, shoot sprung from him, Iphigenia of the tears" (1525–1526). The traditional dirge includes a promise to perform for the dead all the rites and ceremonies of burial. The Chorus, not being kin, cannot make the promise and Clytaemestra will not. Instead, she mockingly says that the cries of woe of Cassandra, while alive, suffice; no further rites are needed. The absence here of the traditional promise is a sign of her impiety and her rejection of all societal norms. It is also the action to which the next play addresses itself.

The Delayed Appearance of Aigisthus

Aigisthus enters for the first time a mere 100 lines before the end of the play. The Chorus have known of Aigisthus but have not spoken of him, nor has he shown himself. This is what the death of the king means: shamefulness will boldly show itself. That he comes on so late in the play and speaks of the wrongs done by Atreus to Thyestes, wrongs done a generation before Troy, reminds us of the endless reach of all deeds.

NOTES

1. *Aeschylus I,* translated and with an introduction by Richmond Lattimore, in *The Complete Greek Tragedies,* edited by David Grene and Richmond Lattimore (Chicago: University of Chicago Press, 1953), pp. 1–2.

2. Lattimore, p. 1.

3. Alan H. Sommerstein, *Aeschylus: Eumenides, Cambridge Greek and Latin Classics Series* (Cambridge: Cambridge University Press, 1989), p. 18.

4. Anne Lebeck, *The Oresteia: A Study in Language and Structure* (Washington, D.C.: The Center for Hellenic Studies; Cambridge: Harvard University Press, 1971), pp. 76–77.

5. Lattimore, pp. 18–23.

6. Colin MacLeod, "Aeschylus, *Agamemnon* 1285–1289," in *Collected Essays* (Oxford: Clarendon Press, 1983), pp. 44–45.

7. Colin Macleod, "Politics and the *Oresteia*," in *Collected Essays* (Oxford: Clarendon Press, 1983), p. 129.

2

Aeschylus
The *Choephoroi*
("The Libation Bearers")

(458 B.C.)

SUMMARY OF THE CHOEPHOROI

The *Choephoroi*, the second play of the *Oresteia* trilogy, is the story of Orestes' return to Argos, his encounter with Electra at the grave of their father, their prayer to Agamemnon, and Orestes' subsequently killing of Aigisthus and Clytaemestra.

AESCHYLUS' USE OF MYTH IN THE *CHOEPHOROI*

The *Odyssey* says that in the eighth year Orestes "came home from Athens, killed his father's murderer, the treacherous Aigisthus" and "ordered a grave mound for his mother who was hateful and for unwarlike Aigisthus." The phrase implies that Orestes also killed Clytaemestra, but no mention is made of his subsequent pursuit by the Furies, which may well have been Aeschylus' invention, as the snakes encircling their heads certainly were.[1] Sophocles and Euripides write plays about Electra, but she is a very different character from Aeschylus' Electra.

The Furies are punishers of matricides and of all who shed kindred blood.

THE RELIGIOUS CONTEXT OF THE *CHOEPHOROI*

Lamentation and Libation

"Choephoroi" are women who carry libations or drink offerings to a grave. Women in Greek culture were intimately involved in the rituals for the dead, obliged to mourn for kin by ritual wailing, to tear their hair, beat their breasts, and score their cheeks. At the grave they poured out liquids such as wine, water, oil, or the blood of sacrificed animals as "drink" for the gods beneath the earth, who included the chthonic Zeus, who often manifested himself as a snake, and for the dead that they might be strengthened, and contact might be established. Libations were accompanied by precise verbal formulas; to speak the wrong word was to open oneself to great harm.[2]

THE PLOT OF THE *CHOEPHOROI*

General Comments

The *anagnorisis* (recognition) that Aristotle describes as central to tragedy occurs at the play's end and is not an intellectual recognition but a psychological one: Orestes' vision of the Furies shows him that deeds of revenge bring torment. Perhaps it might be said that Orestes' *hamartia* (error of understanding) is the belief in the necessity of vengeance.

The plot of the *Choephoroi*, like the plot of the *Agamemnon*, is a revenge plot; but now there is no secondary victim, the avenger suffers pangs of conscience, and the plan is not hidden from the audience. Agamemnon is here remembered as faultless, and Orestes' pained words over the corpses of his victims, Aigisthus and Clytaemestra, form a deliberate contrast to Clytaemestra's exultation over the corpses in the *Agamemnon*. The action is, again, simplicity itself—a resolution is announced and carried through. Minor characters assist rather than obstruct it. Yet the effect of the play is rich and complex, and its structure highly unusual, containing, as it does, the longest single episode in all of Greek tragedy and the most rapid succession of scenes thereafter. The relationship between these two halves of the play is thematically critical, as is the relationship of this second play to the trilogy as a whole. What the *Choephoroi* demonstrates is that revenge undertaken even with the purest of motives, sanctioned by the gods, and urged by "the people" as represented by the Chorus, the Nurse, and Pylades, ends in horror. Character-drawing is "of the simplest," for Aeschylus' interest in Orestes and Electra lies only in their essential purity of heart.[3]

The graveside lament seems to ennoble what follows; the appearance of the Furies at the play's end shows us that no such ennoblement is possible. If sustained lament and prayer are inadequate to purify the act of revenge, nothing is adequate to the task. Thus, the first half of the play is vitally linked to the second half. Aeschylus' deliberate repetition in image and action of the *Agamemnon* likewise reveals that blood revenge, however well intended, remains barbaric. The *Choephoroi* proves the necessity of a radical departure from the ethic of revenge; the *Eumenides* brings that change about.

By repeating both small and large actions of the *Agamemnon* in the *Choephoroi*, Aeschylus ensures that thematic links are suggested. Just as the Watchman in the *Agamemnon* wakes Clytaemestra when he sees the signal flares, so Clytaemestra wakes herself from a nightmare and calls out for lights to be lit throughout the palace. This time her awakening is marked by horror rather than by joy. In the *Agamemnon* Clytaemestra and Agamemnon argue over how he will enter the palace. She prevails and he treads on the purple. In the *Choephoroi* Orestes and Clytaemestra argue before he drives her inside, and this argument, too, is stichomythic. She, unlike Agamemnon, goes inside knowing that death awaits her, and her entry is a direct consequence of his in the earlier play. And again there is a double murder, in this case of two guilty figures, and a display of the bodies by the killer who, instead of rejoicing, appears as a suppliant. Through such parallels as these and many more, Aeschylus not only shows causation, but also unites action across time.

Ironically, Clytaemestra's dream prompts a result opposite to the one Clytaemestra desires: a prayer not for forgiveness for her but for vengeance against her is uttered at the grave by her emissaries. And ironically, we see not one but two scenes in which Clytaemestra and Orestes enter the palace, the shift in order of entry in the second being emblematic of the larger shift in power within the play.

Setting

The *Choephoroi* has two settings: the gravesite of Agamemnon and the palace. The time is the heroic age, approximately eight years after the murder of Agamemnon. In the first half of the play, the central doors of the *skene* seem to represent a covert of trees rather than the palace entrance. The Chorus enter, as is customary, along the *parodos*, not alone but accompanied by Electra.

Dramatis Personae

Orestes	son of Agamemnon and Clytaemestra
Pylades	friend to Orestes
Electra	sister to Orestes
Chorus of Choephoroi	Trojan serving women, loyal to Electra ("Libation Bearers")
Servant	doorkeeper
Clytaemestra	queen of Argos

Nurse ("Cilissa")   servant, formerly Orestes' wet-nurse

Aigisthus   king of Argos

Scene Divisions

Prologue:	1–21	[Orestes, Pylades]
Parodos:	22–84	[Chorus of Libation Bearers, Electra *with them*]
Episode One:	85–584	[Chorus, Electra, Orestes, Pylades]
First Choral Ode:	585–651	[Chorus]
Episode Two:	652–718	[Chorus, Orestes, Pylades, Servant, Clytaemestra]
Second Choral Ode:	719–729	[Chorus]
Episode Three:	730–782	[Chorus, Nurse]
Third Choral Ode:	783–837	[Chorus]
Episode Four:	838–854	[Chorus, Aigisthus]
Fourth Choral Ode:	855–874	[Chorus]
Episode Five:	875–930	[Chorus, Servant, Clytaemestra, Orestes, Pylades]
Fifth Choral Ode:	931–975	[Chorus]
Exodos:	976–1076	[Chorus, Orestes, Pylades]

Synopsis

Prologue: 1–21   [Orestes, Pylades]

Orestes and Pylades, having returned to Argos from Phocia, approach the grave of Agamemnon. Orestes prays to Hermes and performs two ritual acts of hair cutting. In the distance he sees a group of women approaching. He and Pylades withdraw to a covert to observe the women and learn why they have come.

Parodos: 22–83   [Chorus, Electra]

A Chorus of Handmaidens of the household, dressed in black for mourning and bearing libation vessels, enter with Electra, striking themselves in ritual gestures of grief. They have been sent by the queen to appease the angry dead. They bemoan the fall of a great house and its lord.

Episode One: 84–584   [Chorus, Electra; Orestes, Pylades]

In this episode of unusual length, the Chorus advise Electra to pray for all who hate Aigisthus: herself, them, and the absent Orestes. As the women pour libations, Electra sees the locks of hair and a footprint like her own. Orestes enters, declares himself, and reveals Apollo's command that he avenge his father's death. Striking the earth, the Chorus begin the great *kommos*. At its conclusion, Orestes asks why the women have come and learns of Clytaemestra's dream of suckling a snake at her breast. Orestes realizes, as Clytaemestra has, that her dream is prophetic and that he will be her slayer. He describes his plan to gain entry to the palace and calls for the assistance, either through silence or through speech, of the women.

First Choral Ode: 585–651   [Chorus]

The Chorus sing of deadly women, the mother of Meleager, Scylla, Clytaemestra, and the women of Lemnos. The ode divorces the play from immediate time and place, and at its conclusion the setting is understood to have changed from the grave of Agamemnon to the palace.

Episode Two: 652–718   [Chorus, Orestes, Pylades,
                                     Servant, Clytaemestra]

Orestes and Pylades approach the palace and are greeted by Clytaemestra. Orestes says that they bring news that Orestes is dead. Clytaemestra grieves, welcomes the travelers, and says she will summon Aigisthus, as they enter the house.

Second Choral Ode: 719–729   [Chorus]

The Chorus assert that the hour has come for the goddess Persuasion to assist Orestes with her guile.

Episode Three: 730–782   [Chorus, Nurse]

Orestes' childhood Nurse enters weeping. She says that Clytaemestra rejoices in the report of her son's death. The Chorus convince her to alter Clytaemestra's message to Aigisthus so that he may come unarmed to the palace. The Nurse exits.

Third Choral Ode: 783–837   [Chorus]

The Chorus pray that order and right rule be restored to the house.

Episode Four: 838–854   [Chorus, Aigisthus]

Aigisthus enters from the *parodos* and moves toward the central doors of palace. He wonders whether the news of the messengers is true, or simply women's gossip; he says that he will question the messenger closely, for no one can cheat a mind like his own. With this proud claim Aigisthus exits.

Fourth Choral Ode: 855–874   [Chorus]

The Chorus begin a prayer to Zeus that is interrupted by a cry from within the house. Unable to predict who has been killed, they withdraw to one side.

Episode Five: 875–930   [Chorus, Servant, Clytaemestra, Orestes, Pylades]

A servant rushes out crying, "Aigisthus is no more." Clytaemestra enters and calls for an axe that she intends to use to kill her son. At that moment, Orestes appears in the doorway, having come from the inner room. Pylades follows. She argues that her life must be spared, as she is his mother. Orestes hesitates but is shored up in his resolve by Pylades. He drives his mother into the palace at sword point and says she will die by Aigisthus' side.

Fifth Choral Ode: 931–975   [Chorus]

The Chorus express sorrow "for these" and the hope that the fortunes of the house will change.

Exodos: 976–1076   [Chorus, Orestes, Pylades]

Orestes appears with the two bodies. He spreads out the robe used to trap his father as "witness" of his mother's evil. Of Aigisthus he simply says that he has received the adulterer's punishment as the law allows. Orestes suddenly feels himself on the brink of madness and sees before him, invisible to the Chorus, the Furies. He cries out in agony and terror. The Chorus try to calm him, but they cannot. He runs from the stage toward Apollo's shrine at Delphi. The Chorus briefly rehearse the history of the house and ask when calamity will cease.

THE FUNCTION OF THE PROLOGUE[4]

Aeschylus' immediate emphasis on the piety of Orestes is critical to the purposes of this play and of the trilogy as a whole. The *Choephoroi* begins with Orestes' prayer to Hermes and to his dead father to hear him. Verbs such as "beseech" and "cry unto" reveal the depth of his emotion. In fact, the prologue is specially designed to show this second avenger in a way that Clytaemestra is never shown—as without guile. Her motives are always hidden; his are not. She is never seen crying out in grief to her daughter as he does here to his father. She acts for herself, not as agent for another; he will not act alone but rather, he hopes, in concert with the will of his father and the will of the gods. And, in addition to his words, he performs an act of double piety, placing on the grave two locks of hair cut from his head.

The cutting of the hair is a masterful stroke by Aeschylus. There are two occasions on which young men cut a lock of hair: when attaining one's growth, and when mourning one's dead. In the *Iliad*, Achilles cuts a lock of his hair and places it on the grave of Patroclus, whom he mourns as kin. Orestes, in the first action of the play, offers a lock of hair as "return" made by children for their rearing. Immediately thereafter, he offers a second lock, this time as "token of grief." In an ordered world the two offerings should not coincide, and their conflation rouses the audience to an immediate shared sorrow. The lock for growth should be made in the presence of a living and proud father, and the ceremonial coming into adulthood that it represents should not be immediately succeeded by, and equated with, a ceremony of mourning as if adulthood and grief are one. That the locks of hair offered on the tomb have the additional dramatic function of revealing Orestes' identity to Electra is not thematically accidental, for his destiny is one in which adulthood means sorrow. In practical terms, for locks to be cut requires the use onstage of a dagger. Orestes is thus associated with weaponry, but with weaponry in a pious purpose—an emblem of how he would wish to regard the task ahead.

Cutting the hair for growth signifies, for most, the time of leaving home and entering the harsher world. For Orestes, the motion is reversed: having been driven from home while still a child, he now returns home, and the home to which he returns is a place not of maternal love but of savagery and danger.[5]

MORAL CONSCIENCE IN ORESTES AND ELECTRA

That Orestes hesitates when the moment to kill Clytaemestra comes and that he is tormented afterwards suggest a new kind of moral conscience.

Unlike Clytaemestra, Orestes speaks, with pain, of the necessity of his deed and knows that his "victory is a pollution unenviable." In addition, his references to the robe and to his deed in ever more judicial terms suggest that he sees himself on trial in a way that his mother never saw herself. His language is legalistic: the robe "in the day of judgment" is to be present as his "witness" that "with just cause" he pursued his mother's death. He speaks of Aigisthus as having "suffered the adulterer's punishment as the law allows."

Electra's character is also marked by moral purity that the reactions of the Chorus throw into relief. The women embody the culture's norms: they are decent and kind, and yet they tell her and Orestes repeatedly that it is right to pray for vengeance and that it is just that the killer be killed. She is younger than they, but finer in her moral sensibility. That sensibility is expressed at the beginning when she cannot utter the lies her mother has enjoined, when she asks whether she should pray for the coming of an avenger (*dikephoron*) or a judge (*dikasten*),[6] when she asks the Chorus whether it is pious (*eusebe*) to pray for the death of killers, and when she prays that, in return for these libations, Agamemnon may grant that she be "purer of heart and hand" than her mother. Even as the emotion of the scene intensifies, Electra does not abandon the concept of justice. Her cry is "O ye gods, decide aright the plea of right." She, in a sense, belongs to the age of the Court of the Areopagus, an age that is coming, but has not yet dawned.

THE FUNCTION OF SECONDARY CHARACTERS

The Nurse Cilissa

Having heard the false report of his death, the Nurse Cilissa enters grieving for her "beloved Orestes" whom she "took to nurse from his mother at birth" and whose linens she washed.

Aeschylus creates the character of the Nurse expressly for this moment in the play. She is sent to summon Aigisthus to the palace, but the scene needs no such summoner: were Aigisthus simply to appear on stage, announcing that he had been told there were visitors in the palace, neither his arrival nor the absence of an armed guard accompanying him would be noted. Aeschylus specifically draws our attention to the fact that the Chorus and the Nurse countermand Clytaemestra's instruction in order to indicate that Aigisthus and Clytaemestra are hated by the common people, and that Orestes, unlike the avengers of the first play, is acting in a way that all around him fully sanction.

When the Nurse remembers the infant she cared for, we are presented with a different kind of world, one not of unnatural murder following unnatural murder, but of natural affections, even of natural bodily functions of babies, so as to emphasize the enormity of the unnaturalness at Argos. Memory need not be of agonized events or fraught with regret or sorrow; memory can be pleasant, even humorous, and feelings can be very simple: one can love a child simply because one was needed by that child and was constantly changing his diapers. And the Nurse's memory of Orestes does something else as well: it sets up a contrast between the helpless infant and the avenger that that infant has become. Thus, she functions as a reminder of another sort of world that has been lost. The unusual expedient of endowing so secondary a character with a name, "Cilissa," is itself a sign of Aeschylus' wish to emphasize the quotidian nature of the world she represents.

The Nurse has a further function: because she says that Clytaemestra secretly laughs at the report of her son's death, Aeschylus makes Clytaemestra's expressions of grief to her guests sound sincere and at the same time heightens our sense of her canniness and dishonesty. Finally, Aeschylus introduces the Nurse that the audience may measure the real mother who secretly rejoices in the news of her son's death and later, finding him alive, calls for an axe with which to kill him against the surrogate mother who truly grieves. And when the Nurse says that she took him from his mother at birth to nurse, she undermines Clytaemestra's later claim that she nursed Orestes at her own breast.

The Chorus

Insofar as the Chorus function as dramatic characters, they show that the common people chafe under the tyranny of Aigisthus and Clytaemestra, are repelled by their evil deeds, and fully support the revenge undertaken by Orestes. Thus, Orestes is understood to act with the encouragement and approval of all those around him. That the play takes its title from these women emphasizes that very thing. Yet, Aeschylus indicates, even wholehearted communal support is not sufficient to make Orestes' deed correct.

IMAGERY

Of Snakes and the Dead

Among the repeated images that are embedded in the language of the first two plays, in anticipation of their being made dramatically explicit in the third, are images of blood and snakes. The snake is a chthonic creature, for it comes from under rocks and from holes in the earth and raises itself to strike. Thus, symbolically, it comes from the world of the dead, and so

Clytaemestra's dream is rightly interpreted as the anger of the dead rising above ground to kill her. In this regard, the lie that Orestes tells of his own death is a brilliant device on Aeschylus' part, for Orestes, once admitted to the house, is as a dead man restored to life who, in exact imitation of the spirit of Agamemnon and in exact fulfillment of Clytaemestra's dream, rises from the grave to slay the living.

Of Mixed Things

Aeschylus uses images of blood substituting for or mixed into other liquids, and these images suggest unnaturalness, contamination, and horror. In the *Agamemnon* Clytaemestra imagines rain and sperm transformed to blood when she speaks in exultation of blood spurting on her from Agamemnon's body, like rain on the fertile earth. Perhaps in a retributive parallel, or perhaps unlinked to the earlier image, she dreams in the *Choephoroi* of milk issuing from her breast mixed with clotted blood as she nurses a fanged snake.

The Furies, as described by Aeschylus, are themselves monstrous combinations: they are both women and snakes. They are real monsters, as their appearance in the *Eumenides* makes clear, but they are also projections of Orestes' guilty imagination and, as such, they stand for both his mother and himself. They are his mother because they come in her stead to haunt him, and because they contain the blood and snakes of her dream; they are himself because he has been the snake drawing milk, as an infant, and drawing blood, as an avenger, at Clytaemestra's breast, and because snakes and blood characterize the Furies. If they are he, then his own guilt pursues him. He is monstrous in his own mind. And because they are not one but many, Aeschylus indicates the enormity of the guilt Orestes feels. As the Furies writhe and dart within inches of Orestes' body, Orestes' guilt is seen as inescapable.

ASPECTS OF STAGECRAFT

The Central *Kommos*

This *kommos* of episode one is a three-part lament, involving Orestes, Electra, and the Chorus, and a choral sequence of complexity that matches the *parodos* of the Agamemnon. In a sense, there is a fourth figure in this scene, the silent auditor Agamemnon, whose "answer" is understood to be found in the success of the subsequent enterprise.

The *kommos* is often repetitive, and its very repetitiveness imbues it with ritual power. Such repetition is absolutely necessary, for it is part of the goodness of Orestes and Electra that they are not ready to act until they are convinced that their father and the gods have heard them and that they are acting as his and their agents, utterly unlike the avenging pair in the *Agamemnon*. In addition, and movingly, the brother and sister are reluctant to conclude the *kommos*, even when the Chorus declare it sufficient, both because they long to release the grief each has held inside for so long and because, once Orestes takes action, they may never again see each other.

Once the formal dirge begins, neither Orestes nor Electra responds to each other except when Electra, recounting her own confinement, tells her brother to "Hear my tale and grave it on thy heart" (450). The Chorus echo her, saying, "Let it sink deep into thine ears" (451), both their image and hers replicating the penetrative trope of the scene itself—into the earth, into the heart, into the ears. Instead of speaking to each other, Orestes and Electra speak to the dead king, to the gods, and to the powers beneath the earth. Nonetheless, each builds on what the other has said. Their parallel cries, peripherally antiphonal, show the intensity of their individual efforts to contact the dead and the urgency of their desire to do Agamemnon's will.

Its emotional force, intense rhythms, and broad choreographic effects make this scene the most powerful and compelling moment of the entire trilogy, according to scholars who have seen it performed well. At the conclusion of the *kommos*, Orestes and Electra assert that the victory will be Agamemnon's. Whether such assertions are self-delusions masking a desire for revenge is a question that remains unanswered in this play.

The Use of Two Settings

When the scene shifts in the second half of the play to the palace, the funeral mound of Agamemnon, which has been the choreographic and emotional center of the preceding episode, cannot disappear, given the continuous action and complete physical exposure of the Greek theatre. It remains visible to the audience, but it is understood to be far off. It thus becomes emblematic, a visual reminder of Clytaemestra and Aigisthus' guilt, a visual sign that Agamemnon has "heard" the prayers of his children and will now send his aid. In other words, the tomb is not a theatrical liability, but a means of deepening the meaning of the subsequent action.

Costume and Theme

Before the slave women reach the orchestra, Orestes sees them and remarks that they are dressed in black for mourning. At the end of the play, in a terrible parallel, the Furies he sees crowding round him are also black-robed. Blood drips from their eyes. When the women of the Chorus enter, they themselves draw attention to streaks of blood glistening on their cheeks, part of the ritual mourning ordered by Clytaemestra. Aeschylus draws attention through dialogue to the robes and cheeks of the Chorus, for, although they and the Furies seem utterly dissimilar—one group human and real, the other demonic and imagined, one group kindly disposed toward Orestes, the other hating him—their appearances reveal that they are not unrelated. Even if, as Sommerstein argues, the faces of the Furies are dark rather than white, on their faces and the faces of the Chorus are streaks of blood.[7] Both groups of women represent the spirit of vengeance, for the Chorus have been steadfast in urging and justifying vengeance to both Electra and Orestes. Perhaps the similitude suggests that the desire for vengeance may appear relatively harmless at first.

The Display of the Death Robe

Orestes asks that the robe be spread out so that Helios, the sun, may see "the impious work of my own mother" (986). When the robe is displayed in the tableau of the *Agamemnon*, along with the body of Agamemnon and the body of Cassandra, it is displayed as a murder weapon—or one of the murder weapons—the other being an axe or sword. Clytaemestra shows it with pride. To her it represents her guile and cleverness, and in every way diminishes the great warrior king caught in its toils like a hunted and witless animal. And, because of the images in the choral odes of the *Agamemnon*, it also appears as a retributive object: he who "threw a net" around Troy is felled by an open-weave robe that is a net.

The death of Clytaemestra in the *Choephoroi* has nothing to do with a net, and thus it is entirely unexpected that, when Orestes appears in tableau with the bodies, as his mother appeared in tableau in the earlier play, he brandishes the robe. Now it means something else, and that it can mean something further is a tribute to the invention and depth of Aeschylus' art. It is an evocative object. Orestes calls it "evidence" of her crimes, evidence that will speak as "witness" in his "defense." That is its rational, lawyerly function, but more than its rational role is at work here. Vellacott's translation makes clear the psychological force that the net has for Orestes: "since I may not see his body to this treacherous web [I offer my lament]."[8] The net is all that remains to Orestes of his father—it is what his father touched last, and it has his father's blood on it. It also killed his father and is, thus, a thing Orestes both hates and loves. It releases in him a deep and full grief "for him … for deed and punishment and for the whole race." Of the 42 lines Orestes speaks here, 26 are about the net and only 7 describe what he did. How different this is from Clytaemestra's lengthy and exultant description of the actual deed of killing Agamemnon. At this second display of the net, Aeschylus, as he did in the great choral odes in the *Agamemnon*, moves us back in time, not only to the action of the preceding play but further back to the years in which Clytaemestra wove the net, for not until now is it clearly understood to have been her laborious handiwork. We glimpse now, at the moment of their deaths, the monstrous planning of the pair, her patient, steady hatred, this radical distortion of the woman's role of weaver within the household, and that never in the months and perhaps years of its construction were there second thoughts—and our sense of the horror of their deed expands. Aeschylus has saved this earliest detail about the net for last.

NOTES

1. Robert Fagles and W. B. Stanford, "The Serpent and the Eagle," introduction to *Aeschylus: The Oresteia*, translated by Robert Fagles (New York: Penguin Books, 1977) p. 36.

2. Walter Burkert, *Greek Religion*, translated by John Raffan (Oxford: Basil Blackwell Publisher; Cambridge: Harvard University Press, 1985), pp. 192–194.

3. H.D.F. Kitto, *Form and Meaning in Drama* (London: Methuen & Co. Ltd., 1956), p. 47.

4. The opening page(s) of the prologue of the *Choephoroi* were lost in antiquity. Lines 1–9 have been reconstructed from quotes in Aristophanes' the *Frogs* and in other sources. From line 10 on, where Orestes first notices the approaching *Choephoroi*, the text is continuous and uncorrupted.

5. Froma I. Zeitlin, "The Dynamics of Misogyny: Myth and Mythmaking in the *Oresteia*," (originally published, Buffalo, N.Y.: *Arethusa*, 2, 1978), Harold Bloom, ed., *Modern Critical Interpretations: Aeschylus' The Oresteia* (New Haven, Conn.: Chelsea House Publishers, 1988), pp. 47–71.

6. Kitto, p. 41.

7. Alan H. Sommerstein, *Aeschylus: Eumenides, Cambridge Greek and Latin Classics Series* (Cambridge: Cambridge University Press, 1989), p. 91. He argues that the Furies' black masks and black robes are contrasted, in the *Eumenides*, with the whiteness of Orestes' suppliant-wreath and the whiteness of the Pythia's robe.

8. *Aeschylus: The Oresteian Trilogy*, translated by Philip Vellacott (New York: Penguin Books, 1959).

3

Aeschylus
The *Eumenides*
(458 B.C.)

SUMMARY OF THE *EUMENIDES*

The *Eumenides* is the story of the trial of Orestes for matricide before a court of Athenian citizens at which Orestes is acquitted and the Furies agree to become resident deities guarding Athens.

AESCHYLUS' USE OF MYTH IN THE *EUMENIDES*

The myth of the *Eumenides* is an origin myth of the first court of law, the Areopagus, and of the Panathenaiac festival. The Areopagus was both council and court. In Aeschylus' myth, it is created by Athene to try the first case of murder. Midsummer, Athens celebrated the Panathenaia, the holiday of Athene's birth. Citizens of all ages, children, and *metics* (resident aliens) marched in formal and joyous procession. Aeschylus imagines the torchlight procession that ends the *Eumenides* as the first Panathenaia, in which the Furies, newly welcomed to the city, wear the scarlet robes of the *metics* and in which Athene is honored for reconciling the old religion with Olympian worship. The place given the Furies is a reminder that the new city "cannot progress by exterminating its old order of life" but must instead "absorb and use it."[1]

The transformation of the Furies from avengers of those who shed kindred blood to protective deities of the city is reflected in the new name by which they are known, "Eumenides" ("kindly ones"). By the play's end the definition of "kindred" has been broadened to mean *polis*, all of whose citizens are defined as "kindred," and the vengeance of the Furies is directed toward external enemies of the city.

The principle that "the doer must suffer" is no longer axiomatic; judgment must await a trial; verdicts depend on assessments of motivation and consequence, as well as on proof of action. Human jurors replace vengeful Furies, each juror has one vote, and in the case of an evenly divided jury, the court errs on the side of mercy and acquits. The myth of the *Eumenides* is, in this sense, the myth of the beginning of civilization.

THE HISTORICAL CONTEXT OF THE *EUMENIDES*

The Religious Context

Sanctuary was obtained by touching the altar or statue of a god, which rendered the suppliant inviolate. Thus, although the Chorus surround Orestes when he kneels at Athene's altar, they cannot physically touch him. For a state or an individual not to grant a suppliant's request was impiety.

The ancient shrine of Apollo at Delphi offered advice but did not purify. Orestes says he has undergone rites of purification but must also be exonerated by a court of law before he can rejoin human society without taint. Murderers were regarded as carriers of pollution requiring them to be kept apart from all other members of the community.

The Delphic priestess, the *Pythia*, served the god for life. She dressed as a young girl and, while seated over a chasm within the cave and enveloped by the rising vapors, fell into self-induced trances and issued prophetic responses to those who sought Apollo's counsel.

The Political and Social Context

Athens and Argos formed an alliance in 462 B.C., four years before the *Oresteia*; Aeschylus adapts the fact of that alliance to the purposes of the *Eumenides*. When acquitted, Orestes promises a peace between Argos and Athens that is to last for all time. Unlike the war between Argos and Troy that involved all of Greece and that began the cycle of tragedy for the sons of Atreus, the alliance that Orestes creates promises peace and amity between states. It also represents a response of gratitude on the part of a guest—for Orestes, a guest of Athens, was cleansed of guilt there—rather than a response of ingratitude by the guest, Paris, in the palace of Menelaus. Thus, in two ways, Orestes' promise reverses the action that begins the trilogy.[2] As with the Panathenaia and the court of the Areopagus, Aeschylus links mythic past with the Athenian present in ways that celebrate civilized progress.

The *Eumenides* suggests that wisdom and right judgmnet are arrived at largely through social discourse and the institutions of democracy. *Pathei mathos* ("through suffering, learn"), a phrase that appears in the great *parodos* of the *Agamemnon,* expresses an ethos that is particularly "Greek": through such suffering as deeds of revenge bring, society slowly and collectively learns what impulses it must avoid.

THE PLOT OF THE *EUMENIDES*

General Comments

The *Eumenides* is a revenge plot in which revenge is twice threatened and twice abandoned. Its two parts are inextricably linked to each other, for the resolution of the first crisis creates the second crisis.

The stage action consists primarily of efforts at persuasion: in the first half of the play, the Furies and Apollo try to persuade the court to reach particular verdicts; in the second half, Athene tries to persuade the Furies to abandon their rage. These dramatized arguments reflect the possibility of choice, and thus the release of humanity from unexamined premises that have led to disaster. The Furies, for example, make a choice that they did not even know they had.

The protagonist of the *Eumenides* is the Chorus itself. Their rage drives the action of both halves of the play; it is they who experience *anagnorisis,* and it is they whose radical *peripeteia* provides the audience with its extraordinary sense of *catharsis.* They are the focus of the horrified *Pythia* at the play's beginning and of the ceremonial procession at the play's end.

The Unities of Aristotle

Although Aristotle's *Poetics* has convinced some readers that Greek tragedies are built on unity of time, place, and action, that is not so in either the *Eumenides* or the *Choephoroi.* The *Eumenides* has not only two settings, but also a significant and undefined amount of time separating the action in those two settings, for the Furies say that, after leaving Delphi, they have sought Orestes "over every region of the earth." In the *Agamemnon* the time between the sighting of the beacon signals and the arrival of Agamemnon is collapsed. What Aristotle does do, brilliantly, is draw attention to the essential compression of Greek drama and to the tragic effect that such compression produces.

Setting

The setting at the beginning of the play is outside the cave of the Delphic oracle; thereafter, it is the court atop the Hill of Ares in Athens. A third, imputed setting, the place to which the Furies go, is the cave at the foot of the Hill of Ares. Thus, the "old" is geographically the basis of the "new," and the establishment of justice through law "rests upon" the transformed tradition of vengeance.³ The time is the heroic age, shortly after the action of the *Choephoroi*.

Dramatis Personae

Pythia	priestess of Apollo at Delphi
Apollo	
Orestes	son and murderer of Clytaemestra
Clytaemestra Eidolon	ghost of Clytaemestra
Chorus of Eumenides	the Furies
Athene	goddess of Athens
Jurors of Athens	
Citizens of Athens	

Scene Divisions

Prologue:	1–139	[*Pythia*, Apollo, Orestes, Ghost of Clytaemestra]
Parodos:	140–177	[Chorus]
Episode One:	178–243	[Chorus, Apollo, Orestes]
Epi-Parodos and First Choral Ode	245–396	[Chorus, Orestes]
Episode Two:	397–489	[Chorus, Orestes, Athene]
Second Choral Ode:	490–565	[Chorus, Orestes *onstage*]
Episode Three:	566–777	[Chorus, Orestes, Athene, Jurors, Apollo]
Third Choral Ode:	778–891	[Chorus, Athene, Jurors *onstage*]
Episode Four:	892–915	[Chorus, Athene, Jurors *onstage*]
Exodos:	916–1047	[Chorus, Athene, Citizens of Athens, Jurors]

Synopsis

Prologue:	1–139	[*Pythia*, Apollo, Orestes, Ghost of Clytaemestra]

After an opening prayer, the *Pythia* enters the shrine. Immediately thereafter, she rushes out, terror-stricken, declaring that inside is a suppliant, his hands covered in blood, and with him, a throng of monstrous sleeping women, such as she has never seen before. Apollo and Orestes enter from the shrine. Apollo tells Orestes to fly from this place to Athens; there, judges (*dikastas*) will release him from his distress. Apollo calls on Hermes to guide Orestes as they exit separately. The Ghost of the dead Clytaemestra appears. Enraged at their sloth, she tries to rouse the sleeping Furies to pursue Orestes and departs.

Parodos: 140–177   [Chorus]

The Furies issue from the shrine and, seeing Orestes has disappeared, accuse Apollo of stealing their prey.

Episode One: 178–243   [Chorus, Apollo, Orestes]

Apollo orders the Furies away, saying they belong in primitive lands, not at Delphi. The basic arguments of the play are laid out in an exchange in which a distinction is made by the Furies, and rejected by Apollo, between children who kill mothers and wives who kill husbands. His responses are scornful, theirs, angry. The Chorus and Apollo exit in different directions. Orestes then reenters, moves immediately to the altar in the center of the orchestra where a statue of Athene has been placed, and prays. The setting has changed from Delphi to Athens.

Epi-Parodos (second *parodos*) and
    First Choral Ode ("Binding Song"):   245–396   [Chorus, Orestes]

The Furies have "smelled" the blood on Orestes and have followed his scent to Athens. They say they will drag his living body to Hades that he may pay for his murdered mother's agony. For the next hundred lines they sing what is known as the "Binding Song," which holds him hostage at the altar.

Episode Two: 397–489   [Chorus, Orestes, Athene]

Athene enters. She asks who the figures are, and the Furies and Orestes identify themselves. Both agree to her adjudication of the dispute. Athene states the dilemma facing her city: to please the Furies is to reject a suppliant; not to please the Furies is to incur blight on the fields and the land. Thus, Athene adds to the question of motive, which she has already raised, consideration of likely consequence. She finds the matter before her too difficult for a single judge and will "appoint judges of homicide" and will "establish a tribunal to endure for all time." She exits.

Second Choral Ode: 490–565   [Chorus, Orestes *onstage*]

The Chorus fear that if Orestes is acquitted, people will feel empowered to act with license, and woeful deeds will be done by children to parents. This ode presents the Chorus not as barbaric but as protectors of important values that underpin civilization.

Episode Three: 566–777   [Chorus, Orestes, Athene,
                                                 Jurors, Apollo]

The Jurors, led by Athene, enter; Apollo appears as witness and advocate for Orestes, and the trial begins. Orestes admits his crime, but claims the evil of his mother as extenuation. Apollo speaks in his defense and is cross-examined by the Furies who ask how Zeus, who attacked his own father, Cronos, cares for the honor due a father but not for the honor due a mother. Apollo tries to respond to their *ad hominem* charge: the bonds in which Zeus bound Cronos might be undone, but Agamemnon's death was final, he tells them. It is just what the Furies, who turn out to be clever litigators, would wish him to have said, for they reply that Clytaemestra's death is likewise final. Apollo has unwittingly reduced the ground of his defense. He rallies. The battle is entirely verbal but exciting in its shifts of power. Athene then charges the jury. She speaks of the importance of "fear," as have the Furies, and emphasizes the grave importance of the task. As balloting proceeds in stately fashion, the Furies and Apollo descend into squabbling, as litigants sometimes do, lending the Jurors further dignity by contrast. Athene votes for Orestes, ballots are counted, and she announces his acquittal, saying that "the numbers of the casts are equal." Apollo leaves. Orestes pledges eternal friendship between his city of Argos and Athens and departs to reclaim his patrimony.

Third Choral Ode: 778–891   [Chorus, Athene, Jurors *onstage*]

In *epirrhema* (the alternation of choral lyric with iambic speech from an actor) the Furies express their anger and threaten the city, while Athene each time replies with courtesy until they finally respond to her offers.

Episode Four: 892–915   [Chorus, Athene, Jurors *onstage*]

The Jurors accept a permanent and honored home as guardians of Athens who will bless the land.

Exodos: 916–1047   [Chorus, Athene, Citizens of
                                             Athens, Jurors]

Athene and the Chorus, in *epirrhema,* bless the land. Athene summons the torchlight procession that will accompany the Furies to their new home beneath the earth. Attendants apparel the Chorus in festal robes of scarlet and, with Athene at its head, the great procession forms and escorts the Eumenides off the stage.

THE FUNCTION OF THE PROLOGUE

The Prologue begins by emphasizing harmony among the chthonic gods and the gods of Olympus. The *Pythia's* description of the history of the shrine, consisting of the peaceful transition of power from female to male gods, is Aeschylus' adaptation of less peaceful versions of its history.[4] Perhaps Aeschylus intends a comparison to the description in the *Agamemnon* of a different godly succession, Uranus and Cronos overthrown by their sons, to emphasize the ideal of harmony toward which the trilogy moves.

That the *Pythia,* who is accustomed to the uncanny, is so horrified as to rush out on all fours is a sign of how unendurable and how unsanctified the Furies are. Aeschylus uses the *Pythia's* response to measure what Orestes suffers and how fearless and gracious Athene is.

The face and robes of the Ghost of Clytaemestra register the discolorations of death, the robes also being torn and bloodstained where they were pierced by Orestes' sword. The phantom is understood to be the image that the sleeping Furies dream. Aeschylus thus shows what horrors exist in the mind of the Furies and what the impulse of vengeance looks like.

Clytaemestra's scene is both hideous and comic. Again and again she tries to wake the Furies, and all they do is snore, twitch, and call out, dreaming the pursuit that they are not undertaking. The scene is a kind of mocking echo of the great *kommos* of invocation in the *Choephoroi.* Both call forth energy for revenge. Is the Clytaemestra scene anything more than a way of showing the preceding *kommos* for the ignoble thing it did not appear to be and yet was? Other parallels, like the dreams that begin both plays, suggest that Aeschylus intends comparisons that insist on steady revisions of judgment. Vengeance is now embodied in a corpse, suggesting that vengeance is as horrid as death and as deadly to its possessor.

THE RELATIONSHIP BETWEEN THE ARGUMENTS AND THE VOTE

Apollo says that mothers are not parents to their children, and the Furies say that marriage bonds are insignificant; thus, both sides deny central human claims. In fact, Apollo as litigant is less than forthright, not just in arguing for male descent but also in urging the Jurors to ignore their oath and simply follow Zeus' will, which he says he represents, and in offering them what almost amounts to a bribe. Despite Apollo's effort to influence the vote improperly, there are votes in his favor, indicating how thoroughly this Jury apprehends its charge. Not only must the Jury not be bribed, but it must listen calmly even to a litigant who would attempt to bribe it, and, if that litigant's case has merit, it must nevertheless rule in his favor.

The tie vote is, in a sense, a recognition of the inadequacy of both positions. When Athene votes for Orestes, she votes as *Athene Polias*, Athene goddess of the *polis*, because the city and its continuation are contingent on civil institutions and contracted relationships that, like marriage, "link two people of different blood."[5] If the Jury is to be regarded as a single entity whose collective judgment finds good and bad on each side, rather than as six individuals entirely supportive of one side and six individuals entirely supportive of the other side,[6] Apollo wins despite the inadequate parts of his argument, rather than because of them. The weakness of Apollo's argument is suggested by the fact that Athenian law honored the bond between mother and child. For example, "a half-brother and half-sister could marry if they were children of the same father, but not if they were children of the same mother."[7]

The acquittal of Orestes, rather than a sign of support for Apollo's argument for paternity, seems to reflect the view of both male and female characters within the trilogy that the killing of a king and the destruction of marriage are not simply private but societal wrongs. Both the female Chorus of the *Choephoroi* and the male Chorus of the *Agamemnon* decry Clytaemestra's deed, and Cassandra, Electra, and the Nurse are horrified by it.[8]

ATHENE'S METHODS OF PERSUASION

After the Furies become the city's honored guardians rather than its enemies, Athene expresses gratitude to Persuasion (*Peitho*) who "kept ever watch o'er my tongue and lips when I encountered their fierce refusal." Her techniques consist of graduated questions, repetition of points, and recognition and reapplication of the Furies' own premises. She states her purposes openly and holds back irritation. In contrast, the Chorus of the *Choephoroi* pray to *Peitho* to assist Orestes "with guile" as he enters the palace and Clytaemestra convinces Agamemnon that she intends honor when she intends murder. In the third play of the trilogy, the art of persuasion, like so much else, is transformed from a weapon of deceit into a source of amity.

Athene's tone and language to the Furies stand in marked contrast to those of the *Pythia* and Apollo. On first seeing the Furies, Athene registers astonishment but not fear or loathing, and then cautions herself against "speaking ill of one's fellow-creature" who may be innocent. She asks the Furies and Orestes who they are and what they seek. Such identical value-neutral questions convince the Furies she is fair, and indeed she is. She does not try to catch them in a contradiction, as Apollo had immediately tried to do. When she criticizes them for demanding that the case turn on whether Orestes killed, rather than on why he killed, they say, "Well then, question him and pronounce righteous judgment." They have, in other words, placed their case under her jurisdiction. She then does something extraordinary: she asks if they truly will do so. This courteous opportunity for retraction overcomes any lingering reservations; in addition, her question elicits from them a second, corroborating affirmation: "We pay you this deserved respect in return for the deserved respect." The line is critical, for what the Furies are saying is that the principle of like for like that has until now been expressed in blood for blood also means the return of good for good, courtesy for courtesy. It is on this principle of equity that Athene fashions her later persuasion. As she charges the Jury, Athene says Reverence and Fear shall keep them from doing wrong. In this, the Furies hear their own words repeated.

When acquittal is announced, the Furies curse Athens and promise their venom will drop on its soil and nothing will grow, for "Intolerable are the wrongs I have suffered." Again and again they cry out that the "younger gods" have ridden down "the ancient laws." Athene responds with a deliberate and respectful reference to age, saying "I will bear with thy wrathful mood since thou art mine elder, and in that respect thou hast no doubt wisdom greater than I." In the phrase "I will bear with" she also conveys to them, without threat, that she is restraining the power of Zeus' thunderbolts, but that the power exists. They continue to say exactly the same thing in identical stanzas, an indication that they are hearing nothing that is said to them; she repeats the same thing in different ways: "I will not weary ... that thou mayst never say that thou, an ancient goddess, was by me, a younger goddess ... dishonored." The graciousness of her unwearied repetition touches them, as does the articulation of shared values. In addition, she offers them a share of her domain, saying "thou shalt dwell with me."

Most powerfully, Athene persuades them by reapplying their governing principle, "to him that doeth, it shall be done by" (*Cho.*, 313). She promises that if they bestow good upon the land, they will receive honor from it. Athene's offers gradually change the ground of argument, and the Furies can no longer see themselves as injured by Athens. They find that they have two choices, neither of which is cursing the land: they may stay in the land with honor, or they may leave it. Athens has replaced the ill of its verdict with the good of its offer, and it would not, Athene argues, be "just" to return ill for good. Honor no longer seems to demand doing injury. In their crises of decision in the earlier plays, neither Agamemnon nor Orestes could find another option. Options do exist, this play asserts, and the Furies choose to return good for good.

Athene's persuasion is so thorough that the Furies now use stichomythia for comity rather than contention. After bestowing on the land the blessings Athene advises, they themselves pray to the Fates "that lovely maidens may live each to find her mate." The completeness of their reversal is expressed by the fact that they who denied the validity of marriage oaths become protectors of marriage. Rather than blight the land they will ensure its fertility and receive forever first fruit offerings, tokens of both agricultural and marital fruitfulness, from the people of Athens. Their prayer, that there be no faction in the city, echoes and reverses their ancient roles, for they say "may the dust not drink the black blood of its people." Athene's courteous, honest, and wise words persuade the Furies to eternal benevolence. Her goal has been nothing less than the establishment of civilization and the securing of the *polis*, and her means to those ends have themselves been supremely civilized.

THEME IN THE *ORESTEIA*

The tragedy of the *Oresteia* is, in a sense, a cognitive tragedy of the confusion of categories, in which choice is conflated with necessity, one's own will is conflated with the will of the gods, and no clear boundary is maintained between piety and impiety.

Boundaries between pious and impious action are repeatedly transgressed in the *Agamemnon*. For example, incense on the city altars ostensibly celebrates Agamemnon's homecoming but actually celebrates his imminent death. The murderous deeds of Atreus and the equally murderous deeds of Clytaemestra make permeable the boundary between house and human shambles. Iphigenia is conflated with a sacrificial beast at Aulis. Things that should be inviolate are touched or trod underfoot: the carpet, the virgin priestess of Apollo, and the marriage bed. In the *Choephoroi*, the Chorus reveal that the very body of the dead, which at death belongs to the god of death, has been desecrated. The same figure who can dispatch mourners to a gravesite can call for an axe with which to hack her child. The same figure who can cut locks of hair can consecrate himself to vengeance. Categories are not yet clear, and the suffering is great. The third play begins with what seems a graphic conflation of holy with unholy things. Yet, as suppliant in the Delphic cave and beside the statue of Athene, Orestes is safe although terrified. Even the hideous Furies, who have dared to enter Apollo's shrine, respect the suppliant in a way that Agamemnon did not when Iphigenia cried to him and in a way that Clytaemestra did not when she saw Cassandra wearing the garments and emblems of the god. There is something more blatant and yet already less evil at work here, but it is not yet clear how strong that new thing is.

The second great area of tragic confusion occurs when one conflates one's own will with the will of the gods. Doing so is a way of rationalizing one's deepest desires. When Agamemnon assumes that Zeus' will is behind his expedition and says that he acts in "obedience" to the will of Zeus, Agamemnon fails to ask himself whether vanity rather than piety has convinced him. After all, his sense of personal honor, as we see from his appearance onstage, is considerable, and that honor is twice threatened—first by the abduction, and then by the potential embarrassment of a failed enterprise. Clytaemestra can invoke *Zeus Teleios* ("Zeus Accomplisher") when she prepares to murder Agamemnon. Zeus appears to hear, but his *teleios* is beyond her comprehension when she thinks that killing Agamemnon closes the circle, and even beyond her comprehension when, in the *Choephoroi*, facing her son's sword, she understands that her deed of murder has been repaid. She cannot imagine what will follow: the shining beauty of the Court of Law and the raising up of humanity from brute law to civilization. That is what Zeus Accomplisher aims at, and the long arc from Troy to that moment is nothing that those who brought Troy down could have foreseen as Zeus' ultimate purpose. Clytaemestra imagines that there is no gulf between the gods' will and her own. In fact, to some extent she imagines the gods' will as deriving from her own. When asked by the Chorus how she has learned so immediately that Troy has fallen, she replies that her messenger is the god of Fire, Hephaistos himself. When she prepares to enter the palace to kill Agamemnon, she calls out, in triumphant confidence, "*Zeu Teleie*, accomplish these prayers of mine! Let your mind bring these things to pass. It is your will." She describes her deed as holy in that she has "sacrificed yon man" to the Erinyes (the Furies).

Speaking of Agamemnon's spurted blood, she likens herself to the earth receiving heavenly rain, and thus to Gaia sown by Uranus. Clytaemestra's certainty that there is no gap between her purpose and the divine purpose is based not on vanity but on boldness. What Aeschylus will show, with growing emphasis, is that when ego impedes judgment, one has no way of knowing what the gods desire. In this play it is only Cassandra, who wants nothing and seeks neither honor nor vengeance, who can see plainly what the gods intend. In the *Choephoroi*, the problem is more difficult, for evil deeds, Aeschylus suggests, may be done from good motives, as well as from evil ones. As the next play makes clear, Orestes' guide, Apollo, does not seek vengeance, as Orestes believes he does, but rather civil order predicated on marriage and the family, on patrimony properly handed down, and on benevolent rule.

A third category of tragic confusion in the *Oresteia* is choice conflated with necessity. As the text makes clear, Agamemnon reduces his view of his options at Aulis to a single choice, which he then calls "necessity." He repeats this course when urged by Clytaemestra to walk on purple, an action that she takes as replicating symbolically the Aulis deed. It is not convenient, once one has made a choice, to keep in mind the other possibility that was rejected. Orestes does, and he is agonized. It takes a person of exceptional moral rigor to choose a course of action and, rather than grow accustomed to it, continue to regard honestly its negative aspects. Not only is Agamemnon not such a man, but he is not even a man of ordinary moral sensibility. He does not wait until his child is dead to dismiss her from his mind; he does that while she is still alive and before him. Thus, he "prays" to the god that the sacrifice win favor, he instructs his henchmen to place a bit in her mouth to silence her, and he orders that she be held aloft like a goat to the slaughter. The text presents the moment of decision through a deponent verb form because Agamemnon chooses to believe he is compelled to a single decision when two courses actually lie before him. The text metaphorically states that he "donned the yoke of necessity." *Lepadnon*, the word translated as "yoke," also means "harness"; it is a contraption of openings very like a net, and Agamemnon is associated with nets from here on in the play, with the net he threw around Troy and with the net that Clytaemestra traps him in. The net or harness that he willingly puts on he never takes off again. The difference between father and son, an indicator of the movement of the trilogy, is that when the net reappears in the *Choephoroi*, Orestes, who remains mindful that the choice he has made is a choice rather than a necessity, is not enmeshed in the net; instead, he can hold it and contemplate it, as he can contemplate choice and necessity.

One might compare him to Abraham, who was called on by God Himself to sacrifice his child, and who not only took his child to the altar, but let no one else prepare any aspect of the sacrifice, even to the preliminary and menial tasks of chopping wood and saddling the asses. With the child whom one loves and believes will be lost, every contact, even the most peripheral, is precious to the true father. Abraham had no "choice" and yet each moment of his test was for him a moment of choice.

The capacity to make distinctions, to maintain boundaries, and to evaluate one's motives is the capacity to create order out of chaos, to be civilized. Of all the minds in the play, the clearest is Athene's. In the *Eumenides*, as in the earlier plays, Aeschylus presents what seems an unsolvable dilemma: "Either course—to suffer them to stay, to drive them forth—is fraught with disaster and perplexity to me," Athene says. A choice is not made and then rationalized as "necessity," as Agamemnon did, nor is a decision made knowing that it will solve nothing, as Orestes did. The dilemma is acknowledged and a solution is sought from which self-interest is excluded by oath and in which redefinitions create new options. That the Furies, of all deities the most strongly ruled by compulsion, recognize that they can choose to become benevolent protectors of the city clarifies forever the question of choice versus necessity.

The ancient boundaries of piety and impiety, of the human and the divine, of necessity and choice are, in the *Eumenides*, properly restored. The very idea of a jury is dependent on the idea of choice and the establishment of institutionalized boundaries. Thus, the *Eumenides* does not simply embody a *peripeteia* for the Furies; it embodies a *peripeteia* for the action and thrust of both the *Agamemnon* and the *Choephoroi*. That little girls pretend, in their bear masks and saffron robes, to be sacrifices for Artemis but are unharmed, establishes for all time that civilization rejects blood sacrifice and that such acts of piety belong to the realm of symbolic action only. Fighting is relegated to a locus outside the city and must be prompted by more than a woman's lust. Killing is not a holy deed, but a vile one. Staining what belongs to the gods is a travesty, even for a conqueror. This conclusion of the *Oresteia* emphasizes the establishment of proper boundaries of thought and action.

IMAGERY

In this final play of the trilogy, Aeschylus transforms earlier metaphors into concrete physical realities on stage. In addition, images are now associated with actions expressive of the theme of reconciliation.

Of Hounds

The image of the hound—an image of dehumanization, the image the Watchman uses in the opening lines of the *Agamemnon* when he says he lies with bended arm, "dog-like" on the roof of the Atreidae palace, and the image that closes the *Agamemnon* when Clytaemestra speaks of the idle "yelpings" of the Chorus—is introduced into the *Eumenides* when the *Pythia* rushes from the shrine on her hands and feet. It is made more explicit when the phantom Clytaemestra tells the sleeping Furies that they owe her obedience in return for the sacrifices she made to them in the inner shrine of her palace that they "lapped up." She likens their half-awake sounds to the "whimpering of a hound," and the image is transformed into dramatic reality in the *Epi-parodos* when the Furies enter sniffing and tracking Orestes by the blood scent on him. When hound imagery disappears from the text, as it does once the trial begins, its disappearance marks the beginning of the metamorphosis of the Furies. Clytaemestra, however, remains forever associated with hounds, by her own claim of being "watch-dog of the house," loyal to Agamemnon, fierce to his enemies, and by Cassandra's vision, in which Clytaemestra is a "hateful hound, whose tongue licked his hand, who stretched forth her ears in gladness, like treacherous Ate."

Of the Color Red

As the procession forms, Athene instructs the attendants to "apparel [the Furies] honorably in festal robes of scarlet." Most scholars accept the view that the color of the robes put on the Furies is the color of the fabric that Clytaemestra spreads before the feet of Agamemnon. It is also the color of the net that Orestes holds up, drenched in the blood of Agamemnon. But now, in the *Eumenides*, red is no longer the color of sacrilege or murder. It has been transformed into an emblem of honor and welcome. The verb Athene uses, *endutois* ("apparel them"), always denotes additional or decorative garments.[9] Thus, the combination of black robes visible underneath the red garments and signifying that the Furies are daughters of Night is a sign that the ancient and primal can be joined to the rational and restrained.

Of Torches and Brightness

Most important to the conclusion of the trilogy is the torchlight procession that accompanies the Furies offstage to their new and hallowed home. The trilogy's first image of spaced fire appears in Clytaemestra's beacon speech, in which she dubs the islands and mountaintops "torch-bearers" (*lampadephronon*) that signify to her that the moment of revenge is at hand. An etymological repetition comes in the *Choeophoroi* when "lights flare up" (*lampteres*) throughout the palace at Clytaemestra's command. Torches, originally associated with Clytaemestra's power, are now associated with her terror and destruction. The central ode of the *Choephoroi*, the ode about violent women, begins with a reference to "meteors" (*lampades*), a word describing destructive light in nature and formed from the same root. And within that same ode, another murderous mother kills her son, Meleager, by casting a burning brand into the fire. When she appears as Phantom, Clytaemestra again uses words from the same etymological category. She comes to the Furies in their dream when "the mind asleep has bright vision" (*lamprunetai*). Thus, until the conclusion of the *Eumenides*, flaring light is associated with vengeance in all its forms.

At the end of the trilogy, Athene instructs that the Furies be led to their new home "by the light of gleaming torches." Rather than one word, she uses three, each of which expresses the idea of beacons blazing with light. Verbal images finally become physical realities as actual torches are brought on stage in glorious procession. The beacon flares of the *Agamemnon*, beautiful but terrible, are forever superseded and the Furies, daughters of Night, leave the stage surrounded by light.

ASPECTS OF STAGECRAFT

The Number of Jurors and the Action of Voting

An important thematic question turns on stagecraft. If there are 11 jurors, with Athene making the twelfth, rather than 12 with Athene an unofficial thirteenth, Aeschylus is saying that, when Athene withdraws from the court forever, leaving all subsequent juries to the work of mortals, each juror knows that Athene once was among them, and that the juror may well be sitting in her seat. Each juror is then to regard himself as doing what Athene did—casting the deciding vote. With a total of 12 rather than 13 votes, a further purpose is served: it is established that acquittal does not come about only when a majority vote for acquittal; acquittal also comes about with a tie vote. This is a remarkable concept, as is the ultimate construction of the jury with an even rather than an odd number so that a tie is always possible: it is a reminder that doubt—and a tie vote represents significant doubt—is not dishonorable in human affairs, and that doubt favors the accused. Mercy is thereby introduced into the affairs of men.

The jurors vote by walking across the stage and depositing stones in urns. During this process Apollo and the Furies engage in 10 essentially irrelevant stichomythic exchanges of two lines each, followed by a three-line unit, during which time all the jurors must cross the stage to the urns. The longer three-line unit forms a dignified and stately conclusion to a process defined as noble and supremely civilized. Were there a twelfth juror, he would have to rush across the stage to the urns in half the time allotted the others or would have to walk on Athene's lines, a token of disrespect and a theatrically distracting action, as her comments are important. Both thematically and practically, 11 jurors seem likely to have been Aeschylus' intention.

Choreographic Patterns

The normal entry of a Chorus is in stately movement down the *parodos* to the orchestra ground. In the *Eumenides*, the Furies spill onstage from the central doors in random and sporadic movement. In their second entry, a double *parodos* being highly unusual, they perform the "Binding Song" in which they bind Orestes, by incantation and choreographic encirclement, to the spot he has chosen for sanctuary, the altar in the center of the orchestral floor. In the song's final refrain, they say they bring down the heavy-falling force of their feet on the sinner, their metaphor suggesting the power of the accompanying dance movements.

Such choreography suggests the primitive and chaotic. Midway through the play, in contrast, is the orderly entry of the Jurors, led by Athene. Their voting is another orderly choreographic pattern involving 11 identical stage crossings. The play ends with the great torchlight procession of groups of figures. A line forms with Athene at its head, followed by the Furies, the Jurors, and the old and young citizens of Athens. The enlarged procession, an emblem of the *polis* that embraces all as "kin" and of the replacement of chaos by civic ceremony, circles the great orchestral floor and exits, escorting the Furies to their place of honor beneath the Areopagus. A cave has replaced another cave just as one manner of movement has superseded another. The progress from barbarism to civilization is embodied in the contrast between the Furies' entry and their exit and between the use of the orchestra at two different moments in the action. The song that everyone sings concludes with the words, "Raise a glad shout," in which the word for shout, *ololuksate*, is the same word used alone by Clytaemestra (*ep-ololuksato*) when she thought the time of vengeance was ripe. It is now associated with the end of vengeance.

NOTES

1. Richmond Lattimore, *Aeschylus* I, *The Complete Greek Tragedies*, edited by David Grene and Richmond Lattimore (Chicago: University of Chicago Press, 1954), pp. 30–31.

2. Colin Macleod, "Politics and the Oresteia," *Collected Essays* (Oxford: Clarendon Press, 1984), p. 22.

3. Anne Lebeck, *The Oresteia: A Study in Language and Structure* (Washington, D.C.: The Center for Hellenic Studies; Cambridge: Harvard University Press, 1971), p. 149.

4. H.D.F. Kitto, *Form and Meaning in Drama* (London: Methuen & Co Ltd, 1956), p. 54.

5. Bernard M. W. Knox, *The Heroic Temper: Studies in Sophoclean Tragedy* (Berkeley: University of California Press, 1983), pp. 77–78.

6. Kitto, pp. 55–63.

7. Alan H. Sommerstein, *Aeschylus: Eumenides, Cambridge Greek and Latin Classics Series* (Cambridge: Cambridge University Press, 1989), p. 207.

8. Sommerstein, pp. 229–230.

9. Colin Macleod, "Clothing in the Oresteia," *Collected Essays* (Oxford: Clarendon Press, 1984), pp. 41–43.

4

Sophocles
The *Antigone*
(442 B.C.)

SOPHOCLES' LIFE AND REPUTATION

Sophocles was born around 496 B.C. in Colonus outside Athens, the son of a wealthy industrialist, and died in 406 B.C. Sophocles is first recorded as winning first prize in the dramatic competition of 468 B.C. and is believed to have held both diplomatic and priestly office. He wrote until the end of his life, producing two masterpieces at the age of 90. Aristotle describes the *Oedipus Rex* as the finest example of the tragic form. In the year after Sophocles' death, Aristophanes produced the *Frogs* in which Sophocles is represented as "a genial poet and greatly missed by his friends." It is said that when he died, the Spartans who were besieging Athens declared a temporary truce so that he might be buried in Colonus, outside the city walls. A story, perhaps apocryphal, is told that in Sophocles' old age, one of his sons, Iophon, sued in Athenian court to have him declared incompetent in order to seize control of Sophocles' estate. Rather than arguing against the charge, Sophocles recited for the jury the great ode to Athens ("Land of Running Horses") from the *Oedipus at Colonus*, which he was then composing, and the court summarily dismissed his son's case.

CHARACTERISTICS OF SOPHOCLES' STYLE

Sophocles wrote single plays in which a hero confronts his destiny rather than trilogies in which individuals collectively reveal theme. In such single plays, character is sharply drawn, often through the pairing of contrasting figures.

Although no god appears on stage in the three great "Theban" plays of this volume, Sophocles' drama is, in the deepest sense, religious. From the moment the *Antigone* begins, we are conscious of the violation of divine decree and of the withholding from the gods, Death and Love, of what should be theirs. The pivotal role of the blind seer Teiresias in the *Antigone*, the centrality of prophecy to the *Oedipus Rex* and to the *Oedipus at Colonus*, the apotheosis of man into god at the end of the *Colonus*—all these infuse Sophocles' plays with palpable divinity. Humanity is represented as operating against a backdrop of knowledge and intention that is only partially apprehended. This is the natural ground of ironic effect, and Sophocles' plots turn on ironic reversals. In this respect he differs from Aeschylus who, through stunning choral effects, parallel scenes, and complex images, "prepares for the coming events from the beginning."[1]

Sophocles' heroes are single-minded, passionate, guileless, and often angry. At some point in the action, or throughout it, they seek their own deaths.[2] They differ from the heroes of Aeschylean drama by the internalization of their suffering and by the enormity of their endurance.

Aristotle argues that Sophocles' great genius resides in the construction of plots in which every element is essential to the whole, in which *anagnorisis* (recognition) and *peripeteia* (reversal) are central elements.

Sophocles does so many things so beautifully that it is perhaps distortive to point to one single thing, but in studying these plays one cannot but be struck by the fact that Sophocles is also a poet of extreme interiorness. He can ask himself, and find out, what it feels like to be a young girl about to die, what it feels like to be a man suddenly blind, or what it feels like to be wrongfully accused and to find that one's very passion in defense can itself be seen as confirmatory of the accusation against which one argues. Sophocles' psychological penetration, in all its fresh and accurate capacity, must be acknowledged.

A LIST OF SOPHOCLES' PLAYS

Sophocles wrote approximately 120 plays and won either first or second prize in every competition he entered. His seven extant plays are:

The *Ajax*	443 B.C.	
The *Antigone*	442 B.C.	
The *Oedipus Rex*	426 B.C.	2nd Prize
The *Women of Trachis*	429–425 B.C.	

The *Electra*	418–410 B.C.	
The *Philoctetes*	409 B.C.	
The *Oedipus at Colonus*	406 B.C.	produced posthumously in 401 B.C.

Sophocles returns to the story of the royal house of Thebes in the *Oedipus Rex* and in the *Oedipus at Colonus*. In narrative sequence, the *Antigone* covers material that occurs after the *Colonus*. Sophocles did not write these three plays as a trilogy, nor were they meant to be read as a continuous narrative. They appear here in order of composition, with the *Antigone* first. They are sometimes referred to as the "Theban plays" because they all deal with the cycle of legend surrounding the royal house of Thebes, not because of a setting in Thebes.

SUMMARY OF THE *ANTIGONE*

The *Antigone* is the story of Antigone's burial of her brother despite the edict of King Creon and of her death at Creon's order, followed by the suicides of Creon's son and wife.

SOPHOCLES' USE OF MYTH IN THE *ANTIGONE*

Eteocles, the younger son of Oedipus, took the Theban throne from his older brother Polyneices. In retaliation, Polyneices gathered an army from the Peloponnese and brought it to attack Thebes. A successful assault would result in the destruction of the city and the selling of its population into slavery. The attack failed and both Eteocles and Polyneices fell in battle, killed by each other. The remaining children of Oedipus' house were his daughters, Antigone and Ismene. Creon, their uncle, assumed power. In Euripides' the *Phoenician Women* (411–409 B.C.), Antigone is described as a year older than Ismene, but Sophocles makes no mention of relative ages. Creon and Eurydice have two sons, Megareus and Haimon. Megareus leaps from the city walls to his death, in response to an oracle demanding a sacrifice if the city is to be saved.

It is entirely possible that Antigone's death and the subsequent suicides of the play are original to Sophocles, for "in a version of the myth contemporary with Sophocles, Antigone is still alive at the time of the Epigonoi's later attack on Thebes and is burned to death in the Temple of Hera."[3] (The *Epigonoi* are the sons of those who, with Polyneices, attacked Thebes.) In a fragment of a lost play by Euripides, Antigone secretly marries and bears a son to Haimon.

THE HISTORICAL CONTEXT OF THE *ANTIGONE*

One way of understanding the conflict between Antigone and Creon is as a conflict between loyalty to one's clan (Antigone's view) and loyalty to one's *polis* (Creon's view).[4] In fifth-century Athens, for democracy to succeed, civic allegiance had to replace blood ties as the individual's primary loyalty. Creon speaks of forming political alliances in language that more appropriately applies to kinship: decrees about similar issues are called "brother" decrees, and entering a political alliance is called "adopting a friend." Antigone, on the other hand, speaks of blood relationships in political language, saying that if she did not bury her brother, she would be "convicted of treachery." The Athenian politician Cleisthenes reorganized the citizen body into geographical, rather than family units for the distribution of civic privileges and required that one replace one's patronymic with the name of one's deme.

The split between Antigone and Creon also reflects the continuing struggle between the old religion and the new. The gods of the Underworld were traditionally associated with the clan, and thus Creon, the pragmatist, is particularly scornful of Antigone's reverence for Hades and the Dead. Yet there is no question that the Olympians are outraged by Creon's withholding of Polyneices' body from Hades. When Teiresias reports that the gods are refusing altar sacrifices, he is referring to the Olympians. When the Chorus urge Bacchus, "child of Zeus" and "leader of the dance of the stars breathing fire," to come "over the slope of Parnassus," it is the gods of the upper air who the Chorus understand have been outraged by Creon's *hubris*. Through such references, Sophocles indicates that Hades and the Olympians are one, that Antigone is theologically correct, and that Creon's selective view of what the gods require is impiety.

Athenians of 442 B.C. had experience with, and were particularly wary of, tyrants. When Haimon says to his father that a city with only one voice is no city at all, he is speaking of royal Thebes as if it were an Athenian democracy. When Antigone speaks to Ismene of Creon's edict, she says it is a proclamation made by the *strategos* ("general"), the name of the post to which Pericles was elected in 461 B.C. and again from 443–429 B.C.

The *Iliad*, authoritative in all things, ends with the burials of Patroklos and Hector, both delayed, and both insisted on by the gods, the dead, and the dead's kin. Nonburial was a travesty, so much so that "in war, a defeated invader would usually take his dead with him; when this could not be done it was appropriate for the victors to bury them, as the Athenians did after Marathon."[5]

That Antigone takes upon herself the burial of Polyneices is a function of her grief and her recognition that there is no one else to bury him, and is in keeping with the "immemorial duty of the family and especially of the women to wash the corpse, to dress it for burial, and to sing in passionate, self-lacerating sorrow of their loss."[6] That obligation rests on Ismene also.

The intellectual climate of mid-fifth century Athens, with the rise of the Sophists, was one in which distinctions were being made between natural law (*physis*) and man-made law (*nomos*). Creon, however, insists the two types of law are one and are represented in his orders; Antigone separates natural or divine law from temporal legislation and political commands. The climax of her argument with Creon is her insistence on the inviolacy of the "unwritten and eternal laws of god" (the "*agrapta ... nomina*"), which, as Milton said, "nature has ingraven in us." The play's insistence on the burial of even such a man as Polyneices—for Polyneices has been a traitor to his city, and, were his expedition to have succeeded, his city and his kin would have been slaughtered or sold into slavery—reveals Sophocles' "firm conviction" that "divine law was predominant over all political law."[7]

THE PLOT OF THE *ANTIGONE*

General Comments

The plot of the *Antigone* is a double one: it has two protagonists, both of whom experience reversals of fortune, but only one of whom, Creon, experiences tragic *anagnorisis*. The protagonists are presented in separate introductory scenes that reveal both characters to be implacable.

The victor in their conflict seems at first to be Creon, for Antigone is discovered and arrested, refuses to be conciliatory, and, by the end of the apprehension episode, urges exactly what Creon desires, her own death. The scene between father and son is an inverted mirror of the Antigone-Creon scene. Creon and Haimon begin the scene thinking they are in essential agreement, but by its end are permanently divided. The plot is tightly spun: Antigone's suicide produces Haimon's, which produces Eurydice's. The death of wife and son devastate Creon, make Antigone the ultimate "victor," and illustrate the value of kinship, the precise value that Creon rejected. The scene of true *anagnorisis* turns out not to be the revelation of Antigone's culpability, but the more profound scene in the *exodos*, which reveals Creon's culpability. With the exception of Antigone's *kommos* and Creon's *exodos*, every scene of the play is a scene of open conflict (*agon*) between two characters: the prologue shows Antigone and Ismene in disagreement, and thereafter Creon is in dispute with the Sentry, Antigone, Ismene, Haimon, and Teiresias. Each *agon* turns on the issue of burial, thereby emphasizing the unity of action.

Actions are ironically and tragically inverted. Creon keeps a dead man from burial, but buries a living woman in a tomb. Antigone is captured when she performs rituals of mourning for her brother, but goes to her grave with no one to mourn for her. In death Antigone believes she joins her kin, and in death Haimon is said to have joined his bride: the realm of loneliness becomes Creon's realm, the realm of the living. Thebes, threatened by war, is not secured by Creon's actions but is threatened by plague. Having denied Antigone's right to mourn, Creon is himself a mourner at the end of the play, as Antigone was at its beginning. If such symmetry reflects a cosmic order, it is a cosmic order of great harshness wherein reward rests solely in the deed itself.

Creon casts his argument in political terms of order versus anarchy; Antigone casts her argument in religious terms of divine law versus man-made law. The double plot is echoed in the dichotomies with which each protagonist deals. In addition, both Creon and Antigone are motivated by a combination of principle and emotion.

Setting

The play is set outside the royal palace of Thebes the morning after the Argive assault has been repulsed. The time is about 10 years before the Trojan War.

Dramatis Personae

Antigone	daughter to Oedipus, sister to Polyneices
Ismene	sister to Antigone
Chorus of Theban Citizens	
Creon	king of Thebes, uncle to Antigone
Sentry	
Haimon	son to Creon, fiancé to Antigone
Teiresias	blind prophet of Apollo
Messenger	
Eurydice	wife to Creon

Scene Divisions

Prologue:	1–99	[Antigone, Ismene]
Parodos:	100–161	[Chorus]
Episode One:	162–331	[Chorus, Creon, Sentry]

First Choral Ode:	332–375	[Chorus]
Episode Two:	376–581	[Chorus, Sentry, Antigone, Creon, Ismene, Guards]
Second Choral Ode:	582–625	[Chorus, Creon *onstage*]
Episode Three:	626–780	[Chorus, Creon, Haimon]
Third Choral Ode:	781–800	[Chorus]
Episode Four (*Kommos*):	801–943	[Chorus, Antigone, Creon, Guards]
Fourth Choral Ode:	944–987	[Chorus, Creon *onstage*]
Episode Five:	988–1114	[Chorus, Creon, Teiresias]
Fifth Choral Ode (*Paean*):	1115–1151	[Chorus]
Exodos:	1152–1353	[Chorus, Messenger, Eurydice, Creon]

Synopsis

| Prologue: | 1–99 | [Antigone, Ismene] |

Antigone and Ismene emerge from the palace, and Antigone informs Ismene that Creon has decreed that no one shall bury the body of Polyneices, on penalty of death by stoning. Antigone asks Ismene to help her bury their brother. Ismene fearfully refuses and cautions Antigone against such action. Antigone goes off to bury Polyneices outside Thebes.

| *Parodos*: | 100–161 | [Chorus] |

The Chorus of Theban elders enter singing a victory ode.

| Episode One: | 162–331 | [Chorus, Creon, Sentry] |

Creon addresses the loyal men of Thebes whom he has summoned, decreeing that no one shall bury Polyneices. A Sentry enters to report that someone has covered the body with a fine layer of dust, but that there are no footprints or chariot-wheel marks anywhere near the body. The Chorus ask if perhaps some god has done this. Creon orders the Sentry to return and apprehend the criminal or face hanging.

| First Choral Ode: | 332–375 | [Chorus] |

The Chorus sing of humanity's formidable accomplishments and limitations.

Episode Two: 376–581   [Chorus, Sentry, Antigone,
                                             Creon, Ismene, Guards]

The sentry returns with Antigone as his prisoner. He explains that he and his fellows were temporarily blinded by a great dust storm; when the sky cleared, they saw Antigone standing by the body and dust newly sprinkled on it. Antigone tells Creon that she has followed the unwritten, eternal laws of god rather than the decrees of the state. He expresses his anger and orders Ismene brought from the palace. She asks that she be allowed to share the guilt; Antigone refuses. Creon nevertheless sentences both of them to death.

Second Choral Ode: 582–625   [Chorus, Creon *onstage*]

The Chorus describe the great evils that have come to the house of Oedipus and assert that no gift is unaccompanied by ruin. They call wise the "famous saying, that evil seems good to him whose mind the god is driving toward disaster."

Episode Three: 626–780   [Creon, Haimon, Chorus]

Haimon tries to persuade Creon to release Antigone by speaking of the sentiment in her favor and the nature of judicious rule. Creon becomes enraged. Haimon exits as Creon declares that he will bury Antigone alive within a rocky tomb.

Third Choral Ode: 781–800   [Chorus]

The Chorus sing of the "invincible" power of Love, a power to which not only human beings but gods are subject. The ode alludes to the quarrel of father and son and to the feelings of a young bride.

Episode Four (*Kommos*): 801–943   [Chorus, Antigone, Creon,
                                             Guards]

Antigone laments the marriage she will not have and the injustice of her death. The Chorus respond. Creon enters and orders the guards to take her away. She prays that, if she is sinless, Creon's punishment may equal hers.

Fourth Choral Ode :   944–987   [Chorus, Creon *onstage*]

The Chorus sing of three mortals associated with tomb-like caves. The mood is one of sorrow and foreboding.

Episode Five: 988–1114   [Chorus, Creon, Teiresias]

Teiresias enters, led by a boy, to report the unfavorable bird signs and the pollution of the city altars. Shaken by Teiresias' words, Creon, goes off to bury Polyneices and free Antigone.

Fifth Choral Ode (*Paean*):   1115–1151   [Chorus]

The Chorus sing a *paean* to Dionysus, god of Thebes, asking that he intermit the plague that Creon has brought on the city.

Exodos: 1152–1353   [Chorus, Messenger,
                                         Eurydice, Creon]

A messenger announces that Creon, who was once "a man worthy of envy," is now a living dead man, for Haimon has killed himself. Eurydice enters from the palace and hears the report of the deaths of both Antigone and Haimon. She exits. Creon enters with the body of Haimon in his arms. The messenger announces that Eurydice has cursed her husband and killed herself. The play ends with Creon asking to be led away and begging for death. The Chorus have no words of comfort.

THE FUNCTION OF THE SENTRY

The Sentry's contributions to Sophocles' tragic design are belied by the light touch with which he is presented. The Sentry begins with a preemptive, comic confession: "I'll not say that I am out of breath from running." Whether he means that he is not out of breath because he has not run, or that he is out of breath, not from running but from fear, is not clear. He knows messengers are expected to be out of breath. He is at pains immediately to establish his honesty because he fears Creon. That he compounds his slowness in arriving by taking 20 lines to describe that slowness is a function of fright. His narrative irrelevancies—that the guards were so reluctant to carry bad news to Creon that they chose lots, the lot falling to him—demonstrate that the *polis* regards Creon as a tyrant. The Sentry's comic trembling before Creon is, in fact, designed to emphasize Antigone's courage. As the Sentry describes his halting progress from guard post to palace and his Launcelot Gobbo indecisiveness, Sophocles presents the ordinary human state of ambivalence and indecision in contrast to the single-mindedness of both Creon and Antigone. And because the Sentry's internal voices both predict doom, the Sentry's function is also to suggest a fatalistic view of life that the play modifies into a tragic view shaped also by human sin and error.

In Sophocles' skilled hands, the Sentry's second appearance does as much as his first. Because he and his fellow guards have apprehended Antigone, the Sentry is now out of danger. He notes that he has won his freedom at the expense of someone else's but is not greatly troubled by such a trade— another common response that throws Antigone's self-sacrificing love into strong relief. And, having vowed just moments before that under no circumstances would he return to the palace, but finding his fortunes reversed and himself indeed returning, the Sentry says, "My lord, a man should never be too sure of anything." This insight, although submerged in his comic surprise at his own reappearance, is precisely the knowledge that Creon lacks. Creon believes that only he is correct and only he understands the will of the gods, and his *hubristic* insistence on his own correctness shatters him.

When the Sentry reports the capture of Antigone after the dust storm, he says that he hears, in her accents of lament over the body, the cries of a bird whose nest has been robbed. He is not one to feel things deeply or linger over anything that does not directly concern or benefit him, but nonetheless he grasps something of the grief she feels in a way that Creon, to whom she is kin, cannot. The Sentry's graphic details of his and his fellows' attempts to avoid the smell of the body reveal the sheer ugliness of Creon's edict; the Sentry's amazement at the absence of footprints, at the ability of a thin layer of dust to keep off dogs and bird, and at the force of the dust storm suggests the working of the gods on behalf of Antigone, which Creon angrily denies.

When the Sentry first enters, the audience, knowing from the prologue that Creon's edict is being countermanded even as he announces it, expects to hear a report of Antigone's having buried the body. Instead, Sophocles creates a delay in which the audience is made to think about themes and about the nature of both protagonists, that their confrontation, when it comes, may be the more acute.[8]

THE FIRST ODE: 332–375

"Many things are formidable" (*polla ta deina*) the ode begins, "and none more formidable than man." Yet, "against death he has no device." Just as man is master over his environment, so god is master over man. Pious persons are mindful of their place in the divine hierarchy.

The ode concludes with a warning: human beings' formidable powers must be used in accordance with "the laws of the earth and the justice of the gods," a phrase suggesting that nature and the gods are one. If humans do not act in accordance with such law, their skill destroys them. Through that "if" the ode asserts that we have the power to choose the course we will follow. In a line of stunning ambiguity, the ode says that man "comes to nothing without resources." Either it means that there is no challenge ("nothing") to which a person comes without resources, or that, despite all one's resources, a person comes to death ("nothing"). Both readings are not only compatible within the ode but also necessary to the theme, for Creon's rise and fall illustrate first the one reading and then the other. The word *deina,* often mistranslated as "wonderful," likewise conveys the same duality, for it means both "formidable" and "dreadful."[9] Thus, this first ode sets the terms of the play's movement.

ANTIGONE

The prologue introduces Antigone's character through contrast with Ismene's. Antigone is presented as active: she draws her sister out of the house, she already knows of Creon's edict, and she has decided what she will do in response.

Ismene's fear of Creon, like the Sentry's, reveals the daring of Antigone. Antigone's character is further defined when she finds Ismene's claim that she is only a "woman" and Ismene's promise to "remain silent," contemptible. The swiftness with which Antigone forms judgments and the untemporized nature of her reactions are indicated by the quick shift from expressions of love for her sister at the beginning of the scene—"O own kin, own sister Ismene"—to expressions of near-hatred, *ectharei* and *ecthra,* at its end. That Ismene responds with two words of love, *philois* and *phile,* is a matter of indifference, or perhaps even of disgust, to Antigone, who departs in silence. When the sisters next meet Antigone rejects Ismene, and in the *kommos,* as she is about to be led to her tomb, Antigone cries out that she has "no kin" to mourn her. In her mind, all ties with Ismene have been severed by Ismene's hesitation. As her reaction to Ismene reveals, Antigone responds to each present instant. That Polyneices attacked the city is no longer relevant; what is relevant is that now his body lies unburied.

That she has loved Ismene until this moment and that Ismene continues to love her mean nothing. Antigone's nature is sharply contrasted to her sister's: Ismene forgives Antigone's mockery when Antigone tells her to "proclaim this to all," using the same verb (*keirukseis*) that earlier in the scene described Creon's edict or "proclamation" (*keirugma*) and thus suggesting that Ismene is Creon's lapdog. That Ismene can love one whose values are different from her own throws Antigone's nature into relief, for Antigone can love only those—at least only those among the living—who share her values. Ismene's reply, "It would not be as fitting as for him and for her," to Creon's crude statement that one bride is as good as any other reflects this, for Haimon, Antigone's fiancé, stands up to Creon as Antigone has, and, like Antigone, does so on behalf of one he loves.

Antigone's reactions are absolute: she does not balance feelings and values against each other or against their consequences, but gives herself wholly to feeling. She frequently uses words that describe sensations, such as "sweet" (*hedeus*) or its opposite, "bad-tasting," to describe situations and actions.[10] Her use of sensory language demonstrates a direct and almost childlike apprehension of right and wrong and something close to a physical inability to act in contravention of those precepts. And as with sensations, she does not come to decisions in graduated steps, but entire and whole.

An inability to forgive also drives Antigone's actions. She says more than once that she could not face herself, not forgive herself, were she not to do what she must for her brother. The harshness she applies to others she also applies to herself, and that very harshness steadies her course. That others regard her as reckless reflects as much on them as on her, for the sort of integrity she exhibits requires a measure of recklessness. Although Sophocles does not allude to Antigone's youth until the *kommos*, Antigone's qualities are the qualities of the young. She is proud, fearless, focused on the present, absolute in her judgments, passionate, and selfless. Her very flaws, what Creon and the Chorus regard as her "highly emotional" and "overly forward" nature,[11] make possible her greatness.

In her first scene with Creon, Antigone speaks of the unwritten laws of god that supersede the laws of the state. "God's ordinances," she says, "are not of today and yesterday; they live forever … these are the laws whose penalties I would not incur … through fear of any man's temper."

When what might be construed as the means of mitigating her punishment are presented to her, in Creon's question and in Ismene's confession, Antigone scorns excuse. We see in her a perfect fusion of word to action: she says what she will do and she stands by what she has done.

To use the Sophist vocabulary of Sophocles' day, Antigone recognizes only law (*nomos*) that is in accord with nature and natural feeling (*physis*). In the Sentry's description and simile of the dust storm, Sophocles links Antigone to nature and the gods. The Sentry describes the dust storm as unrelated to any weather signs, and as coming from the gods. It blinds all the watchers and enables Antigone, undetected, to approach her brother's body. It reverses the guards' action by recovering the body of Polyneices with dust. Thus, the dust storm acts in league with Antigone. It tears leaves from the trees in mid-summer, a time when leaves do not fall. In fact, the literal rendering of the phrase usually translated as "tormenting the foliage" is "tearing the hair."[12] The Sentry's personification describes nature as doing to itself what a woman in the traditional act of mourning does to herself. Thus, Sophocles suggests that all nature and the gods echo Antigone's grief and honor Antigone's actions. She is seen to be acting in accord with impulses of *physis* and, given the mystery of these occurrences, with the will of the gods.

Immediately after the dust storm, the Sentry hears Antigone cry "with a sound like the piercing note of a bird when she sees her empty nest robbed of her young." Her work of burial has been destroyed and only a thin layer of nature's dust covers the body. The Sentry's simile likens Antigone's cry to a sound beyond speech, such as an animal would utter. Teiresias' later report of birds clawing each other and vomiting onto the altars of the city coincides with the moment of Antigone's entombment and death, and is perhaps another sign of nature's affinity with Antigone. Imagery manifests Antigone's relation to natural laws and her role as "defender" of them.[13] As she goes off to her death, she likens herself to Niobe, who turned to stone and merged with nature.

Antigone's fear and sadness in the *kommos* are not demanded by the plot and do not illuminate the issue of divine law versus human law. They are simply hers and are emphasized so that we may feel this moment to be real and so that we may learn the cost, in human terms, of doing right. Stage time and real time coincide here: each minute she remains with the Chorus is a minute more of life; when she leaves the stage, her life is over. Thus, each moment of the scene is invested with a special urgency.

Sophocles has presented her, in conflict with Creon, as principled, reverent, and resolute—in other words, as the embodiment of adult virtue. Now he shows her as the very young girl she is, alone at the moment of death, and desiring life. We see how very young she truly is when the Chorus address her as *technon*, "child," while she is before them and, after her exit, apostrophize her as *O pai*, "my child." In fact, the placement of an entirely unexpected vocative, *O pai*, at the end of what seems to be a narrative ode makes all of it into direct address to the absent child. By this simple device, Sophocles both sustains and deepens the feeling of the preceding *kommos*, whose sorrow has, until this point, been confined to Antigone alone. That the staid and conservative Chorus continue to hold her in their minds after she is led off is a mark of deep and unexpected grief, and is overwhelming to the audience.

The Ode to Eros that precedes the *kommos* emphasizes, among other things, that Antigone was to have been a bride. Appearing just as the ode concludes, she becomes the young girl whose "soft cheeks" at night Eros visits and the "young bride" whose eyes "enthrone desire." The language of the *kommos* is emphatically bridal. She mourns that she has "known nothing of marriage songs," and the Chorus say she is "passing to the bridal chamber where all come to rest." Her yearning, the yearning of the unwed girl, now so strongly stated, cannot be a sudden desire of hers; rather, we must understand that she has always desired this, and we must measure her sacrifice by the strength of her desire.

That against this context she says that she buries her brother because, with parents dead, she can get no more brothers, but that she would not have undergone this punishment to bury a husband or child because one can always remarry and bear more children, may be simply an assertion of the primacy she attaches to blood ties. It is more likely, however, an attempt to shelter herself in an illusion that what she has missed, a husband and a child, were not so essential after all. The thought lasts only a moment, but it reveals, even by the very implausibility of its premise, her pain and her strenuous effort to carry on without breaking down.

Antigone regrets what she will not have, but she never regrets what she has done. To the last she understands that she has "shown reverence for reverence." She wants not to be forgotten, and so she begins the *kommos*, "See me, O citizens of my native land," and ends in exactly the same way: "Look rulers of Thebes, upon the last of the royal house," and we think, perhaps, of the need of each of us, like Didi and Gogo, to be "seen," to have our existence confirmed.

It is a deliberate irony that in the *kommos*, at the very moment when Antigone is about to leave this world, Sophocles makes her part of the nexus of human relationship rather than part of the world of the dead that she has imaginatively inhabited. His achievement here is to create profound sorrow without sentimentality, and our final impression of Antigone is of courage, that, to the victim, seems not to be courage at all.

CREON

When Creon delivers his edict, he seems to speak soundly. He begins by speaking of the "ship of state," which must be sailed in a "straight course."

He says that a man is revealed by how he governs. He decries those who, out of fear, fail to speak out on issues of importance. His next statement, that no one should "rate a dear one higher than his native land," is a proposition more potentially complex in its application than the two preceding statements, but an idea that would strike Athenians in Sophocles' audience as in accord with the reforms of Cleisthenes. What he says next, that in consonance with these "rules" (*nomoisi*, from *nomos*) he now prohibits burial of Polyneices, bears no logical connection to the principles he has espoused. Allowing such burial is not "rating a dear one higher than his native land" because such a principle applies only when there is a necessary choice to be made, when, in other words, one's "native land" will be damaged by some favor or advantage given to the "dear one." Thebes is safe; Polyneices is dead; the principle Creon invokes is inapplicable.

The personal anger that underlies Creon's decree is evident in the hyperbole and repetitions of his language. He speaks of Polyneices as planning "to drink the people's blood" and "to burn ... the gods of his race," and he uses coordinate expressions, as if a single word will not do, to describe the outrage that he hopes will be perpetrated on the corpse: no one shall be allowed to "bury or lament" Polyneices, who will remain "unburied"; "birds and dogs" will "devour and savage" his body. Thus, the highly emotional climax of what begins as a purely rational speech reveals Creon as a ruler governed not simply by civic concern but by deeper and darker feelings. This same mix of seemingly solid principles, shaky application, and excessive anger becomes Creon's pattern of argument and is apparent in his speeches to the Sentry about money and to Haimon about insubordination within a household or a city.

Sophocles uses the action of the prologue to create reservations about Creon in the audience's mind. The prologue concludes with Antigone's going off to bury Polyneices; thus, when Creon enters a few moments later and proclaims his edict, the audience reacts with concern for Antigone and a sense that Creon has been outwitted. He does not know what most nearly pertains to him—that his decree, even as he pronounces it, is being subverted. He is thus shown, from his first appearance onstage, to be overconfident in his expectations and assumptions. Perhaps he often thinks he knows more than he does. Indeed, it will become clear that he thinks he knows what is best for the city when he does not, and that he thinks he knows whom the gods would wish to punish, when he does not.

Because the prologue clearly establishes that Antigone acts alone and that her motives are ones of piety and personal loyalty, when Creon later accuses others—first the Sentry and then Ismene—of the deed, he reveals how limited his thinking is. His inability to conceive of any motive for burial other than greed or any burier other than a male is another indication to the audience of his constricted sensibility. That he has noticed so little of the different natures of Antigone and Ismene as to conflate them and so little of the nature of his own son as to suggest that Haimon might blithely seek another bride demonstrates how incapable he is of making refined judgments. Creon reaches conclusions too quickly and adopts them too forcefully. Ironically, he is proud that he is headstrong, as his description of the ideal ruler shows. Nor does he wish to hear anything but agreement from his people.

Creon summons a Chorus whom he flatteringly describes as you who have "reverenced the power of the throne of Laius" and been loyal to successive regimes. Such loyalty is often hard to manage and requires from subjects a certain agility. Such subjects are quickly acquiescent. That it is these whom Creon assembles reveals a good deal about the sort of ruler he is and the sort of citizenry he values.[14] They are more pious than he, as their attribution of the Theban victory to the gods and as their comment about the mysterious dust on Polyneices' body indicate, but not pious enough to argue forcibly against the violation of the corpse. He wants no genuine opposition, such as he later receives from his son.

Creon's speech is heavily metaphoric.[15] He frequently equates men with beasts being harnessed and reined in, images from a mind bent on controlling others. When the news that Polyneices' body has been covered lightly with dust is brought to Creon, Creon likens the citizenry to draught animals "unwilling to keep their necks beneath the yoke." To Antigone he says threateningly, "spirited horses are controlled by a small bridle." In his anger he adds image to image, likening her also to "iron" that will "crack" and "shatter." As a woman, she is no more than a "furrow … [to] be ploughed." He orders Ismene and Antigone into the house, saying that neither is to be "loosed to roam freely." And when Creon determines that he can immure Antigone with just enough food to keep the city from a technical charge of murder, he uses the word "fodder." In the *parodos*, gods, not humans, harness humans and in the fourth ode both Danae and Lycurgus are described as bowing to the "yoke" of necessity, the yoke of the gods. In the great first ode, which describes man's control over nature, a proper hierarchy is observed: people catch birds and fish, not men, in nets and tame beasts, not other people. Thus, the odes suggest that Creon's impulses are not only tyrannical but impious. Creon shows himself most impious in withholding from the Gods of Death and Love their due: from Hades he withholds the body of Polyneices; from Aphrodite he withholds the marriage of Antigone and Haimon.

HAIMON AND CREON

Haimon's dialogue with his father comes at the exact midpoint of the play and is the pivot on which it turns. Instead of Antigone, who is not interested in, and does not address, questions of proper rule, Haimon speaks to his father on his father's own ground of argument, and he speaks not simply as political ally but also as loving son. This scene most conclusively reveals Creon to be a tyrant and misogynist. He is given a second chance to reflect and consider; he chooses not to take it, and his rejection of rationality shows his willfulness and unfitness for rule.

Haimon's purpose is to save Antigone, but toward that end he articulates the Athenian ideal of open debate and democratic governance. "A city is no city if it has in it only one voice."

Haimon speaks with tact and deference,[16] scrupulously avoiding words of blame. He says, "retreat from your anger," as though such anger is his father's enemy on a field of battle; he calls his father's insistence that his "opinion and no other must be right" a "garment of one mood only" which he urges his father not to wear, just as kings do not wear the same robe all the time. These rhetorical distinctions are designed to offer Creon a graceful means of retreat. Applying Creon's own nautical metaphor, Haimon speaks of a ship's commander who *never* slackens his sails and is overturned by the sea and wind. Haimon's phrasing implies, even while suggesting an error on the part of such a captain, that much of the time a seaman is correct in keeping his sails taut. Thus, Haimon presents an argument that is wise and kindly. Creon's only reaction is fierce resentment at the impertinence of a young man presuming to teach something to an elder. His nature is revealed, especially when measured against Haimon's restraint, to be irredeemably tyrannical.

Creon repeatedly expresses contempt for women, mere "furrows," and believes any concession made to a woman is a diminution of manliness. At the conclusion of his first speech to Haimon he says, "We must never allow a woman to vanquish us." If it may be said that Haimon, in going to Antigone's tomb, takes on the role of the bride who, in marriage, enters her groom's house,[17] then Haimon's action (which in symbolic terms is also an enactment of the groom's entry and in literal terms is an attempt to rescue or share the terror of one he loves) is a reply to Creon's misogyny, although to make such a reply is hardly his concern at the time. Haimon's action causes Creon to be "vanquished" by a woman, for Antigone's death causes Haimon's and Haimon's destroys Creon. And as the third ode makes clear, the "woman" who vanquishes Creon is not simply Antigone but also Aphrodite: "Victory (*nika*) goes to the visible Desire that comes from the eyes of the beautiful bride, a Desire that has its throne beside those of the mighty laws, for irresistible in her sporting is the goddess Aphrodite."

That the name "Haimon" means "blood" (*haima*) is emphasized in the *exodos* by the Messenger's bitter pun, "Haimon is dead [*haimon ololen*]; his own hand has shed his blood [*autocheir d'haimassetai*]." The etymology of his son's name should urge on Creon the recognition that blood ties and obligations to

one's kin are powerful. In denying "Haimon" in all senses of the word, Creon
brings doom to himself and those he loves. The Chorus request clarification,
asking whether "his own" means Haiman's hand or Creon's, for they know
what Creon has failed to understand—that one's kin are indeed "one's own."
Haimon, too, knows that, for he kills himself, not out of chagrin at his failure
to kill his father, and not out of fear that, having made that attempt, he will
himself be executed, but out of "anger against his father." It must follow, then,
that he understands his wounding as a means of wounding his father and that
his suicide asserts the reality of kinship. That he dies embracing Antigone and
that that embrace is reported by the Messenger as a marriage embrace means
that Haimon's death is also an assertion of the power of Aphrodite and romantic love. Thus, because his death is linked to both Creon and Antigone, it is
a terrible reminder of the need for reconciliation of the oppositions that have
shaped the play's conflict. In his death, Haimon teaches Creon that the blood
ties Creon has denied have become the only things truly valuable to Creon.

THEME IN THE *ANTIGONE*

Sophocles tells us what the *Antigone* means in the final lines of the play:
"Good sense is by far the chief part of happiness; and we must not be impious towards the gods. The great words of boasters are always punished with
great blows, and as [those who boast and are arrogant] grow old [those blows]
teach them wisdom."

Sophocles opens the play with Ismene choosing a course different from
Antigone—a divergence that the plot does not demand—to establish, at the
very outset, the idea of choice and free agency. That in her next appearance
Ismene regrets that choice is also central to Sophocles' design: actions have
consequences and although we may regret those consequences, we cannot
avoid them. Thus, Ismene's regret foreshadows Creon's inability to cancel his
actions when he finally wishes to. That Antigone, as she goes to her death,
filled with sorrow, nonetheless does not regret what she has done, although
she wishes the consequences were different, makes her truly heroic: the
essence of being human is to choose and to act, and then, to accept the consequences of one's actions. The suffering that often follows is, to Sophocles,
the price of human dignity and freedom.

ASPECTS OF STAGECRAFT

The Staging of the Prologue

Antigone's lines, "I summoned you out of the gates of the courtyard because
I wished you to hear this alone," suggest that Sophocles may have intended

Ismene and Antigone to descend from the playing platform into the great open space of the orchestra, a space perhaps "eighty feet in diameter."[18] Two small figures in a huge space is a visual reminder of the difficult task before them. Their scene stands in stark contrast to the one that follows: Creon, surrounded by guards and addressing a full Chorus of citizens in the same space. If the sisters do come down into the orchestra, then they must also exit from it. "Each of them has some thirty yards to walk."[19] Ismene returns through the same doors into the palace; Antigone goes off by the *parodos* to her task of burial. The different trajectory of each and the time it takes to traverse the orchestral space, a time of silence, suggests not only the breaking of their connection with each other, but also the loneliness in store for each.

The *Ekkyklema* and the Death of Eurydice

Eurydice, after hearing the report of Haimon's death, says nothing. She turns, slowly and silently, and reenters the palace from which she has come. That exit is stunning in performance. Everything stops. There is neither sound nor movement anywhere on stage. The inwardness of the moment is emphasized by two visual emblems associated with her death, both reported by the Messenger: the inner altar where, the Messenger says, she kills herself and the fact that "with her own hand she struck herself beneath the liver, so that she experienced the suffering of her son." Eurydice becomes a new emblem of love and grief, for, in her love for Haimon, she wishes to know his pain in the most inward way, in her own body. That Sophocles imagines this as the act of woman whose husband has valued the *polis* over the hearth and the altar is an ironic contrast of the most searing sort.

Her body is displayed on the *ekkyklema*. The Chorus say to Creon, "You can see it. It is no longer hidden indoors," and Creon responds, "Alas, I, wretched, see this second disaster." Sophocles' purpose is not sensationalistic: the tableau is necessary, for only through the deaths of his son and wife does Creon "see." The *ekkyklema* is essential to this most harsh *anagnorisis*.

Creon's Carrying of the Body of Haimon

Creon enters bearing the body of his son, and continues to hold him throughout the *exodos*. By that very posture he acknowledges both the ties of love and kinship that he has denied and his responsibility for what has come to pass. The Chorus emphasize the meaning of Creon's posture when they say that in holding Haimon, he holds "a reminder" that "his ruin came not from others, but from his own error." His language as he carries the angled body alludes directly to his earlier assured references to the "ship of state." The "port" to which he has sailed his vessel is, he says, the "port of Hades," and the voyage, like everything he has touched, has not been "straight" but "crooked."[20] Creon's *anagnorisis*, coexistent with his *peripeteia*, is embodied in this simple stage action: he now understands the reality of death, the force of love, and the consequences of pride. Unlike Oedipus, the hero of the next Theban play, Creon has been genuinely culpable, but Sophocles nevertheless is able, through the searing imagery and stagecraft of this final scene, to make Creon the object of cathartic pity and terror.

NOTES

1. Karl Reinhardt, *Sophocles* (Oxford: Basil Blackwell Publishers, 1979), pp. 94–95.

2. Bernard M. W. Knox, *The Heroic Temper: Studies in Sophoclean Tragedy* (Berkeley: University of California Press, 1983).

3. Charles Segal, "Antigone: Death and Love; Hades and Dionysus," *Modern Critical Views: Sophocles* (New York: Chelsea House Publishers, 1990), p. 188.

4. Knox, pp. 62–116.

5. Victor Ehrenberg, *Sophocles and Pericles* (Oxford: Basil Blackwell Publishers, 1954), p. 29.

6. Knox, p. 87.

7. Ehrenberg, p. 30.

8. H.D.F. Kitto, *Form and Meaning in Drama* (London: Methuen & Co., Ltd., 1956), p. 152.

9. Cedric Whitman, *The Heroic Paradox: Essays on Homer, Sophocles, and Aristophanes* (Ithaca, N.Y.: Cornell University Press, 1964), p. 110.

10. Robert F. Goheen, *The Imagery of Sophocles' Antigone* (Princeton, N.J.: Princeton University Press, 1951), p. 76.

11. Goheen, p. 26.

12. Whitman, p. 118.

13. Whitman, p. 116.

14. Cynthia P. Gardiner, *The Sophoclean Chorus: A Study of Character and Function* (Iowa City: University of Iowa Press, 1987), p. 86.

15. Goheen, p. 25.

16. Sir Richard Jebb, *The Antigone of Sophocles*, abridged by E.S. Shuckburgh (Cambridge: Cambridge University Press, 1902), p. 152.

17. Segal, p. 188.

18. Kitto, pp. 149–152.

19. Kitto, p. 150.

20. Martha C. Nussbaum, *The Fragility of Goodness* (Cambridge: Cambridge University Press, 1986), pp. 62–63.

5

Sophocles
The *Oedipus Rex*
(426 B.C.)

SUMMARY OF THE *OEDIPUS REX*

Oedipus Rex is the story of Oedipus' discovery, through a process of relentless inquiry, of his true identity and of the fact that he has unwittingly fulfilled the oracles of Apollo that he sought to avoid.

THE PLAY'S TITLE

Aristotle in the *Poetics* calls this play "*Oedipus*" with no word for "king" appended to the name of the hero. The absence of "king" preserves the tragic ironies that surround the figure of Oedipus. In Greek, *basileus* was the word for the hereditary descendant of the royal house, and *tyrannos* was the word for someone who came to power through means other than lineal descent. A kind of usurper himself, the *tyrannos* usually feared usurpation, as Oedipus does from Creon. Oedipus is, of course, both at once: he thinks he is *tyrannos*, learns he is *basileus*, and at the very moment when the Chorus call him "true king," he is filled not with joy but horror, for he learns he is the pollution of his "true" city. From the moment he is proven *basileus*, he can no longer be even *tyrannos*. The difficulty about what to call Oedipus is echoed in other ways as well. The last words Iocaste speaks on stage are "Alas, alas, wretched one! That is all that I can say to you, and nothing any more!" Iocaste, now knowing everything, cannot call him "husband," cannot call him "son," because he is both and therefore neither. He is "wretched one," "unhappy one," describable only in terms of what awaits him or in terms of the destiny he has fulfilled, but not in terms of any relationship, because the signifiers of relationship are tainted by the multiplicities they must signify.

SOPHOCLES' USE OF MYTH IN THE *OEDIPUS REX*

The Myth in Homer and in Other Classical Sources

The broad outlines of the story of Oedipus were fixed in Homer's day. In the *Odyssey* Iocaste, called "Epikaste," hangs herself but Oedipus continues to rule in Thebes, suffering "all the sorrows that are brought to pass by a mother's furies." Homer states that all happens by the bitter designing of the gods, in keeping with the governing principle of the *Odyssey* itself. Of the moment of Oedipus' discovery of his identity, the focus of the *Oedipus Rex*, Homer says only that the gods "made it all known." No mention is made of the blindness of Oedipus nor of Teiresias, who appears in the same book of the *Odyssey* as Epikaste, and whose use in the *Oedipus Rex* may be entirely Sophocles' invention.

In Aeschylus' the *Seven Against Thebes*, Oedipus blinds himself. In an extant fragment from a lost play by Euripides, however, the charioteers of Laius blind Oedipus, so even this part of the legend was "free for variation."[1] In Euripides' the *Phoenician Women*, Iocaste does not hang herself, and that direct contradiction of Homer's account suggests the latitude a playwright had. Oedipus journeys to Delphi, and after encountering Laius on the road and killing him, travels back to Corinth to make Polybus a present of Laius' chariot and horses. To bring these spoils to Corinth is to fail to avoid the place of prophetic danger. An Oedipus who knows of no oracle or who makes no resolve to avoid Corinth and the oracle's fulfillment, is very different from Sophocles' pious hero whose acquisition of oracular knowledge and the action he takes to avoid the prophecy cause its fulfillment and his own destruction.

THE HISTORICAL CONTEXT OF THE *OEDIPUS REX*

Law Courts and Litigation

Athenians were litigious and the investigative methods of the law courts—initiation of a murder inquiry by the next-of-kin, careful pursuit of each clue, reliance on witness report—are reflected in the play. When Oedipus begins the inquiry, he says, in terrible legal irony, that he "takes the son's part" in pursuing the investigation. Acceptable methods of eliciting testimony from a reluctant witness included the use of force such as the Theban Shepherd is threatened with:[2] Oedipus in that scene would not be regarded as violent. That laws of Athens recognized accidental homicide and homicide in self-defense as legally exculpatory actions places Oedipus' profound sense of guilt in a noble light.

Religious Supplication

The play opens with Suppliants—old men, youths, and young children—seated by an altar. By tradition, an *hiketes* ("suppliant") was one who sought protection, and whose laying of an *hiketeria* ("olive branch") bound with wool on an altar or hearth rendered that person inviolable; an *hiketes* is also specifically one who seeks purification from the sin of homicide. Thus, although the Suppliants' function is to seek relief from the plague, their very appearance subtly foreshadows Oedipus' fate.

The Plague

The *Oedipus Rex* opens with a description of plague. Thucydides, in Book II of *The History of the Peloponnesian War,* describes a terrible plague in Athens in the years just before the writing of the *Oedipus Rex.* Beginning in the east, it reached Piraeus and passed up the Long Walls to Athens. Because Athens was under siege by Sparta, the population of the surrounding countryside moved to huts within the Walls. There, in conditions of heat, overcrowding, and filth, that population was decimated. Athens lost one third of her people; the great leader Pericles died of plague in 429 B.C. The plague, which seemed to abate, returned in force the next year. The Priest's description would immediately touch the audience.

THE PLOT OF THE *OEDIPUS REX*

General Comments

Aristotle says that the plot of the *Oedipus Rex* achieves the maximum tragic effect possible because we see in Oedipus a protagonist of noble character and renown who falls from good fortune to bad, not through evil and depravity, but through some kind of error of understanding (*hamartia*). In Aristotle's judgment, plot is the defining element of tragedy, and in the plot of the *Oedipus Rex* not only are the moments of recognition and fall simultaneous, but each action follows from the preceding action. These qualities, Aristotle argues, make the *Oedipus Rex* most able to excite the tragic emotions of pity and terror that, together, create *catharsis*.

The plot of the *Oedipus Rex* is the most profoundly ironic in all of Greek drama. The stunning ironies of Oedipus' history, the rumors at the Corinthian banquet and Oedipus' subsequent journey to Delphi, seem to be Sophocles' invention, for what an audience can be relied on to know, like the riddle of the Sphinx, can be passed over while new content must be narrated.

Oedipus learns in the play that in seeking to avoid his fate, he has brought it about. The terrible paradox is that to seek to avoid his fate is to try to circumvent the will of the gods and thus to be guilty of impiety and *hubris*. Not to seek to avoid that fate is to be guilty of the unnatural and dreadful deeds of incest and parricide, and thus to be guilty of another sort of impiety. The actual action we see onstage is also profoundly ironic. An investigation reveals the investigator to be the criminal the investigator seeks.

Oedipus' destiny is ordained, yet every action Sophocles dramatizes shows Oedipus exercising free will. In contrast to him are Creon, Teiresias, and Iocaste. Each, by his or her behavior, presents a less noble alternative to Oedipus' openness, assumption of responsibility, or decision to endure. Both Teiresias and Iocaste urge that Oedipus forego his search. Oedipus chooses to defy them. Thus, Sophocles creates a situation of maximum ironic dissonance between destiny and action to suggest that human beings are nonetheless free, within a limited sphere, to act with responsibility. It is an assertion of the dignity of man.

The ironies and paradoxes extend, of course, to the conflation of sight and blindness. Normally, "physical sight is equated with knowledge and light and truth, darkness with their opposites,"[3] yet Teiresias, the blind prophet, sees what Oedipus, the sighted man, does not. When Oedipus finally sees, he blinds himself.

The climactic scene of the play is itself a masterpiece of ironic construction as is, to a lesser degree, Iocaste's attempt to allay Oedipus' concerns about prophecy. The Corinthian Shepherd comes bringing Oedipus a desirable thing, a throne. He expects his revelation about Oedipus' parentage will relieve Oedipus' fears. Instead, although his revelation makes return to Corinth possible, it makes return to Corinth irrelevant, turns Oedipus' fears into dreadful certainties, and reveals that what is anticipated has already been accomplished. Kitto adds that "an act of mercy, tinged with a perfectly honest shrewdness, leads the Corinthian to the verge of what is, for him, greatness; as he stretches out his hand, eagerly and with confidence, it turns into horror."[4] Thus, not only is the scene of the Corinthian Shepherd a reversal for the principal figures; it is also a reversal for the secondary ones.

Finally, the pattern of the *Oedipus Rex* is that of a foundling story, a comic pattern of "the lost one found."[5] In such stories, the restoration of the lost one is a moment of triumph; here it is a source of the deepest grief.

Setting

The setting is outside the doors of the royal palace of Oedipus at Thebes. The time is two generations before the Trojan War.

Dramatis Personae

Oedipus	king of Thebes
Priest	
Creon	brother to Iocaste
Chorus of Theban citizens	
Teiresias	blind prophet of Apollo
Iocaste	queen of Thebes
Corinthian Messenger	a shepherd
Theban Shepherd	
Palace Messenger	
Suppliants	
Antigone and Ismene	daughters to Oedipus

Note: In the text, sometimes the gods are referred to by name, sometimes generically as "god."

Scene Divisions

Prologue:	1–150	[Suppliants, Oedipus, Priest, Creon]
Parodos:	151–215	[Chorus]
Episode One:	216–462	[Chorus, Oedipus, Teiresias]
First Ode:	463–512	[Chorus]
Episode Two:	513–862	[Chorus, Creon, Oedipus, Iocaste]
Second Ode:	863–910	[Chorus]
Episode Three:	911–1085	[Chorus, Iocaste, Corinthian Messenger, Oedipus]

Synopsis

Suppliants assemble before the doors of Oedipus' palace and ask his help against the plague that is ravaging the city. Creon, whom Oedipus has already sent to Delphi, returns and says that the city must expel the killer of its former king. Oedipus reassures his people.

The Chorus of Theban elders enter and invoke the gods to save them.

Oedipus enters and makes a proclamation ordering anyone with information to come forward and threatening severely anyone who withholds information. (The text is slightly corrupt in this passage. Its meaning is that if the killer fears death by coming forward, let him know that he will only be exiled. Anyone with information, who is himself guiltless, will be rewarded. However, if the murderer does not come forward, when he is subsequently discovered, to him is forbidden reception at any hearth or speech from any citizen or participation in any religious ceremony.) Teiresias, having been summoned by Oedipus, enters, but refuses to speak. Oedipus insults him and, in return, Teiresias accuses Oedipus of the regicide. Both men exit.

The Chorus urge the killer to flee faster than the winds, for he is pursued by the son of Zeus and the dread spirits of death. They assert that, like a mountain bull limping with sore-wounded foot, he is unable to leave far behind the prophecies coming from earth's center. They can neither believe nor deny what Teiresias has said. They can recall no past quarrel between the royal house of Corinth, from which Oedipus has come, and the royal house of Thebes that would prove Teiresias correct in charging that Oedipus of Corinth has killed the King of Thebes. They again praise Oedipus for rescuing them from the Sphinx and refuse to judge him criminal.

| Episode Two: | 513–862 | [Chorus, Creon, |
| | | Oedipus, Iocaste] |

Oedipus accuses Creon of engineering Teiresias' accusations in order to usurp the throne. Iocaste interrupts their angry exchange; Creon protests his innocence and leaves. Iocaste presents to Oedipus her "proof" that prophets and prophecies are worthless: an oracle said that Laius would die at the hands of their son; instead, Laius was, it was reported, killed by highwaymen at a crossroads.

Oedipus remembers such a place and also remembers having struck and killed a traveler there who hit him with a goad. To Iocaste he describes his doubts about his paternity, his journey to Delphi, the god's words, and his determination never again to return to Corinth lest he kill his father and marry his mother, as the oracle predicted. He asks to question the servant who survived the roadside killing, and Iocaste promises to summon him. They enter the palace.

| Second Choral Ode: | 863–910 | [Chorus] |

In this central ode dealing with a central question of the play, piety, the Chorus pray that an evil fate may overtake the *hubristic* (arrogant and violent) man who does not reverence the gods.

| Episode Three: | 911–1085 | [Chorus, Iocaste, Corin |
| | | thian Messenger, Oedipus] |

Iocaste places offerings on the altar of Apollo and prays for his assistance. A Messenger arrives from Corinth bringing news of Polybus' death and offering the throne to Oedipus. When Oedipus explains that he cannot return to Corinth because he fears fulfilling the oracle regarding his mother Merope, the Messenger explains that there is nothing to fear, as Polybus and Merope are not Oedipus' real parents. He himself, the Messenger, once tended sheep on Mt. Cithairon outside Thebes, where he received an infant from a Theban Shepherd attached to the house of Laius and brought that infant to the royal house of Corinth, where the childless king and queen adopted him. Oedipus, he declares, is that infant. Iocaste, silent until this moment, begs Oedipus to cease his inquiry. He refuses and she exits into the palace.

Third Choral Ode: 1086–1109   [Chorus, Oedipus *and*
                                          Messenger *onstage*]

The Chorus impute divine birth on Cithairon to Oedipus, imagining him the child of a mountain Nymph and some god.

Episode Four: 1110–1185   [Chorus, Oedipus, Corin-
                                          thian Messenger, Theban
                                          Shepherd]

The servant who witnessed Laius' death arrives; he is identified by the Corinthian Messenger as the very man (the "Theban Shepherd") who gave him the baby years before. Under threat of torture the Theban Shepherd answers Oedipus' questions, and through incremental steps it is revealed that he received the child from Iocaste herself. Oedipus cries out in grief that "All is now clear" and that he is damned in his birth, in his marriage, and in blood he shed. He rushes into the palace as the Messenger and the Shepherd depart.

Fourth Choral Ode: 1186–1222   [Chorus]

The Chorus sing a lament for Oedipus and for humankind in general, noting the confluence of glory and pain in Oedipus' kingship.

Exodos: 1223–1530   [Chorus, Palace Messenger,
                                          Oedipus, Creon, Antigone
                                          and Ismene]

A Messenger from the palace describes Iocaste's death by hanging and Oedipus' self-blinding. Oedipus enters. He gradually regains rationality and begs to be led away. Creon, now king, orders that Oedipus return immediately to the house and refuses to make any decision about exile until the oracle can be further consulted. Oedipus begs Creon to give Iocaste proper burial and asks to see his daughters who, with Creon's permission, enter. The Chorus say that no one should be called fortunate until it can be said that that person has ended life without grief.

OEDIPUS' CHARACTER

Oedipus is a man of moral and intellectual excellence. The prologue immediately establishes his heroic nature. His first words are words of compassion, "My children," and, without ceremony or intermediaries, he makes himself available to them. Everything here reveals his openness and his assumption of kingly responsibility for his people. His sending to Delphi, before being asked, demonstrates initiative, piety, and concern for his people, as does his insistence, despite Creon's suggestion, that the oracle be heard by everyone and not filtered through policy decisions made "indoors." Once the oracle is reported, Oedipus responds with directness and resolve. He does not exclude himself from the strictures of his edict and becomes enraged at Teiresias when Teiresias refuses to reveal what Oedipus believes will help the city. In all but name, he is a *basileus*, a true king whose subjects are literally defined as his "children."

Oedipus' nobility is defined through the contrasting responses of Creon. Arguing that he is no potential usurper, Creon states that he prefers the prerogatives of power without the responsibilities. Such an attitude, self-protective and self-aggrandizing, is inconceivable for Oedipus. His views, unlike Creon's, are nowhere formally stated in the play, but they inhere in all that he does in the play and has done before it. Oedipus is the hero king, the risk-taker, the man who seeks glory and accepts "grief." Creon, on the other hand, is "one who is safe from tragedy."[6]

Creon is, indeed, the nonheroic mirror through whom Sophocles makes clear the nobility of Oedipus. When at the end of the play Oedipus begs to be sent away that he may rid his city of the pollution he carries, Creon, despite the oracle that he himself heard, refuses to act without further confirmation from the god. We feel how pusillanimous and small his spirit is in contrast to that of Oedipus who has reacted with immediacy and pity. In addition, Creon's lack of emotion sets Oedipus' strong emotion in noble relief, for Creon interrupts Oedipus' farewell to his children and when Oedipus pleads for more time, Creon says, "Do not wish to have control in everything!" as if such a request had anything to do with power.

Through Iocaste Sophocles also reveals Oedipus' nobility of spirit. When Oedipus enters the palace, he himself finds Iocaste dead in a noose of her own fashioning. The alternative of suicide is directly before him. He takes up her golden pins and, driving them again and again down into his eyes, blinds himself. It is Sophocles' point that Oedipus sees two possibilities and chooses the harder and more painful course: heroic endurance, the continuation of mind and memory, and submission to whatever the gods now intend. Iocaste escapes the consequences of her deeds; Oedipus does not.

The Flaw in the "Tragic Flaw"

Those who misapprehend *hamartia* as "tragic flaw" and then seek a flaw in Oedipus' character generally settle on "rashness" or "anger." Sophocles carefully crafts the cautious character of Creon to demonstrate that Oedipus' open, emotional, and impulsive nature is not "rash." In like manner, Sophocles presents an infuriated Teiresias, whose anger in no way leads to, or can be understood as meriting his destruction, to forestall a charge of "anger" against Oedipus.

Sophocles' inclusion of Teiresias in the play is brilliant: Teiresias is a physical image of Oedipus' future, blind not sighted, impoverished not regal, carrying a tapping staff not a scepter. Furthermore, his riddling words to Oedipus, the solver of riddles, introduce the question of Oedipus' identity and, perhaps, plant a fear in Oedipus' mind that makes him especially responsive to Iocaste's glancing reference to "a place where three roads meet." Most important, however, Teiresias is shown in the scene with Oedipus to have a temper as violent as Oedipus' own, a clear sign that Sophocles does not regard anger as in any way deserving of dreadful punishment, for Teiresias is surely not punished for his anger. Anger is, if anything, a concomitant of nobility of spirit. Oedipus' anger at the roadside is both princely and natural, he having been struck by a goad, a detail that appears in no other extant telling of the story.

The most serious objection to the notion of a "tragic flaw," a notion that claims Oedipus somehow "gets what he deserves," is that such a thought misapprehends the nature of these gods. Sophocles' is not a *quid pro quo* universe in which niceness is rewarded and badness is punished. The gods create design but people are blind to the design of their lives and unable to insulate themselves against tragedy. Sophocles' universe is a profoundly religious one in which, by their actions alone, people cannot secure purchase.

In addition, to argue that he "gets what he deserves" is to find rashness or anger deserving of a life of torture, shame, and agony, of blindness and unending guilt. It is an equation that is morally monstrous.

Sophocles had the option of making the oracle to Laius conditional (*if* Laius has a son, that son will kill him) or unconditional (Laius *will* have a son who will kill him). Both Aeschylus and Euripides write plays in which Laius' oracle is conditional; Sophocles, like Pindar,[7] chooses to make Laius' oracle unconditional and thus removes culpability for his sins from Oedipus, for he could not have done other than what he did, no matter what action he took.

THE SPHINX AND THE RIDDLE

The Sphinx is alluded to several times in the play, but never is her riddle stated or her myth fully told. Such omission means that it can be assumed that Sophocles' audience knew the story well: a creature with the head of a maiden and the body of a winged lion appeared at Thebes and prevented all entrance to and egress from the city. Freedom from her constricting grip would come only by answering her riddle. The enigma she posed was "What is the creature which is two-footed, three-footed, and four-footed, and weakest when it has most feet?"[8] The answer Oedipus makes is "Man." What appears to be an answer to an abstract question is, although Oedipus does not realize it at the time, his own personal destiny: as infant, he moved on "four feet"; as a man, on "two"; not aged, but blind, Oedipus will carry a staff and move on "three." *Oidipous* means "swollen foot," the legacy of the piercing carried out in his infancy, and *oidi* is also a form of the verb "to know"; thus his name is itself a bitter and hidden riddle, for if he "knew" the circumstances of his "swollen foot," he would also know his identity.

In the original Sphinx myth, Hera, jealous that Zeus has impregnated Semele of Thebes, sends the Sphinx to punish the whole city. Sophocles alters the myth to fit his plot. The Sphinx is sent by the gods so that Oedipus' doom may be fulfilled; the punishment of the city is simply instrumental to the larger design. In an additional irony, the Sphinx's arrival derails the inquiry into Laius' death until the investigator can become Oedipus himself. When the Priest says, "It was some god breathed in you to set us free," he speaks more than he knows, for the gods do "inspire" Oedipus with the answer, but only so that he may enter the grateful city, be hailed as its hero, and marry its widowed queen. Oedipus, to discredit the accusations of Teiresias and Teiresias' prophetic powers, boasts of having solved the riddle that Teiresias failed to solve. Teiresias replies, "It is that very happening that has been your ruin." Answering the riddle required great daring and inductive intelligence, qualities sometimes spoken of as typically "Athenian,"[9] and Oedipus ironically regards that, as do his people, as his greatest achievement. What seem to be chance and nobility of character are actually the long and terrible design of the gods. Appearances are utterly deceptive.

WHEN TWO EQUALS ONE[10]

One might argue that there are, in the action of the plot, "two" Oedipus figures, the searcher and the object of the search, the solver of the riddle and the riddle itself, and that in the imagery of the play Oedipus is likewise "two": the healer of the city and its disease, the hunter and the hunted, the ship's captain and the storm, the sighted and the blind, the husband and the son. Two equals one.

Whether or not to put faith in oracles becomes a critical question in the play, which Iocaste finesses by saying, in effect, that the will of the gods and the words of an oracle or seer cannot necessarily be equated. Yet, it turns out that two do equal one. When the Corinthian Shepherd explains that he received the baby from a servant of Laius, and Oedipus seeks to have that man brought to him, the Chorus say that they think the man "is none other than the [witness] whom you were eager to see before." Two equals one.

In this play, numbers and measurement, as signs of a person's ability to know the physical world, associate Oedipus with the precision and clarity of thought that were deemed to adhere in the new sciences of fifth-century Athens. The greatness of Sophocles' art is that, in his hands, these tools of rational inquiry uncover that which is beyond rationality—the realm of destiny and the gods' inscrutable power.

THE BLINDNESS OF OEDIPUS

The Use of Iocaste's Golden Pins

It may well be that use of the brooch pins for the blinding is Sophocles' own brilliant invention. By using the ornaments of Iocaste's gown, Oedipus not only punishes himself painfully, but also punishes himself on Iocaste's behalf, making her possessions the instruments of his self-mutilation. In addition, the text says he drives the pins into his *arthra* ("sockets"), the same word used by Iocaste for the baby's pinned ankle sockets. In even this sense, Oedipus executes upon himself the original justice designed for him, rendering himself "helpless as the baby was rendered helpless."[11]

The *Kommos* of the Blind Man

In the *kommos*, Sophocles brings the newly-blinded figure of Oedipus onstage and yet avoids bathos and sensationalism. Sophocles' art makes us look not *at* the blind man, but through the blind man's eyes *at* the world, at Oedipus' state of disorientation and imprisonment, at his acute helplessness.

In technique, Sophocles concentrates on the physical realities as he imagines them for Oedipus.

Oedipus enters and asks, "Where am I being carried?" "Where is my voice borne?" It is as though, without his eyes, he cannot ground his being. In utter darkness, everything is space, and he floats. There are no markers. He can locate neither others nor himself. His voice reaches beyond where he is, and he wants his eyes to follow it, but they cannot. He has no physical equilibrium, no sense of up or down, no depth of field. Another question follows: "Ah, god, how far have you leaped?" Movement through space and time is one, for this god has "leaped" from Oedipus' past, through time, through all the misunderstood actions, to this moment, and has "leaped" on and into him: boundaries are permeable.

In this way Sophocles establishes and imagines blindness. The interrogatives are those of a sightless man: "Where?" and again "Where?" and "How far?" The *Oedipus at Colonus*, too, begins with the questions of a blind man about where he is, where he has come to, where he must step, but they are different sorts of questions: they have a concreteness and a practicality.

Questions that are really cries give way to declarative fragments. He senses other things moving in space and time, swirling about him, as he remains unable to move: "cloud of darkness ... coming over me ... sped by an evil wind." A "cloud" sped "by wind" suggests that his reality is intangible. The darkness he exists in he calls "irresistible" and of a degree of horror for which there is no language—"unspeakable." The blind man has only language, and these things exceed language. Oedipus next expresses his pain in images that are tactile and thus describable by a blind man: this goad "stings" and "sinks" into him.

The Chorus say, "it is no wonder that you should lament," and the confirmatory kindness of these words brings Oedipus to his first recognition that he is not in a black, swirling void. He calls out, "Ah, friend, you are still remaining to protect me." In Greek the personal pronoun is part of the verb form, but he expresses the "you" (*su*) separately, emphatically, because human contact is so precious now. And then he says, "I recognize your voice, though I am in the dark."

Sophocles imagines this recovery in the most exquisitely incremental steps. When the Chorus ask him, "Which of the gods set you on to blind yourself?" he not only replies but adds something: Apollo brought this to accomplishment, but "my own hand and no other" was the instrument. Slowly, a sense of autonomy and a sense of identity ("my," "no other"), together with a sense of form (a "hand," an "eye"), return to him. He uses the plural rather than the singular for "friend" when he speaks to the Chorus: the world around him is less empty, fuller. The components of rational discourse gradually return to this man who was the emblem, in his logical thinking, of all rationality.

He continues, "What was I to look upon or cherish?" And then, no more can he rehearse his thoughts at the moment of crisis. He begs now for a conclusion to his life. The Chorus pull back: we wish we had never known you. He does not blame them but curses the Shepherd who released him from the cruel fetters of his feet, "for if I had died then, I would not have been so great a grief to my friends or to myself." A sense of how he is perceived by others begins to return.

Increasingly, Oedipus is integrated into a shared pattern of song and communication, able to continue and repeat choral rhythms. The grammatical construction of his speeches is more sustained. He begins a negative contrafactual ("For if I had died then, I would not have been so great a grief to my friends or to myself") that the choral response interrupts, after which he continues with two more result clauses ("I would not have come to be my father's killer, nor would I have been called by men the bridegroom of her that gave me birth"). Even his capacity for grammatical continuity grows.

The Chorus agree with his assessment: "I too wish it had been so." It is an unsentimental reaction, one that makes us not criticize them, but wish for something more generous. But they are right, it seems. Then the Chorus say he would be better dead than living and blind. The *kommos* ends and Oedipus replies in a sustained counterargument in regular meter of almost 50 lines. He disagrees with them and in disagreement the self is reasserted: I was right, not wrong, to have blinded myself, he says, and he presents his reasons. He utters the painful words "father," "mother," and "children" now for the first time; and he lists the physical features of the city, its "wall," "statues," "temples," and "houses," things he has, through blindness, consciously removed from his sight as being not worthy to look on. The terrible void is being repopulated.

Finally, Oedipus can take thought for others, for Iocaste and her burial, for his young daughters whom he loves and embraces as long as Creon allows him to do so. The distance traveled from his entry with bloodied eyes to the end of the play is, in a sense, as far as a distance as he travels to his *anagnorisis*, and as noble. It is made vivid for us by Sophocles' extraordinary feat of imagining what it must be like to become blind and under such circumstances.

THEME IN THE *OEDIPUS REX*

The *Oedipus Rex* suggests that the human condition is subject to forces and events beyond human comprehension and control. Good intentions do not necessarily produce good results. From the character of the protagonist we learn something else: intelligence and generosity of spirit, energy, and resolve, however much they cause their possessors pain, are also the sources of human greatness, and the attainment of self-knowledge "may be the most difficult and lonely of all forms of heroism."[12]

After Oedipus' questioning of the Theban Shepherd has revealed his identity, Oedipus asks what is not part of the strict logic of inquiry: why, given the prophecy, did you save the child? The answer is, "I felt sorry for it, my lord." Sophocles thereby reveals that anything—good intentions, ordinary intentions, self-serving intentions—can become grist for the mills of the gods to produce what they will. Even in this way, the play reasserts "the traditional religious view that man is ignorant, that knowledge belongs only to the gods."[13] None of us can see ahead, nor can we trust that what we intend kindly will issue in kindness; we are all, like the Shepherds, no different from the great Oedipus.[14] When we think we know with certainty, we come closest to proving that we know nothing at all, that nothing can be relied on, for "in a sense every man must grope in the dark as Oedipus gropes, not knowing who he is or what he has to suffer; we all live in a world of appearance which hides from us who-knows-what dreadful reality."[15]

Oedipus' cognitive discovery, as terrifying as the discovery of pollution within oneself, is that all that he has believed to be true, all that he has felt to be reliable and sure, all that he has based his sense of himself on, all his happiness has been an illusion. He has lived in a world of phantom forms and not known it. The play is a tragedy of cognition in which Oedipus' self-blinding is the overt and belated confession of the recognition, "I have been blind." The victory over the Sphinx was an illusion; the view of himself as heroic savior is a mockery; the belief that he was protective of his father and mother is a delusion; his notions of who he is and where his home is are wrong; the life he has lived with his wife and children, his cherished children dining with him at the table, appeared to be one thing but was, all that time, quite another—shameful, vile; finally and most dreadfully, his view of himself as free is false.

SIGMUND FREUD AND SOPHOCLES

Freud believed that he had found in the *Oedipus Rex* a literary analogue to the process of psychoanalysis, for it is a play that concerns the "gradual discovery" of "a deed long since accomplished," that discovery coming about through a "skillfully prolonged enquiry." In addition, Freud believed the play's message to be, "In vain do you deny that you are accountable, in vain do you proclaim that you have striven against these evil designs. You are guilty, nevertheless," and that that message expressed the essential guilt that burdens humanity. Freud coined the term "Oedipus Complex" and the adjective "Oedipal" to describe what he believed was the motivation behind the play's action.[16] Iocaste's famous lines, "Many have lain with their mothers in their dreams too," seemed to Freud an uncanny reference to the operation of the Unconscious in dreams, the expression of repressed desires, which he called "dream-work." Freud further interpreted Oedipus' self-blinding as "a symbolic self-castration" through a displacement upward, in punishment for illicit desire.[17]

ASPECTS OF STAGECRAFT

The Use of the Third Actor

Aristotle credits Sophocles with the introduction of a third actor, by which he means an actor who is not merely present, as Pylades is for much of the *Chophoroi*, but an actor to whose responses we play close attention. In the scene with the Corinthian Messenger, Iocaste is that third actor. She does not speak until just before her exit, but we are conscious throughout the scene that she is hearing and understanding what Oedipus is not. Her silence is active, rather than passive, and expresses horror, shame, and supreme self-restraint as she balances her own feelings against the need to keep Oedipus ignorant of what she now knows has occurred. Sophocles' use of the third actor deepens the tragic values of scenes such as these.

The Absence of the *Ekkyklema*

When Oedipus reenters in the *exodos* wearing a mask with bloodied eyes, the effect is overwhelming, despite the preparation of the Messenger's graphic speech. The audience would more likely have expected an *ekkyklema* to have been wheeled out, on it Oedipus and, beside him, the body of Iocaste.[18] What Sophocles does here instead is extraordinary. By bringing Oedipus onstage, Sophocles turns the stage convention in which the victims are passively displayed into an act of willed self-exposure. The extraordinary openness that we saw in Oedipus at the beginning of the play, when he appeared before the people and when he insisted that Creon's news be delivered publicly, we see now in a far harsher test. When most reduced, Oedipus is dignified through action and will.

NOTES

1. Richmond Lattimore, *Story Patterns in Greek Tragedy* (Ann Arbor: University of Michigan Press, 1965), p. 4.

2. Bernard M. W. Knox, *Oedipus at Thebes* (New Haven, Conn.: Yale University Press, 1966).

3. W. C. Helmbold, "The Paradox of the *Oedipus*," *American Journal of Philology* 72 (1951), 293.

4. H.D.F. Kitto, *Greek Tragedy* (Garden City, N.J.: Doubleday & Company, 1954), pp. 145–147.

5. Richmond Lattimore, *The Poetry of Greek Tragedy* (New York: Harper & Row, 1966), pp. 82–102.

6. Karl Reinhardt, "Illusion and Truth in Oedipus Tyrannus," *Modern Critical Interpretations: Sophocles' Oedipus Rex* (New York: Chelsea House Publishers, 1988), p. 101.

7. Odes, Olympian II, 42 ff.

8. Sir Richard Jebb, "Introduction" to *The Oedipus Tyrannus of Sophocles* (Cambridge: Cambridge University Press, 1978) (originally published, 1885), p. xiii. Jeffrey Rusten, *Sophocles: Oidipous Tyrannos*, "*Commentary*" (Philadelphia: Bryn Mawr Greek Commentaries, 1990), p. 4, cites Askelpiades of Tragilos (fourth century B.C.) as the first extant source of the riddle.

9. Knox, *Oedipus at Thebes*.

10. Sophocles' use of the language of mathematics is discussed at length in *Oedipus at Thebes*.

11. Lattimore, *The Poetry of Greek Tragedy*, p. 86.

12. Cedric Whitman, *Sophocles: A Study in Heroic Humanism* (Cambridge, Mass.: Harvard University Press, 1951) p. 139.

13. Knox, introduction to *Sophocles: The Three Theban Plays* (New York: Penguin Classics, 1984), p. 152.

14. H.D.F. Kitto, pp. 145–147.

15. E. R. Dodds, "On Misunderstanding the Oedipus Rex," *Modern Critical Interpretations: Sophocles' Oedipus Rex* (New York: Chelsea House Publishers, 1988). p. 48.

16. Sigmund Freud, *Introductory Lectures on Psycho-analysis*, trans. J. Riviere (London: George Allen and Unwin, 1929), p. 278.

17. G. Devereux, "The Self-Blinding of Oidipous in Sophokles: *Oidipous Tyrannos*" *Journal of Hellenic Studies* 93 (1973): 36.

18. Reinhardt, p. 99.

6

Sophocles
The *Oedipus at Colonus*
(406 B.C., performed 401 B.C.)

SUMMARY OF THE *OEDIPUS AT COLONUS*

The *Oedipus at Colonus* is the story of the arrival of Oedipus and Antigone at the grove of the Furies just outside Athens on what is later revealed to be the day of his death, the effort of Creon and Polyneices to force him back to Thebes, and his death, apotheosis and eternal blessing of Athens.

THE HISTORICAL CONTEXT OF THE *OEDIPUS AT COLONUS*

The Political and Social Context

In 406 B.C., when the *Oedipus at Colonus* was written, Athens was in desperate straits, its treasury empty and its population starving. The representation in the *Colonus* of Athens as a place of honor and reverence, and as eternally protected by resident deities, must have been poignant to the play's first audience in 401 B.C.

Although the play is set in the heroic age, in Sophocles' lifetime, too, relations between Athens and Thebes alternated between hostility and cordiality. Realignments were always possible, and, perhaps in part for that reason, Sophocles does not associate Thebes directly with the depravity that Creon exhibits. Nonetheless, when Sophocles' audience heard Theseus, in naiveté and goodness, ask Oedipus, "And how could war arise between our two cities?" they knew that bitter hostility had marked Theban policy toward

Athens for much of the century and they would, therefore, have been immediately inclined to see prophetic wisdom in Oedipus' words.

Sophocles, like Homer, presents the condition of exile as one of destitution and indignity, as Oedipus' bitterness at those who have forced his exile and as Oedipus' love for Theseus who has given him Athenian citizenship reveal. The horror of exile can also be inferred in that both Creon and Polyneices couch their offers as the opportunity for Oedipus to end his exile.

Hero-Cults

The *Oedipus at Colonus* is "an enactment of a cult-legend." The hero-cult was the worship of heroes, real and imaginary, at their tombs. The locales in which such bodies were buried were believed to be specially protected and blessed by the power of the hero after death.[1] Such a grave was always passed in silence. Within the play the grove itself must not be looked on; the site and manner of Oedipus' death cannot be spoken of.

Blood sacrifice at heroes' tombs was sometimes a component of such cults. When Oedipus says to Theseus that, should hostilities break out between Athens and Thebes, "My corpse shall drink hot blood," what he means is that, buried in Athens, he will protect Athens in battle and vanquish her enemies, whose blood will be spilt unto the earth. It is important to note that the date of composition of the Colonus, 406 B.C., was at the dire final moment of the Peloponnesian War.

Rites for the Dead

The next of kin had three obligations to the dead: the washing and arraying of the body with fresh garments, the pouring of libations at the grave, and the wailing/formal lament at the tomb. These obligations were absolute.

The *Colonus* contains the "most detailed description of a libation ritual" in classical literature.[2] The great *kommos* of lamentation at the end of the *Colonus*, sung by Antigone, Ismene, and the Chorus, stands in the place of the formal cultic lament and, as such, contains these traditional components:

- The prefatory announcement that one has come to perform the lament.
- The description of the manner of death and the circumstances of death.
- The expression of the desire to join the dead in Hades.
- The expression of an inability to carry on without the dead.
- A direct address to the dead.
- A statement of the benefits of death.

- An acknowledgment of the death as the gods' will.
- The assertion that death is humanity's shared fate.
- The concluding claim that one has properly performed the rites of lamentation due the dead.
- The promise that one will perform sacrifice and libation to the dead.

Antigone's anguished pleading that she be allowed to visit Oedipus' grave is owing in part to the fact that she cannot properly perform her lament unless she can be at her father's gravesite. Any variation by the playwright on the formula has dramatic weight. Twice the text says that Oedipus' death in the grove was "without wailing or lamentation," and thus Sophocles emphasizes the holiness of the site and Oedipus' readiness and calm at the moment of his death.

THE PLOT OF THE *OEDIPUS AT COLONUS*

General Comments

The *Oedipus at Colonus* is a story of the transformation of the man Oedipus into a cultic hero. It is the only known play in which such apotheosis is "the purpose and the main significance of the whole action."[3] The *Colonus* is the last, the longest, and, perhaps, the most beautiful of all Sophocles' plays. Although classified as a tragedy and treating of a noble subject who suffers and dies, it ends in happiness. In ways somewhat different from those spoken of in Aristotle's *Poetics*, the *Colonus* is cathartic and arouses in the audience both pity and terror, but terror of the sort felt in the face of the sacred and divine. Pity is aroused for the protagonist, but turns into wonder and joy at his transformation and is redirected to the lesser figures of Antigone, Ismene, and Polyneices, who must continue to move in a world of human blindness and limitation, the world that we all occupy and that Oedipus leaves.

Oedipus' view of his innocence and guilt is vastly different in the *Colonus* from his view in the *Oedipus Rex*. Secondary figures are different here as well: Creon is a villain and Antigone is a devoted daughter and sister, not a firebrand.

The *Colonus* appears episodic but is tightly integrated. The plot opens with an assertion of its proper result, Oedipus' cultic burial at Colonus; closes with that result achieved; and in between presents proofs that that result is appropriate. Its construction is, in this sense, rhetorical. The proofs come in the form of encounters that reveal the worthiness or lack of worthiness of the various contenders for Oedipus' blessing. Theseus' actions, taken in response to the actions of Creon and Polyneices, prove Athens worthy of Oedipus' blessing; Creon and Polyneices' efforts to secure that blessing prove them undeserving.

Actions recur in intensified form, as when the grove is entered briefly at the beginning of the play and then permanently at the end, or when, in subsequent scenes, Oedipus must argue against ignorance and untruth.

The Creon scene is "the most traditional in construction" and is a scene of reversal.[4] It is built on *dissoi logoi,* the back and forth of argument. Its climax, which seems to come in the kidnapping, turns out to come in the revelation of Creon's true character.

A Note about Language

Metaphor is infrequent in this play. Creon twice calls the girls "sticks" that help Oedipus walk and once calls them "prey" that he, through his guards, has captured. Oedipus refers to Creon reductively as a "mouth" who "has come here" with "much mouthing" and as one who later speaks with "unholy mouth." Set against a backdrop of simple and direct language, these occasional figures of speech are made to stand out.

The god's call to Oedipus, "You there, Oedipus, why do we wait to go? You have delayed too long!" is an example of Sophocles' simplicity of means. Critics note that the use of first person plural effortlessly joins the man to the god. In addition, the lines themselves, although spoken by gods, are so ordinary as to seem nearly colloquial, and indeed that is Sophocles' intention, for he has the Chorus speak to Oedipus in the same way when they grow impatient to hear Oedipus' name: "The delay is long; hurry up!" By simple iteration Sophocles shows how far Oedipus has traveled, from outcast to blessed.

A Clarification of the Oracles

In the prologue Oedipus refers to an oracle, pronounced years before by Apollo, that his death would be in the land of the dread goddesses, the Furies, and that its sign would be earthquake, thunder, or lightning. Apollo's oracle also promised that Oedipus would bring advantage by his burial to the land and people who received him and ruin to those who had sent him away. The prophecy expresses in general terms what the new oracle that Ismene brings makes more explicit: that if Oedipus is not buried at Thebes and if the Thebans come in hostility to the place of his burial, they will suffer defeat and death, for Oedipus' wrath will reach them from his grave. Ismene also brings news: from fear of the oracle, Creon is coming to take Oedipus back to Thebes. He will claim to be bringing Oedipus into the city itself, but will actually hold him prisoner just outside the city walls, so that Oedipus may not be buried elsewhere. Thus, Oedipus will be forever an exile, even in death, for he will be denied burial in Theban soil and the acknowledgment of identity that such burial confers. In addition, Ismene brings news that her brothers are quarreling for the throne and that Polyneices is mustering an army in Argos to lead against his own city.

The significance of these oracles of Apollo is that through them the god is asserting that Oedipus is not a pollution and should be restored to life and honor in Thebes.[5] The oracles also imply that the male kin—Polyneices, Eteocles, and Creon—who drove Oedipus into beggarly exile have now the opportunity to right that wrong. They wish to bring Oedipus only so near to Thebes, however, as to ensure that his *nekros* (dead body) will protect them and not their enemies. At the same time they wish to spare themselves the embarrassment of openly admitting, by bringing Oedipus into Thebes proper, that they acted shamefully in driving him out. Their solution will continue the deprivations and indignities of exile, add the shame of imprisonment, and use Oedipus to their material advantage. Oedipus understands all of this. To do this to anyone, let alone a king and father, is dreadful. A son who can subscribe to such a plan, who by law, custom, and religion is obliged to support and honor his father, is *kakon kakiste* ("of evil men, the most evil"). Polyneices would, in addition, make his father complicit in his attempt to slaughter his brother and enslave his city—for the Argives who join Polyneices will expect Thebes as spoil. This is the son of a man whose ruling passion was love of Thebes.

The Proximate Causes of Oedipus' Exile

Oedipus progressively describes his sons as more culpable and injurious. First, he says that both sons "agreed that the throne should be left to Creon," and then, that "they did not prevent" Oedipus' being "uprooted, and sent away, and proclaimed exile." Next, he describes them as actively driving him out, and, finally, he says that Polyneices "held the scepter and the throne" and acted alone in making his own father "cityless." Kitto argues a pattern of increasing "definition and certainty" from which "we are made to feel more and more the power of Oedipus."[6]

The Significance of the Grove

Oedipus moves from polluted to sacred status, and that movement is implicit not only in the new oracles of Apollo but also in the simple theatrical fact that nothing terrible happens to Oedipus when he treads on the sacred ground: the Furies whom he addresses in friendly prayer in the prologue are not aroused to anger against him. They are female deities, whose special province is the punishment of wrongs done to mothers and to blood kin, and it is their grove that the gods have decreed to be Oedipus' destination. His entry there, if a symbolic reenactment of his ancient crime of entering the forbidden maternal space, is the purest imaginable sign that pollution has gone from him. Thus, what is at first a surreptitious act, interrupted and reversed, repeats itself at the end of the play as a stately and hallowed procession.

The Setting

The setting is just outside the sacred grove of the Furies in the deme of Colonus, near Athens. The time is about 20 years after the action of the *Oedipus Rex* and a few days before the attack against Thebes led by Polyneices. The *skene* has before it a painted backdrop representing the grove, in front of which are rocks and a statue of Colonus, the hero, astride a horse. The grove of the Furies to which Oedipus comes at the beginning of the play is the grove that, in the *Eumenides*, becomes their permanent home under the earth. The play assumes the prior action of the *Oedipus Rex*.

Dramatis Personae

Oedipus	a beggar and exile
Antigone	daughter to Oedipus
Stranger of Colonus	
Chorus of Elders of Colonus	
Ismene	daughter to Oedipus
Theseus	king of Athens
Creon	emissary of Thebes
Guards	
Polyneices	elder son of Oedipus
Messenger	

Scene Divisions

Prologue:	1–116	[Oedipus, Antigone, Stranger]
Parodos:	117–253	[Chorus, Oedipus, Antigone]
Episode One:	254–667	[Chorus, Oedipus, Antigone, Ismene, Theseus]
First Choral Ode:	668–719	[Chorus, Oedipus *and* Antigone *onstage*]

Episode Two:	720–1043	[Chorus, Oedipus, Antigone, Creon, Guards, Theseus]
Second Choral Ode:	1044–1095	[Chorus, Oedipus *onstage*]
Episode Three:	1096–1210	[Chorus, Oedipus, Theseus, Antigone, Ismene]
Third Choral Ode:	1211–1248	[Chorus, Oedipus, Antigone *and* Ismene *onstage*]
Episode Four:	1249–1555	[Chorus, Oedipus, Antigone, Polyneices, Theseus]
Fourth Choral Ode:	1556–1578	[Chorus]
Exodos:	1579–1779	[Chorus, Messenger, Antigone, Ismene, Theseus]

Synopsis

| Prologue: | 1–116 | [Oedipus, Antigone, Stranger] |

Oedipus, old, blind, and led by Antigone, who has accompanied him in his wanderings, enters and sits on a rock. A Stranger appears and orders the blind man to move from ground that is sacred to the "all-seeing" Furies. Oedipus declares that he will never leave this place and asks that the king be summoned to receive a boon. The Stranger summons the elders of Colonus, as Oedipus prays to the Furies, asking them to grant him "a passage" and "a conclusion of my life" within their sacred precincts, in accord with Apollo's will. Oedipus and Antigone hide in the grove.

| *Parodos:* | 117–253 | [Chorus, Oedipus, Antigone] |

The Chorus enter in great agitation at the report of the Stranger. They insist that Oedipus leave the grove and promise him sanctuary, a promise they retract when they learn who he is.

| Episode One: | 254–667 | [Chorus, Oedipus, Antigone, Ismene, Theseus] |

Oedipus justifies his actions as having been done in ignorance and says that he brings "advantage to the citizens here." They agree to summon Theseus. Meanwhile, Ismene arrives with news from Thebes. The Chorus tell Oedipus the rites of purification he must perform, and he appoints

Ismene his surrogate. Theseus enters and welcomes Oedipus, who explains, in a speech of extraordinary beauty, that time changes all things, including friendship between cities. He predicts war with Thebes and promises that when that war comes, his body, buried here, will protect Athens forever, if what the gods speak is true. Theseus offers the hospitality of his own hearth to Oedipus who, knowing that his end is near, asks only to be allowed to remain at the grove.

First Choral Ode: 668–719   [Chorus, Oedipus *and* Antigone
                                                  onstage]

The Chorus sing the great ode to Colonus ("Land of running horses").

Episode Two: 720–1043   [Chorus, Oedipus, Antigone, Creon,
                                              Guards, Theseus]

Creon arrives from Thebes with armed guards, but assures the Chorus that he intends them no harm, saying he comes only to persuade Oedipus to return with him to Thebes. Oedipus exposes Creon's real intentions, the two men argue, and Creon announces that his guards have secretly seized Ismene and will now arrest Antigone. They bear her off, to the agony of Oedipus and the outrage of the Chorus. Theseus enters, having been interrupted in his sacrifices to Poseidon by the cries of the Chorus. He orders an immediate pursuit of the girls and charges Creon with dishonoring Thebes and Athens. Creon's responses are conciliatory at first but grow more strident. Theseus orders Creon to show him where the girls are as they exit.

Second Choral Ode: 1044–1095   [Chorus, Oedipus *onstage*]

The Chorus express their longing to be at the scene of the fight. They predict victory for the Athenian horsemen and pray to Zeus for aid.

Episode Three: 1096–1210   [Chorus, Oedipus, Antigone,
                                               Ismene, Theseus]

Antigone and Ismene are reunited with their father. Theseus announces that a suppliant seeks audience with Oedipus. Oedipus realizes the man is his son Polyneices and refuses to meet with him but is convinced by Theseus and Antigone to grant the interview.

Third Choral Ode: 1211–1248   [Chorus, Oedipus, Antigone
                                       and Ismene *onstage*]

The Chorus sing that not to be born is best and compare the suffering man Oedipus to a promontory that great waves break over and forever batter.

Episode Four: 1249–1555   [Chorus, Oedipus, Antigone,
                                    Polyneices, Theseus]

In this two-part scene, Polyneices professes shock at the condition of his father, reproaches himself, and urges Oedipus to join him in the campaign to unseat his brother Eteocles. Oedipus accuses Polyneices of driving him from Thebes and prophesies that Polyneices and Eteocles will die at each other's hands. Polyneices ignores Antigone's plea and sets off alone for Thebes.

Suddenly, there is thunder. Knowing that his time of death has come, Oedipus asks that Theseus be fetched immediately. He prays that he may remain clear-headed to repay Theseus for his kindness and fulfill his promise of the eternal protection of Athens. Oedipus leads his daughters and Theseus offstage without assistance, as the thunder continues.

Fourth Choral Ode: 1556–1578   [Chorus]

The Chorus pray to Persephone and Hades that Oedipus may die without pain. To the goddesses of earth they pray that the stranger "may walk clear" and easily when he comes to the plains of the dead below.

Exodos: 1579–1779   [Chorus, Messenger, Antigone, Ismene,
                               Theseus]

A Messenger reports the death of Oedipus. Antigone and Ismene enter and, with the Chorus, sing a *kommos* of lament. Theseus enters. Antigone pleads to be taken to Oedipus' grave, but Theseus, having sworn not to reveal its location, refuses. She accepts her father's will. Theseus promises to send her and her sister to Thebes to try to avert the coming conflict between their brothers. The Chorus urge an end to lamentation as they exit.

THE SIGNIFICANCE OF THE POLYNEICES SCENE

Those who argue either that the construction of the *Oedipus at Colonus* is fragmented and episodic, or that the character of Oedipus is unjustifiably wrathful, cite as evidence the scene between Polyneices and Oedipus. The questions that must be answered, and that provide clues about Sophocles' meaning and artistry are: (1) Why include this scene at all? (2)Why place it after the scene with Creon? (3) Why precede it immediately with a scene of reunion? (4) Why show Oedipus angry and risk loss of sympathy for him? If such a risk indeed existed, why was it essential to take? If it did not, how do our attitudes differ from those of Sophocles' audience, for the religious and secular attitude of our age elevates the ideal of forgiveness and defines as primitive the heroic ideal of rewarding one's friends and punishing one's enemies. Thus it can initially seem to a modern audience that Sophocles has "left it possible for us to abhor the implacable father more than the heartless children."[7]

When Oedipus is called to his death in the second half of episode four, just after the Polyneices scene, Sophocles wishes him to be a figure whose stature and integrity mark him as rightly chosen by the gods for the mystery that will be uniquely his. As the Creon scene concludes, Oedipus is a sympathetic but weakened figure. He has had his children ripped from him and he has had to rely on Theseus to return them. In writing a scene of supplication, Sophocles restores Oedipus' power, for Oedipus now becomes the dispenser of reward and punishment. Theseus urges Oedipus to hear the suppliant, and Sophocles removes Theseus from the stage so that Oedipus may be the sole judge of his son and the sole authority present. Both the decision to hear Polyneices and the decision to answer him are dramatized separately to emphasize Oedipus' exercise of free will.

In scenes of supplication, sympathy is usually with the suppliant; Sophocles uses the Chorus to direct sympathy away from Polyneices. When they tell Polyneices they "take no pleasure in his former journeys" from Thebes to Argos to Attica, by which they mean they take no pleasure in the deeds that have caused those journeys, and wish him to "now return with all speed," they have wholeheartedly adopted Oedipus' position and rejected Polyneices' claims on his father. They do not urge a compromise: right can be wholly on one side and not on the other. Thus, they guide the audience against the tendency to distribute blame and assist the audience in seeing that Oedipus is correct.

The moral standard that underlies this play and this culture is absolute obligation to one's parents. Polyneices' deeds are exposed in the scene, and long before the scene Oedipus says to Ismene that it is his sons who have injured him. If the gods have punished Oedipus so sorely for unintentional injury to parents, what does Polyneices deserve, who violates every natural feeling and every blood tie and has knowingly and intentionally injured his father?

Oedipus' curse on Polyneices is viewed through the lens of the preceding scene with Creon. That scene provided absolute validation of Oedipus' judgment and integrity. In the Polyneices scene, Sophocles presents a hypocrite of a different sort, and this time Sophocles withholds from the play all tangible evidence of his villainy. In addition, Sophocles makes Antigone sympathetic to Polyneices and gives Polyneices words of repentance that border on the sincere. Sophocles takes great dramatic risk and thus must have been sure about what he intended. Indeed, the absence of verifiable evidence forces us, finally, to take Oedipus at his word and to rely on what we know of his character. The reliance that Sophocles makes us place on Oedipus' judgment is itself a device that elevates Oedipus in our minds above ordinary human stature and readies us for the scene of apotheosis that will follow. In other words, Sophocles *needs* to make this scene dependent on assertion, just as he needed to make the Creon scene dependent on evidence, establishing Oedipus' judgment in the Creon scene that he might make us infer it here.

The Polyneices scene also must follow the Creon scene because Polyneices' offer is revenge: bless me, march with me, and together we will punish Thebes and my brother and, implicitly, Creon who is allied with Eteocles. If Oedipus were driven by vengeance, even such partial vengeance as Polyneices offers would be tempting. Oedipus rejects the offer utterly. He will not support one villain against another, and his realities have no connection to the petty rivalries and resentments that animate Polyneices.

The Polyneices scene is also one of strained reunion intended to stand in sharp contrast to preceding scenes of joyful reunion, Ismene's arrival from Thebes, and Antigone and Ismene's restoration to Oedipus. These earlier reunions establish Oedipus as a man capable of great love so that Polyneices, and not Oedipus, is understood to be the source of dissonance in this scene. Indeed, the second and more emotional reunion, in which Sophocles emphasizes through dialogue and physical embrace the abiding love between Oedipus and his children, immediately precedes Polyneices' entrance.

If the Polyneices scene were omitted, the conclusion of the play could not stand in tonal contrast to what preceded it, nor would the desirability of such peace as death brings be as strongly felt. Polyneices' persistence in marching to Thebes reminds us of how much of life consists of self-willed error, and the pain the interview causes Oedipus demonstrates the truth of the third ode, which asserts that life is pain. Against both of these states, death stands as a desired release. This scene, which follows the third ode and illustrates the pains of earthly existence to which the ode alludes, is tied to the theme of death. Polyneices, going offstage, urges Antigone to "place me in my tomb with funeral rites." It is a remarkable moment, for we have thought of Oedipus' death throughout the play; the universality of death is suddenly demonstrated by Polyneices' words.

Finally, in speaking of the future that Polyneices himself creates, Oedipus is revealed as having prophetic power and as being able, through his curses, to call down the very future he foresees. Oedipus' divine transformation begins to be felt, and it is this that Sophocles wishes to present. It is fitting therefore that the scene of apotheosis follow right after the Polyneices scene.

SECONDARY CHARACTERS

Theseus

Theseus represents the two great virtues of Athens, its reverence for the gods and its kindness to strangers. Indeed, Oedipus says to Theseus, "I have found in you alone among mankind piety and fairness and the absence of lying speech." By his conduct Theseus demonstrates that Athens deserves Oedipus' blessing and, thus, that Oedipus judges correctly.

Sophocles makes no allusion to Theseus' past, except in the single word, "exile," by which Theseus describes himself to Oedipus. According to myth, Theseus is brought up in Troezen, ignorant that his father is Aegeus, king of Athens. On arriving at manhood, he travels to Athens, is acknowledged by Aegeus as his heir, and again becomes an exile when he is taken to Crete in a tribute ship. There, he kills the Minotaur and, after many years, returns to Athens.

The virtue of Theseus is apparent in the delicacy of his first address to Oedipus, which Sophocles places immediately after the relentless and intrusive questioning of the Chorus. Theseus avoids any reference that may shame Oedipus: he says he knows Oedipus by his "clothing," but does not describe his garments as either ragged or dirtied, by his "eyes" and by his "stricken face," alluding only to the pain Oedipus has inflicted on himself and endured after his crimes, not to the crimes themselves. In addition, he uses the normal and honorable patronymic, "son of Laius," which acknowledges Oedipus' royal lineage and dispels any sense that Theseus considers Oedipus guilty of anything that the spirit of Laius would not forgive. Immediately thereafter Theseus asks what he or his city may do to assist Oedipus, introducing the subject to relieve his guest of having to do so. Then Theseus says, "I have not forgotten that I myself was brought up in exile, as you were, and that in my exile I struggled against such dangers." He, a great king, not only equates himself to the polluted man but, by referring to the exile of Oedipus' youth in Corinth rather than to his current exile from Thebes, avoids referring to Oedipus' shame. Even his saying "I have not forgotten," rather than "I remember," is a mark of moral fineness: it is not the presence of Oedipus that makes him suddenly "remember" his own suffering; rather, it is ever before him. Theseus concludes his short speech, saying, "I know that I am a man, and that I have no greater share in tomorrow than you have." Not simply as exiles, but as men, they are one and their destiny is one. Even Theseus' grammar in this speech, which consists of subordinate clause linked to subordinate clause, reflects in syntactic terms the way in which Theseus connects one experience with another and links his destiny to that of others.

Theseus questions Oedipus' judgment at certain moments, suggesting that Oedipus is overly passionate in his refusal to return to Thebes and to hear Polyneices, and overly pessimistic in his prediction of war between friendly nations. Oedipus replies fully to Theseus' question about the outbreak of hostilities, and all that he says proves to be true, not in future time, as Oedipus' own words suggest, but within moments, with Creon's arrival and seizure of Oedipus' daughters. Theseus' skepticism, however, is dramatically necessary, for his subsequent rejection of that skepticism and assertion of faith in Oedipus' judgment become a demonstration, repeatedly enacted within the play, that Oedipus' perceptions of truth and falsity are absolutely sound. That Theseus does not undertake war against Thebes, when Creon violates his hospitality by kidnapping, presents a stark contrast to Polyneices, who acts solely out of vengeance and knowingly injures his city. Theseus is able to separate his judgment of the city of Thebes from his judgment of its emissary.

Theseus' piety is emphasized in two ways: by his repeated association with the offstage altar of the gods and by his urging Oedipus not to dishonor the god before whose altar Polyneices has seated himself by refusing to hear the suppliant. Theseus' piety is emphasized again when Theseus tells Antigone that he cannot reveal Oedipus' burial place because "the god heard me promise this, and the lord of oaths, the son of Zeus who hears all words." Yet he interrupts his rites of sacrifice to welcome the stranger and to rescue the girls. Although the Chorus are torn between reverence for the gods and kindness to strangers, their king sees no such division.

The disparity in age between Theseus and Oedipus is emphasized by Theseus' question about war "between our nations." Oedipus' response, in perhaps the most exquisite words of advice in tragedy, begins "Most beloved son of Aegeus" with *philtate,* the adjectival superlative, expressing both Oedipus' love for Theseus and the dead Aegeus' love for Theseus. In this moment, Oedipus speaks to Theseus as father would to son, explaining age and time and death. At the end of the play, Oedipus guides Theseus to the grove and passes to him, as to a beloved and deserving son and lineal descendant, his blessing. Theseus stands as a model son against whom Sophocles would have us judge Polyneices.

Creon

Creon is a skillful rhetorician who uses his gifts to manipulate and distort. His veneer is one of civility and concern, and he pretends to be an upholder of the civilized values of dedication to one's *polis* and kin, propriety and decorum, moderation and hospitality. Among Creon's rhetorical ploys are the justification of an action by selectively describing its cause, the use of blatant flattery, the pretense of helplessness and the subtle attempt to draw pity away from Oedipus and toward himself, which he accomplishes in part by repeatedly referring to himself, and not Oedipus, as "an old man." Creon speaks of the pity he feels for Antigone and thereby actually shames both her and her father by drawing deliberate attention to the fact that "anyone who sees her can take her."

When Creon's mask of affection for Oedipus drops, he says to Theseus, referring to Oedipus whom he wants to take to Thebes, that the rulings of the Areopagus do "not permit such wanderers to live together with this city." His choice of the word "wanderer" is particularly duplicitous, for "wandering" can be an act of choice on the part of the wanderer, and using such a term mutes the sense of Theban culpability for Oedipus' exile.

Creon accuses Oedipus of prideful anger and moments later, having taken both daughters, says, "I shall no longer resist my violent anger but will carry this man away" also. His impiety is revealed not only in his unholy seizure of both girls, but in that by seizing Ismene, he interrupts her acts of propitiation of the Furies and Theseus' sacrifices to Poseidon. He is, in a sense, an immoral analogue to Theseus, for "everything which in Theseus is genuine in Creon appears as part of his disguise."[8]

Polyneices

Polyneices' right to the throne of Thebes is highly suspect, for Ismene indicates that only if rule passes from Laius' line can "pollution of the city be avoided." Even if that were not the case, it is traitorous to lead a force against one's own city. Antigone expects that he intends to destroy it. What booty will go to his Argive comrades is not explicitly stated, but Sophocles' audience would understand that definite recompense would have been expected and would have come from the Theban treasury. Out of personal vanity, he will, by his own report, lie to those same comrades, for were they aware that he received from his father a curse rather than a blessing, they would abandon the expedition. His military actions show him to be one who, in seeking to punish his enemies, is not above injuring his friends.

In the play Polyneices is explicitly compared to his sisters. Oedipus says they "bear the burdens" of their father's sorrows while Polyneices and Eteocles, in the Egyptian manner, "sit in their houses working at the loom, and their consorts provide the necessities of life out of doors." Ismene recognizes that Oedipus and Antigone's suffering is acute and therefore declines to speak of her own. The kidnapping of the two girls is further evidence of the suffering they endure for their father. In contrast to them, Polyneices has offered no assistance all these years and has in fact been the cause, either by initiation or by acquiescence, of Oedipus' expulsion and beggary. He exaggerates the details of his own travails and equates them with his father's. Once his plea that Oedipus march with him to Thebes is rejected, the concern he has expressed for his father's condition vanishes, and all his words to Antigone refer to himself and his future. At the end of the scene, he explains that he cannot turn his army back because "to flee," using the same word that means "to be an exile," is "shameful." He has conveniently forgotten that he forced precisely this fate on his father. Antigone's words, "I supplicate you," do not remind him that he has just appeared as a suppliant before the altar of the god and that he has just said that he and his army "supplicate" his father.

Polyneices is compared not just to his sisters but to Oedipus himself. At the beginning of the scene, the great Oedipus has yielded to the request of Antigone to see Polyneices; at the end of the scene, the paltry Polyneices does not yield to the request of Antigone to disband his army. Oedipus, bound by destiny and circumstance in ways Polyneices could not possibly comprehend, values and insists on his ability to act according to his own will. Polyneices, who has all his life been free of the constraints of destiny, does not value that freedom at all and behaves as though he has no freedom, so bound is he by the vanity and ambition that he deludes himself into calling his "honor."

Polyneices asks his father, disingenuously, if he will not even explain why he is angry. Polyneices' expressions of remorse move immediately, with no relaxation of emotion, to a self- absolving expectation of mercy, both from the gods and from his father. Polyneices, the evil son, stands in contrast to Theseus, who acts as true son to Oedipus. Theseus wishes to assist Oedipus; Polyneices wishes Oedipus to assist him.

DEATH

The *Colonus*, a play about the coming of death, defines a good death, such as comes to Oedipus, as marked by readiness and love, the sort of death that all humans might wish for themselves. "Death had been presented in ... the *Antigone* as the experience of being torn away, voluntarily but painfully, ... from youth and family. But that now lies in the past."[9] Death now is felt as a moment when the boundary between the human and the divine is dissolved.

In scene after scene death is kept before us: in Oedipus' words to Theseus about the changes that time brings to all things, in Polyneices' anticipation of his own death, in the choral odes and the great *kommos* that concludes the play.

The odes collectively move us toward reconciliation with the idea of death, but none so well as the ode to Colonus. The beauty of Colonus turns on elements reminiscent of death. The narcissus in Greek myth "is *the flower of imminent death*, being associated, through its narcotic fragrance, with *narke* [numbness]." It is also, in the *Hymn to Demeter*, "the *last* flower for which Persephone is stretching forth her hand when Pluto seizes her." The crocus was associated with the Eleusinian cult of death and resurrection and, according to Juvenal, was "planted on graves."[10] The nightingale is a bird of lamentation. The description of Colonus as "never vexed by the sun or by the wind of many winters" echoes Homer's description of Elysium.[11] The ode to Colonus also suggests timeless continuity in its repetition of words such as "never" and "ever." The ode ends with images of continuous motion, of horses, boats, and waves. Thus Colonus, the place of Oedipus' death, is associated with beauty and is both death-filled and deathless; by extension, its beauty becomes death's.

At Oedipus' death all things necessary and proper are done: the washing of the corpse and the putting of white garments upon it. Things that for all other persons occur after death occur for Oedipus while he still lives and give his dying a special sanctity and honor. That the offices are performed by Oedipus himself, as the phrase "gave him the bath and the raiment that is customary" suggests, demonstrates his absolute readiness, as does the fact that his death occurs "without lamentation."

Free will is precious to Oedipus, given his history, and Antigone finds comfort in knowing that "he died where he chose to die." Of the injunction of silence, she says, "If this accords with his wish, that is sufficient." Oedipus' death is marked, then, not only by readiness and love, but also by choice. Theseus says, "Cease your lamentation, children," for "it is for Oedipus a treasure." It is hard to think of Sophocles or of any of us wishing a better sort of death.

THEME IN THE *OEDIPUS AT COLONUS*

"In the world of time things become their opposites."[12] Allies become enemies, and time transforms everything. Oedipus is a figure who embodies a profound paradox: outwardly, he is ragged and filthy, a worthless beggar; inwardly, he is of inestimable worth. He is the polluted man who is holy and the guilty man who proclaims his innocence. He is the pariah, the outcast, who protects the city and the land; he is the man tortured by the gods who becomes a god himself; he is the feeble man who can withstand the thunder of the gods until Theseus arrives, that he may fulfill his promise. He embodies "the everlasting contradiction of inner and outer value."[13]

To Oedipus is assigned the task of unmasking hypocrisy and reviling evil. It is an heroic task, although not in the way that encountering a monstrous Sphinx is heroic. Its realm is everyday life, for the evil Oedipus faces is plausible evil, masquerading as kindliness or regret. It is the evil perhaps most common in life and hardest to combat, in which one person must stand against many and appear to be impolite, overly emotional, a disturber of the social harmony that the plausible villain seems to advocate and that the community seems to prefer. Oedipus struggles to assert truth against skillful lies, to an audience that assumes that excess is suspect and that "right" is surely present on both sides. Such a view reduces the ideal of moderation to a principle that justifies the avoidance of real distinctions and that is wary of both passion and certainty.

Truth and ease of speech do not necessarily go hand in hand. As Oedipus says of Creon and himself, "I have never known an honest man to speak so well under all conditions."

Language is subject to corruption, and, thus, it is fitting that in the *Colonus* much is made of silence and of the inviolability of the secret that Oedipus passes to Theseus. Yet we also hear Antigone's reassurance to Oedipus, and the poet's vindication of his art: "Actions evilly devised are exposed by words."

"METATHEATRICS" AND THE PSYCHOLOGY OF THE VIEWER

Through inspired dramatic invention, Sophocles makes his audience experience, at first- and not second-hand, the mystery of death and transformation. As Oedipus, who before needed assistance with every step, bids Theseus to follow him, he says, "I am led by the escorting Hermes and by the goddess below." In other words, he "sees" the god, as neither his companions on stage nor the audience does. It is a remarkable statement, for it asserts that, visible to him, is not merely the path into the grove, which we all can see, but that which we cannot see, the god himself. It is at this moment that Oedipus' recovered "sight" is shown to us not only as miraculous but also as greater than our own. Thus, his apotheosis is credible.

Oedipus is a character of extraordinary endurance, and the physical emblem of that endurance is his uninterrupted presence on stage. By keeping Oedipus steadily before our eyes, Sophocles so accustoms the audience to his presence that his exit is a void sharply felt just as the void death creates is sharply felt. In other words, by the simple expedient of keeping his protagonist on stage at all times, Sophocles has made real for his audience the fiction of loss and attached that fiction to both the character and the actor who portrays that character.

There is in all of us an impulse desiring the completion of any action and a feeling of tension at its interruption. Because attention throughout the play is drawn to interrupted ritual, the completed rituals associated with Oedipus' death bring to the audience a release of tension and a sense of peace that replicate what Oedipus is imagined to experience. This occurs even though the rituals of death are different from the rituals of purification and sacrifice. All ritual is performed off stage, but much stage time is given to speaking of ritual, first, in the lengthy instruction of the Chorus to Oedipus and Ismene about purification, and then when we hear that Ismene has been interrupted in performing those rites. Ritual action is again interrupted, for Sophocles emphasizes that Theseus, in order to rescue the girls, must leave off his sacrifice to Poseidon. A third interruption of ritual comes from the gods themselves: the thunder forces Theseus to leave the altar of Poseidon. The death of Oedipus, as the Messenger reports, is attended by rituals fulfilled and thus by a release of tension.

The *kommos* sung by Antigone, Ismene, and the Chorus is of unusual length because what Sophocles puts before us is not representational but actual: we hear the dirge for the dead in all its fullness and are thus made participants in the final ritual act of the play. Sophocles makes stage time approximate real time, as if we were actual attendants at the rites for Oedipus. The experience of sorrow and its cathartic resolution create an ending that conveys, not only through what we observe but also through what we are made to participate in, the full meaning of death and apotheosis.

That Theseus cannot and will not reveal the burial place of Oedipus to Antigone and Ismene, nor the manner of Oedipus' death, works on the audience precisely as does the full lament: by excluding the audience along with the survivors, and by asserting the existence of a secret through the knowledge of the initiated Theseus, Sophocles helps his audience feel itself in the presence of the sacred—of that which cannot be touched or trod upon or spoken of or known, and our sensing the immanence of the divine makes the conclusion transcendent.

ASPECTS OF STAGECRAFT

Onstage Action: Walking

Almost everything that Oedipus says in the prologue draws attention to his need for assistance: "Come, my child, seat me." When the Chorus insist he leave the grove, for him to do so requires a string of questions with guiding answers from Antigone. Their dialogue occupies some 30 lines of text: "Take hold of me, then! Further then? Further? Lead me, then, daughter. Like this? Shall I sit down? Ah me! Alas for my ruinous affliction!"

That Sophocles would risk so slow a dramatic pace so early in the play reflects not poor playwriting but the considered decision of a master playwright who designs a moment of tedium to set up a stunning climax later. And so, when Oedipus, hearing and feeling the thunder run through him, knows he is called by the god, no special effects, no *mechane*, nothing is needed, but for Oedipus to walk firmly, unaided, leading others into the sacred grove. Sophocles' dramatic climax consists of his hero's simply walking across the stage.

Onstage Action: Forbidden Contact

The seizing of Antigone by Creon's guard and the dragging of her offstage is a moment of shocking physical violence in the play. In his actions, as in his speech, Creon "touches" what he should not touch. In sharpest possible contrast to that act of forbidden contact is Oedipus' immediate recoil and checking of his own impulse to touch Theseus. In gratitude Oedipus says, "Stretch out your right hand to me, king, so that I may touch it and may kiss your face, if it is permitted." Oedipus is immediately overwhelmed by a sense of his own unworthiness and by the thought that, however free of guilt he knows himself to be by law, he still feels a taint that he would not pass on to a man of Theseus' great goodness. The scrupulosity and humility of Oedipus' action, set beside the *hubristic* insolence of Creon's, form a powerful contrast.

The other form of forbidden contact in the play, in fact its pervasive form, deals with treading on sacred ground.

Of the *Geron*

The stage figure of the *geron* (the "old man"), as the comic Chorus of feeble and foolish old men in the *Lysistrata* demonstrate, was a figure of fun, especially when angry. That Sophocles makes just such a type, an unkempt old man, perhaps his greatest hero means that Sophocles knows exactly what will and will not arouse laughter. Polyneices speaks of himself and his father as subjects of Eteocles' mockery, but although Polyneices may, indeed, be ridiculous, Oedipus never is. He is severe and generous, vulnerable and steadfast, terrifying and god-designated. Such a figure, even in rags, can never be the object of derision.

NOTES

1. Walter Burkert, *Greek Religion*, translated by John Raffan (Oxford: Basil Blackwell Publisher; Cambridge, Mass.: Harvard University Press, 1985), pp. 203–208.

2. Burkert, p. 72.

3. Karl Reinhardt, *Sophocles*, first printed in German in 1933 (Oxford: Basil Blackwell Publishers, 1979), pp. 193–194.

4. Reinhardt, pp. 209–212.

5. Sir Richard Jebb, *The Oedipus Coloneus of Sophocles*, with a Commentary, first printed in 1903; abridged by E. S. Shuckburgh from the Large Edition (Cambridge: Cambridge University Press, 1955), "Introduction," p. ix.

6. H.D.F. Kitto, *Greek Tragedy* (Garden City, NY: Doubleday & Company, 1954), pp. 414–415.

7. Jebb, p. 21.

8. Reinhardt, p. 211.

9. Reinhardt, p. 224.

10. Jebb, p. 150.

11. *Odyssey*, 4.563 and 6.42.

12. Cedric Whitman, *Sophocles: A Study in Heroic Humanism* (Cambridge, Mass.: Harvard University Press, 1951), p. 198.

13. Whitman, p. 190.

7

Euripides
The *Medea*
(431 B.C.)

EURIPIDES' LIFE AND REPUTATION

Euripides was born to Athenian citizens about 485 B.C. and died in Macedonia in 406 B.C., having moved there a little more than a year before. Aristophanes' the *Frogs* pits Aeschylus and Euripides against each other in a drama competition in Hades and lampoons them both. It was performed a year after Euripides' death and offers the reliable biographical detail that Euripides possessed an extensive library at a time when no one else did. Scurrilous contemporary reports call Euripides a misogynist—a charge that the sympathetic portrayal of women and indeed of all victims of society in his plays disputes—and impugn him as the son of a vegetable seller, but the esteem in which he was held is evident from the fact that when news of his death reached Athens, Sophocles dressed himself in black and instructed his Chorus not to wear their customary garlands in the *proagon* (pre-competition) procession.

Aristotle calls Euripides "the most tragic of all the poets" and scholars regard both Roman comedy and modern European drama as having their true roots not in Aeschylus and Sophocles, the poets of high tragedy, but in Euripides, who, as Aristophanes concedes in the *Frogs*, made characters speak "in human fashion" and "showed scenes of common life," and whose attention to human psychology and motive is the precursor of theatrical realism.

CHARACTERISTICS OF EURIPIDEAN DRAMA

Minor figures, such as the Nurse and Tutor in the *Medea*, and the Herdsman in the *Bacchae*, have characteristic modes of speech and are associated with realistic settings. And while its chief feature, like that of Aeschylean and Sophoclean drama, is plot, Euripidean drama presents in detail and with complexity the emotional life and the sexual and psychological motivations of its major figures. He is the first dramatist "to make the conflict inside an individual central in a play."[1] His methods and sensibilities are consistently ironic, and his plays tend to have "paired antagonists"[2] rather than a single hero.

Often "the sympathy invoked for one character is suddenly alienated and shifted to another; the victim and the oppressor change places."[3] Euripides draws on the same body of myth as Aeschylus and Sophocles, but he sometimes presents figures—villains and heroes—"in a new light of innocence or guilt."[4] In fact, such character degeneration of heroes "was a device favored by Euripides as a means of communicating the seemingly infinite potential of human fallibility."[5] In addition, like Pentheus in the *Bacchae,* and with the exception of Medea, the characteristic Euripidean hero "suffers rather than acts."[6]

Euripides sees humans as lacking the rationality needed to make the distinction the Sophists insisted on between *physis* ("nature"), that which is immutable in the universe, in human nature, and therefore in society, and *nomos* ("law" or "convention"), that which human beings have created and which can be modified.[7] His plays show that the consequences of such irrationality are broadly destructive.

Euripides makes fuller use than his predecessors of another aspect of Sophist teaching, *dissoi logoi* ("double argument"), the rhetorical method of constructing opposing arguments for a single question that has become the basis of Western political debate and jurisprudence.

The gods, whether through direct intervention, as in the *Bacchae,* or through human agency, as in the *Medea,* are operative and powerful, and oversee this pattern of human destruction, even when represented with radically diminished dignity. Their will "is no longer, as in Aeschylus, revealed in time as beneficent."[8]

Euripides, like his predecessors, alternates dramatic episode with choral song, but the divisions are less sharp; they "merge into one another with perfect smoothness."[9] One way in which that merging is accomplished is through choral odes that make explicit reference to surrounding action.

A LIST OF EURIPIDES' PLAYS

Of the 90 or so plays that Euripides wrote, only 4 won first prize and 2 of those 4 prizes were for the plays performed after his death. A total of 17 (or 19 if the *Rhesus* and the *Cyclops* are regarded as legitimate attributions) survive. The relatively large number of preserved dramatic manuscripts of Euripides indicates his strong popularity with successive generations. His extant plays are:

The *Rhesus*	before 440 B.C.	
The *Alcestis*	438 B.C.	2nd Prize
The *Medea*	431 B.C.	3rd Prize
The *Children of Heracles*	429 B.C.	
The *Hippolytus*	428 B.C.	1st Prize
The *Andromache*	430–424 B.C.	
The *Hecuba*	ca. 425 B.C.	
The *Cyclops*	ca. 425 B.C.	
The *Suppliant Women*	ca. 423 B.C.	
The *Heracles*	ca. 420 B.C.	
The *Trojan Women*	ca. 415 B.C.	2nd Prize
The *Iphigenia among the Taurians*	414–410 B.C.	
The *Electra*	413 B.C.	
The *Helen*	412 B.C.	
The *Ion*	ca. 412–411 B.C.	
The *Phoenician Women*	ca. 411–409 B.C.	2nd Prize
The *Orestes*	408 B.C.	
The *Bacchae*	406 B.C.	1st Prize, produced posthumously in 405 B.C.
The *Iphigenia in Aulis*	406 B.C.	1st Prize, produced posthumously in 405 B.C.

SUMMARY OF THE *MEDEA*

The *Medea* is the story of the Colchian princess and sorceress Medea who revenges herself on her husband for his abandonment of her by killing their sons and his new bride.

EURIPIDES' USE OF MYTH IN THE *MEDEA*

Jason sails on the ship *Argo* to Colchis on the Black Sea in quest of the Golden Fleece. Aeetes, whose father is Helios, the Sun, and whose daughter is the princess Medea, requires Jason to yoke the fire-breathing bulls and sow a field with dragon's teeth. Through the magic of Medea, who has fallen in love with him, Jason completes each task and steals the Fleece. To deflect the attention of Aeetes from their escape, Medea kills her own brother. The *Argo* returns to Iolcus, where Pelias refuses to relinquish the throne to Jason, contrary to his promise. Medea contrives to have Pelias' unsuspecting daughters kill their father. She and Jason flee to Corinth, where they have two sons. Jason subsequently abandons Medea to wed the princess of Corinth, who in other retellings of the myth is called Glauke or Creusa; Euripides leaves her nameless. Her father is Creon.

It is at this point that Euripides' play begins.

Legends vary about what happens next but all seem to agree that Medea slew Jason's bride and her father and that Medea placed her young sons in the Temple of *Hera Akraia* ("Hera dwelling on the heights") for safety but that "either accidentally by Medea or deliberately by the Corinthians"[10] her children were murdered. Medea's deliberate killing of her sons may well be Euripides' invention—Aristotle in fact writes that "Euripides ... made Medea kill her children,"[11] as may be her encounter with Aegeus and the device of Helios' winged chariot. Medea fled Corinth, Jason died years later when a rotted timber from the *Argo* fell on his head, and Medea became King Aegeus' consort in Athens and later tried to kill his son Theseus.

THE HISTORICAL CONTEXT OF THE *MEDEA*

The Political and Social Context

Three weeks after the Great Dionysia of 431 B.C. when the *Medea* was performed, the truce between Sparta and Athens was broken and the Peloponnesian War began. The decades just before the play were a time of "overwhelming destruction of the mythical and coherent world-order."[12] The lines in the first choral ode, the ode that comes between the appearance of Creon and the appearance of Jason, express the same sense of moral upheaval: "Good faith has gone, and no more remains in wide Hellas a sense of Shame. She has flown away to the sky."

The *Medea*, despite its essential emphasis on passion and revenge, and despite the fact that its story is set in the heroic age, is alive with issues debated in fifth-century Athens. It reveals that Euripides "loved Athens but loathed her arrogant exclusiveness, loathed her subjection of women, loathed her imperialist ambitions."[13] Women had no legal or economic power. They were dependent, first, on their husbands; if abandoned or divorced, on their fathers; finally, on their sons. Medea, with young sons, a father whom she has betrayed and a husband who has deserted her, is utterly helpless at the beginning of the play, as the casual manner in which Jason casts her off indicates. She has become his wife through mutual oaths rather than through the traditional steps[14] of *pherne* ("dowry" brought by the bride), *engue* (the moment of "betrothal" when the father or guardian hands over or "entrusts" the bride to the groom), and *ekdosis* (the formal "conveyance" of the bride from her father's home to the home of the husband). Medea's initial action of coming out of doors, an action urged on her by the Chorus, itself challenges the tradition of the *gunaikeion* (literally, "women's apartments," figuratively, the secluding of wives indoors),[15] as does the Nurse's being outside, for the Tutor draws immediate and somewhat disparaging attention to it.

Jason's claim that he has abandoned Medea to join his sons to the Corinthian royal house and secure for them the benefits of Greek citizenship in Corinth would surely have resonated with Euripides' audience and raised questions in the minds of some about the exclusionary law passed in Athens in 451 B.C. limiting Athenian citizenship to children of parents who were both citizens of Athens. Jason assures Medea that he has more than compensated for whatever pain his abandonment may have caused her by having brought her, a foreigner, a barbarian, to Greece. His claim is invalidated by the fact that, if Jason represents Greek culture, then such a culture hardly refines one's sensibilities, and his "claim" is valueless.

The Religious Context

Zeus is *Zeus Horkios* ("guardian of oaths"). To break a sworn oath is not simply to violate a contractual obligation and to deal dishonorably with one's fellows and with the gods; it is also to be guilty of impiety and *hubris*, the proud self-assurance that denies the greater power of the gods altogether.[16] Neither Jason nor Creon respects oaths: Jason blithely casts aside the oaths he has sworn "with his right hand";[17] Creon is complicit in Jason's oath-breaking when he contracts a new marriage between Jason and his daughter. "The commonest form of oath called down *exoleia*, root-and-branch destruction with loss of all progeny, on the swearer if he should fail to keep his oath."[18] That neither Aegeus nor Medea spells out the *exoleia* indicates that the consequences of oath-breaking are so well-known as not to need specification.

What Aegeus, the just and diplomatic man, doesn't anticipate when he promises sanctuary is that Medea will kill a royal king and her own children.

Yet the fact that she leaves for Athens at the end of the play without any doubt about her reception there establishes the holiness of the oath—she is confident that not even her having murdered her two sons will keep Aegeus, a man to whom children are particularly precious, from fulfilling his oath.

That Zeus is also *Zeus Xenios* ("protector of strangers") makes Creon's exile of Medea an act of impiety, for she, as yet, has done no wrong in Corinth to merit such a measure.

The Intellectual Context

Socrates argued that human beings desire happiness and that when rational creatures behave in ways that do not lead to happiness, it is because they have failed to understand where happiness lies. Medea's decision to kill her sons is a decision whose consequence, unending sorrow, she fully understands. No aspect of the play receives more emphasis than her decision to kill her children. She weeps when she sends them off to the palace; she argues both sides of the question not once, but twice, in her climactic monologue; she touches and embraces her sons in a scene of unbearable sadness. And yet she kills them. That she chooses vengeance over everything else is not to say that vengeance is her happiness; it is not. In making Medea the killer of her own children and in focusing the second half of his drama on that act, Euripides denies the claims of the Socratic school that human beings are rational. The Messenger concludes his report by saying that "those mortals who pass for philosophers and subtle reasoners are most to be condemned. For of mortals there is no one who is happy."[19]

THE PLOT OF THE *MEDEA*

General Comments

The plot of the *Medea* consists of the working out of Medea's revenge on Jason and on Creon."[20] The first half of the play is expository: Jason's treachery and Medea's grief and anger are revealed, narratively by the Nurse and Tutor, then dramatically in Medea's scenes with Creon and Jason. The Aegeus scene divides the play into two halves, for after that scene Medea announces a change in plan: she will let Jason live but kill his sons. The steps of her revenge are such that, once set in motion, each makes the next inevitable.

At no point in the play does Euripides use a third speaking actor in a scene. What he achieves by this starkness is a heightening of the sense of *agon*, of contest between two figures, one of whom is always Medea. That there is no scene in which she is not present and which does not bear on her immediate situation suggests the preternatural resolve with which she pursues her revenge.

Medea's and Jason's fortunes mirror each other. In a chiasmic *peripeteia*, her fortunes fall with Creon's edict and Jason's acquiescence to it, while Jason's rise. The pattern then reverses. Medea successfully executes her plan and escapes punishment, while Jason's fortunes steadily fall. She always knows where she stands and what she has lost; he, until the very end, does not, and even then, his *anagnorisis* lacks self-definition.

There is not an episode in which Medea does not know more and is not planning more than her auditor understands; in fact, her whole "design" depends on her ability to fool others into underestimating the danger she poses.

The Creon Scene

The standard ironic situations in which a character unwittingly touches on a truth, or in which expectations are reversed, both appear when the Tutor returns from the palace with news that he expects will please Medea. That what in a normal situation and by a normal person would be regarded as a good thing causes such dismay as she expresses is an ironic indication that in this tragedy, a tragedy created not by fate but by character, normal expectations, like those of the Tutor, are invalid.

In Medea's scene with Creon, the audience is informed of Medea's purposes retrospectively. This variation on the stock method of anticipatory irony gives the audience a clear sense of how very clever and dangerous Medea is, for we are fooled, too. Euripides grounds his irony in the vanity of his characters, in a way that Aeschylus and Sophocles do not. Creon's desire to think himself a good fellow, despite his lack of respect for oaths and his violation of the laws of hospitality, makes him grant Medea the extra day that allows her to destroy him. Jason's susceptibility to flattery makes him the instrument of Medea's destruction of all his hopes.

The Aegeus Scene

Aristotle dismisses Aegeus' timely arrival as improbable. Arguments in favor of the Aegeus scene include (1) the unanticipated arrival of a savior illustrates the operation of divine will "beyond our judgment," of which the Chorus speak at the play's conclusion; (2) the scene emphasizes the sacredness of oaths and thus justifies the aid Medea receives from the gods, Zeus and Helios, who punish Jason, the oath-breaker, through Medea; (3) the scene, by revealing good will toward her from a prudent and objective man, reaffirms the evil of Jason and Creon and indicates that she was well regarded before she was forced to be brutal; (4) by emphasizing the importance men in Medea's culture place on having children, the scene gives Medea the idea to kill her sons; (5) and the scene facilitates her murders by providing Medea with a place of refuge, although it can be argued that she has already expressed, in her monologue following Creon's exit, indifference to the personal consequences of revenge.

The Setting

The play is set in Corinth outside what has been the house of Jason and Medea but is now the house of Medea only. The time is the generation before Troy.

Dramatis Personae

Nurse	female servant to Medea
Chorus of Corinthian Women	
Tutor	to Medea and Jason's children
Sons of Medea and Jason	
Medea	abandoned wife to Jason
Creon	king of Corinth
Jason	husband to the princess of Corinth
Aegeus	king of Athens

Scene Divisions

Prologue:	1–130	[Nurse, Tutor, Children]
Parodos:	131–212	[Chorus, Nurse, Medea *offstage*]
Episode One:	214–409	[Chorus, Medea, Creon]
First Choral Ode:	410–445	[Chorus]
Episode Two:	446–626	[Chorus, Jason, Medea]
Second Choral Ode:	627–662	[Chorus]
Episode Three:	663–823	[Chorus, Aegeus, Medea]
Third Choral Ode:	824–865	[Chorus]

Synopsis

The Nurse's prologue describes the consequences to Medea of Jason's abandonment; the Tutor enters with the children and reports that Creon has decreed exile for Medea and her sons. Meanwhile, cries of despair are heard from behind the doors of Medea's palace. The Tutor and the children exit into the house, while the Nurse warns the boys to stay far from Medea.

The Chorus of Corinthian women enter with words of pity for Medea. They urge the Nurse to fetch her so that they may offer advice to temper her grief.

Medea speaks to the Chorus of the inequities women suffer and of her additional helplessness as a foreigner abandoned by her husband. She wins from them a promise to keep silent about whatever revenge she may contrive. Creon appears and announces his decree of banishment. Medea supplicates him to rescind his edict, fails, and then begs for one more day in Corinth to gather provisions. Creon agrees; at his exit she exults, declaring that she will use this day to kill Jason, Creon, and Creon's daughter.

The Chorus express the wish that traditional roles of men and women might be reversed, that men may be recognized as the breakers of oaths and that poets might no longer slander women. They sing of their sympathy for Medea.

Jason arrives and tells Medea that the blame for Creon's edict rests on herself and her violent temper. He offers her money and introductions to friends in her exile with their sons. She lists all she has done for his sake and decries his violation of their sworn marriage vows. He says Aphrodite and Medea's own lust made her help him and claims he has repaid her with the far greater benefit of residence in civilized Greece and has married Creon's daughter out of a self-less desire to ensure the welfare of his and Medea's sons. She scorns his money and he calls the gods to witness that he has behaved admirably.

Second Choral Ode: 627–662   [Chorus]

The Chorus express the view that love is best when joined to moderation. They hope that they may be spared its excesses and the pain of exile.

Episode Three: 663–823   [Chorus, Aegeus, Medea]

Aegeus enters. He is traveling from Delphi to Troezen in hope of finding a cure for his childlessness. In return for her promise of assistance he vows that if she can make her way to Athens without his aid, he will give her sanctuary. He departs and Medea reveals her new plan: she will kill her children and thereby destroy Jason's line and his hopes. The Chorus beg her to reconsider. Embarking immediately on her plan, she orders that Jason be summoned.

Third Choral Ode: 824–865   [Chorus]

The Chorus sing of the beauty and holiness of Athens and ask how such a place can receive a murderer. They insist Medea will be unable to kill her children.

Episode Four: 866–975   [Chorus, Jason, Medea, Children]

Jason arrives and Medea convinces him that she now thinks his judgments were correct and that she is reconciled to his new marriage. She calls the children and asks Jason to bring them and her gifts to the princess that the princess may intercede with Creon and save the children from exile. They, unaware of her plot, depart carrying the poisoned robe and crown to Jason's bride.

Fourth Choral Ode: 976–1001   [Chorus]

The Chorus sing that there is no hope left, and they express pity for the children, the bride, Jason, and Medea herself.

Episode Five: 1002–1250 [Chorus, Tutor, Children,
                                                 Medea, Messenger]

The Tutor returns with the children and cheerfully announces that the princess has accepted Medea's gifts. Medea sends him into the house and in a tortured monologue argues for and against her decision to kill her children. They remain silently onstage as she embraces them. She concludes that her anger is stronger than her afterthoughts and sends them inside. The Chorus call those blessed who never have had children or known the griefs of parents. A palace Messenger arrives with news of the death of the princess and Creon, and urges Medea to flee. Instead, she asks for a slow and full account of exactly how her two enemies died. She then prays that her heart and hand may be steadfast and enters the house to kill her sons.

Fifth Choral Ode: 1251–1292   [Chorus, Children *offstage*]

The Chorus call out to Earth and Sun to stop Medea. Their song is interrupted by cries of the children within. The doors are barred and the Chorus cannot enter. They allude to what they take to be the comparable tale of Ino, who killed her children and then destroyed herself.

Exodos: 1293–1414   [Chorus, Jason, Medea]

Jason arrives to save his sons from the vengeance of Creon's friends. As he batters at her door, Medea appears aloft in a winged chariot sent to her by Helios, her grandfather. With her are the bodies of her two sons, whom she will not let Jason touch. She announces the establishment of a cult in the Temple of *Hera Akraia* in their memory and prophesies Jason's ignominious death. Jason calls on the gods to witness Medea's evil. The Chorus assert the primacy of divine power, as the play ends.

ANALYSIS OF MEDEA'S SPEECHES

Medea's Speech to the Corinthian Women: 214–266

Medea immediately establishes herself as sharing the women's attitudes and concerns. She begins with an apologia that indicates she values their good opinion. She says that she has come outdoors because she would not be thought proud, thereby emphasizing her complete internalization of the Greek concern for reputation. She cautions against conflating appearance with reality, as it is easy to mistake reticence and a desire to remain indoors for pride, thereby also deferring to the tradition of the *gunaikeion*. She suggests that the Women's expectations of communication from her are entirely appropriate, for she says that not only foreigners but also citizens must adapt to the customs of the country. Her statement simultaneously draws attention to her situation and asks for no special quarter. Medea thus establishes herself as a nonthreatening presence very much like the Women of Corinth. This occupies about 11 lines.

Within this exposition is a short description, just five lines, of her state of mind. Medea cleverly makes her own woes not the focus of her speech. She is circumspect in her emotional expression because moderation is regarded as a virtue by her audience and admits the one emotion, despondency, that is sure to elicit sympathy rather than wariness. She avoids all reference to the vengeance she cried out for offstage when she said, "May his whole house be shattered." Her diction is nonspecific in describing Jason's treachery: what he has done is simply "this thing." That which drives her to rage and fury, the discovery that her husband is "wholly vile," is not presented as her concluding point, but as an illustration of the intellectual problem that supposedly occupies her mind: the difference between appearance and reality, now applied not to the problem of knowing one's neighbor but to the problem of knowing one's spouse and his true nature.

Medea then, in a two-part exposition, speaks first of the inequities that all women suffer. Cleverly, she merges her situation with theirs, casting her comments into first-person plural ("we women"). She is able to lead them to question what they have never before dared examine openly, the traditional role of women, precisely because she has, in the preceding section, asserted her absolute respect for tradition. The climactic moment of this portion of her speech is her reference to the almost insurmountable difficulties a young bride faces when brought to her husband's home, knowing neither him nor the customs of the household. Brilliantly, without an explicit statement, Medea suggests the correspondence between what a foreigner coming to a strange land experiences and what a young bride coming to a new household endures.

The second part of her exposition turns from the general to the particular and rebuts what she has striven to establish: their similitude. This is perhaps her masterstroke. Everything to this point has worked to convince the women of Corinth that they and she are alike. They are expecting a further discussion of women's shared lot. Instead, Medea shocks her hearers by suddenly asserting an essential difference: they have the recourse of home and friends; she has nothing. Having established herself as their sympathetic spokesperson and advocate and having aroused in them self-pity and indignation, she then, by an *a fortiori* argument, arouses even greater pity for herself.

Medea's conclusion is a request for their silence in the face of any revenge she may choose to exact. Her use of the hypothetical rather than the actual future form is clever in allowing them to imagine that they may be agreeing to nothing at all. That her final words speak of women in general dreading "cold steel" but, "when once wronged in the matter of love," having thoughts "of blood," reminds them of their own suppressed anger, which they conflate with hers. Thus, she has turned women who came to exhort her to acquiesce to her abandonment into emotional allies who, as the next Choral Ode vividly demonstrates, suddenly desire a different world-order for men and women.

Because she is so powerful and accurate in her description of women's subjugation, the Chorus is hard put to regard her speech as calculated oratory. That what she says is neither pure manipulation nor pure truth is a mark of Euripides' genius: in this speech he conveys the complexity of her nature and suggests that human beings can simultaneously be righteously outraged and self-regarding. To trust anyone too far is therefore dangerous. Medea's rhetorical skill is a warning and a foreshadowing of what she can accomplish.

Medea's Speech after Aegeus' Departure: 764–810

Medea's speech of triumph after Aegeus departs is particularly important in terms of theme and plot. It outlines all that will follow in the action of the play and makes subsequent scenes and exchanges deeply ironic. Whether Medea thinks of her plan only after Aegeus departs or earlier is unclear. If after, we are struck by the rapidity of her thought; if before, by her duplicity. The very fact that we do not know is itself a mark of her dangerous unpredictability. From this point on, the Chorus, whose support she won in her first speech, oppose her, their opposition gradually turning from sorrowful to horrified.

As she sets out the details of her plan, Medea says that the princess "will die a painful death ... with such poisons will I smear these gifts." In the Choral Ode that precedes this scene, the Women use the same verb (*chriso*, "to smear, anoint, dip") when they beg that Aphrodite may never "smear with desire" one of her arrows and let it fly "against my heart from your golden bow." Euripides' use of *chriso* in these two very different contexts reveals with great subtlety that keen erotic betrayal lies beneath all that Medea does.

Although this speech has roughly the same number of lines as Medea's address to the Corinthian Women, its excited tone makes it seem half the length. Medea is not concerned here with how others regard her, and in her single-minded ferocity she follows one point rapidly with the next; her sentences are relatively short, their grammatical subject is "I," their verbs future indicative. Even her comment that what she says will be unpleasant to hear, a momentary recognition of audience attitude, is cast in Greek in the imperative: "Hear, then, words that will give you no pleasure." Sentences tend to be constructed as breathless catalogues with many direct objects. Her excitement is conveyed not only by her initial celebratory cry to the gods, but also by her repeated use

of "now" at the beginning of lines: "Now I shall be victorious over my foes ...
Now I may confidently expect that my enemies will pay the penalty."

In her jubilation, Medea, who does not usually speak metaphorically, says
that Aegeus is the "harbor" where she will "tie her stern cable." For Medea,
nautical imagery is significant—it recalls the *Argo* and all that is heroic
and manly, and, while such imagery alludes to the voyage that was for her
and Jason a time of love, her imagery also displaces Jason as captain: just a
few moments before he had claimed that he would debate with her in the
manner of a captain reefing sail before a storm. Now she is the captain, not
out on the open sea, but in sight of a harbor.

Most important, however, is her use of the diction of the Greek hero: "I shall
be victorious over my foes," she cries. "My enemies will pay the penalty."
By casting her action in such terms, terms that she repeats with far greater
emphasis at the end of the speech when to the idea of vengeance she adds
the heroic Greek ideal of fame, "Let no one think me weak ... No, quite the
opposite, hurtful to foes, kindly to friends. Such persons live a life of greatest
glory," Medea sheds her feminine nature and debases the heroic ideal. That
Medea's children must die undercuts any claim she has to be acting justly.
She is not good to her friends: she has tricked Aegeus, who likes her, and she
will kill her children, who love her. Her assumption that *Themis* ("Justice")
has sent her a "harbor" so that Medea can repay evil without suffering further
evil herself reveals the essential solipsism of her thinking.

Medea's Speech to Her Children: 1019–1080

In this extraordinary speech of *dissoi logoi*, Medea is her own interlocutor as
she states reasons why she should and should not kill her children. As she hesitates a second time, she even imagines her heart arguing against her hand.

The speech is also an anticipatory lament for her dead children. First, she
imagines a future without them. As she cries out, "O children, children," she
for the first time imagines with searing specificity all that will never be. Her
mind naturally moves to the central and defining events of life: birth, marriage,
and death. Against this eternal context, we feel the desire for revenge pall.
That Medea does also, but by the end of her speech overcomes such a feeling,
is a measure of the violence of her fury, a fury that, as she says, "overbears" her
reason. Not even her achingly vivid awareness of the living bodies of her young
sons can stop her.

Before that conclusion Medea twice falters in her murderous resolve.
Medea's opening words to her children, "You have a city and a home, and
when we have parted, there you both will stay forever ... I must go to exile
in another land," conflate Corinth with the Land of the Dead. That her

meaning is hidden from her sons emphasizes the loneliness of the course on which she is embarked. These linguistic ironies diminish as her mind moves to the more profound and universal irony of the "travail" of bearing and raising children who will die, of finding that "all was for nothing." From her awareness of loss comes her resolve not to kill the children, a resolve that contains the speech's only appeal to reason and the only place where action is measured on an objective scale of value: "Why should I hurt them, to make their father suffer, when I shall suffer twice as much myself?"

The Medea of unbridled vengeance returns, as does the self-justifying diction of "enemies" who will "laugh" at her. She calls on her heart to pity the children, but nothing is stronger than her vengeful fury. Her sense of the power of her own *thumos* ("rage") is expressed in the series of brief, desperate apostrophes to her heart, for she understands that only emotion can drive out emotion—reason is too weak. The rationalizing language of "enemies" and "insolence" again reasserts itself, and so, with infinite sorrow at what she cannot stop herself from doing, she moves to the other perception that deep and imminent loss arouses, the acute awareness of the physical presence of the ones who will be lost; and she notices for the last time the hands, the lips, the skin, the very breaths of the living bodies before her.

Her speech concludes with an *anagnorisis* that summarizes the *agon* of the speech and that expresses, in agonized personal terms, the fact that one can know what is right and not do it or, as here, not be able to do it.

When in the *exodos* Euripides places before us a Medea surrounded by the lifeless, bloodied bodies, she is harsh, unreachable, and unrepentant. The woman we have heard here has disappeared. Perhaps Euripides writes this speech so that we, reflecting on it later, may know that vengeance deadens emotion.

REALISM IN SECONDARY CHARACTERS

Euripides' characters are naturalistic. When Jason and Medea speak, they repeat, modify, and embellish their statements, they discuss their motives, they describe their feelings, and they make and reconsider decisions. Actions that in no way advance the plot, or that threaten to give away the secrets on which the plot depends, such as the weeping Medea cannot check in her second scene with Jason, and the hesitation and wavering in her final speech to her uncomprehending children, invest her character with psychological reality. Lesser figures such as the Nurse, Tutor, and Messenger are particularized by personal traits and by the details of place and situation to which they themselves refer.

Realism in the Characters of the Nurse and the Tutor

The Nurse's speech begins with what are in grammar called contrafactual ("against-the-fact") statements. Through the childlike wistfulness of her "If only ... not," and the simplistic ascription of a devastating and distant result—Jason's desertion of Medea—to an irrelevant proximate cause, the hewing of the pine in the forests of Pelion to make oars for the *Argo*, Euripides presents the Nurse as a loyal servant whose mind is simple and sympathetic.

The Tutor's cranky opening question, by drawing attention to the fact that the play has begun with the artifice of a monologue, turns that artifice into a moment of realism: the Nurse explains her breach of decorum, saying, "It was too much, I couldn't bear it; I had to come out here and tell my mistress's wrongs to earth and heaven." The Tutor then draws attention to himself as the bearer of important news, which he wishes to have coaxed out of him. Through details of characterization, Euripides focuses attention on the news that will be delivered and begins to suggest, in the Nurse's emotion and in the Tutor's self-containment, a little of the contrast that will be revealed in the natures of the primary female and male figures, Medea and Jason. When the Tutor finally decides to speak, he tells where—"the gaming tables where the old men sit"—and how—"they thought I was not listening"—he came by the news of Creon's edict, his irrelevancies rooting the tragic plot in common life.

Interspersed throughout the Tutor's and the Nurse's speeches are homely adages. The Nurse's commonplaces lack the slight smugness and rhetorical edge of the Tutor's; they are straightforward, born of the simple observation of pain: "That's what keeps a life free of trouble, when a wife obediently accepts her husband's will," and "To trusty servants it is a disaster when the dice of their masters' fortunes fall badly." These phrases, with their duplicated grammatical subjects and everyday metaphors, have the ring of colloquial speech.

Realism in the Messenger

The Messenger rushes on with a specific dramatic purpose. He has not come to report the deaths but to save Medea: "Medea, flee! flee! The sea vessel and the chariot that treads the ground—do not refuse them!" he cries. Only at Medea's urging does he describe what he has seen. He begins slowly, with colloquial phrases, and presents a portrait of normal servants "below stairs": gossiping, taking sides, expressing affection for the children of their masters, noting details about their masters' private lives. Then, as the Messenger begins to describe "his mistress," he realizes that that title must offend Medea, and he interrupts his narrative to clarify and excuse himself: he means she "whom we honor now instead of you," and in his apology stumbles again, forgetting that the present tense is no longer appropriate for the princess. The realism of his speech reaches its apogee when he describes the bride who, after putting on the golden crown, stops to "arrange the curls of her hair in a shining mirror" and who notes "her straight leg" as she "paraded" about in the robe, just as, when in new clothes, we all admire our own bodies and not simply the clothes themselves.

Only after establishing so firmly realistic a base does Euripides allow the Messenger to recount his story of unbridled horror: the sight of a body melting as it is burnt alive and of parental love and concern turned to desperate self-preservation. After his graphic account the Messenger says he and the other servants "were all afraid to touch the corpse." The collective response, too, is a tiny brilliant stroke. And, when the Messenger's narrative ends, he adds to it a commonplace of his own—a class resentment, perhaps, aimed at the "propounders of wise theories," who in their intellectuality fail to understand what the simple Messenger and his fellows know, that "happiness is a thing no man possesses." Thus, through the subtlest of techniques, Euripides creates a real speaker and a realistic context to lend credibility to inherently fantastic deaths.

JASON'S CHARACTER

Euripides enjoys "tracking out the lines of thought and feeling which really actuate men."[21] Jason thinks in categories: women, Greeks, foreigners. He therefore regards all behavior he sees as exemplifying the traits he has ascribed to the group to which he assigns each individual, and never as reflecting individual circumstances or individual qualities. No woman is different from any other. Medea's reactions, he is certain, have nothing to do with him and everything to do with the simple fact that she is a woman. It is a way of thinking that absolves him of all responsibility and relieves him of the need for self-reflection. His entrance line, "This is not the first time," expresses his sense that he's seen this before and that he's got a category in which to place it. Because he generalizes about women, "the last thing a woman of character can stand,"[22] Medea knows just what to say when she wants to convince him that she regrets her angry words. She need only remark, "Well, women are what they are." To encourage him to ask the princess to intercede for the children, Medea's ploy to explain the children's bringing the poisoned robe and crown to her, Medea simply says that he will succeed with the princess, "if she's like other women."

Jason, while thinking of himself as irresistible, regards the sexual act as something dissociated from his emotional life. In a sense, Euripides presents Jason's greatest breach of his marital relationship not by his having taken another wife, but by his separating himself from his passion and speaking to Medea of hers. It is as if he strips her naked before him. In his mind, women are the eager pursuers, men the objects of desire. Even if Medea is correct when she scornfully says he must be eager to bed his bride, he is not moved by lust; he compartmentalizes it, and what he thinks about in his nonsexual moments are wealth, status, and reputation. When he speaks of sexuality, he calls it, with distaste, "that domain."

Jason is not especially intelligent, and assumes that all people share his values. That Medea might value something other than a tenuous tie to the royal house of Corinth never occurs to him because such a tie is what he values. He repeats his offer of material assistance because he cannot imagine anyone, from pride, rejecting such an offer. He explains to Medea that she has him to thank for having become famous in Greece, for fame is what he seeks.

Jason's mind is neither logical nor self-critical, and so when he says that the opportunity to marry a local princess is a stroke of great luck, he forgets that he is speaking to a woman to whom he made another expedient marriage. He regards himself as Medea's moral superior, patient and forgiving, and so he says, "Call me names if you like, be angry at me; I can never be angry at you." He has, of course, no cause to be angry, for he has not been injured. He speaks of his own travails, as a "stateless exile" from Iolcus, to the woman who left her home and kingdom to sail with him and who now faces beggary. And when he says, within five lines, that she does not "need" more children and that he has married to have more, he does not even notice the gross indelicacy of his words or what they imply about his view of marriage.

He regards himself as loyal because he has come to offer assistance to his "loved ones" and believes that his assessments are balanced, and that his niggardly concessions are compliments: "So far as you did help me, you did well" and "I admit, you have intelligence." Even in the final moments of the play his understanding and his imagination remain circumscribed. When he arrives to find the Chorus frantic, his thought is for himself. As he cries out, we see in Jason a capacity for pain but no capacity to understand that pain. Indeed, Jason's wish at the end of the play to have not begotten children, as if fatherhood were the source rather than the vehicle of his suffering, reveals how inadequate his understanding is.

THEME IN THE *MEDEA*

Theme turns in part on what Medea's escape in the dragon chariot means. Is Euripides, by placing her in the *mechane*, the stage machine by which "gods" descend, implying that she is turned into a god? If so, is that apotheosis a sign that she has behaved rightly and punished the destroyers of marriage, the violators of oaths and the oppressors of the weak, as the gods would have her do?

Or is her apotheosis a comment about the gods themselves, arguing that they, like Dionysus in the *Bacchae*, are as brutal as she? Is her apotheosis a comment on the dehumanizing effect (because gods are not human) of vengeance?[23] And if her escape is not an apotheosis, is it a theatrical joke, a wry reminder from Euripides that to imagine that dire actions do not have dire consequences is to be a fabulist? In political terms, is the escape to Athens, which the dragon chariot guarantees, Euripides' means of indicating that it has become a city that shelters evil?[24] Or that to it has come, in 431 B.C., "a spirit of vengeance"?

Perhaps the meaning of the *Medea* is to be found not in what happens to Medea, but in what happens to Medea and Jason jointly. At the end of the play, their positions are inverted: it is Jason who is now bereft and homeless, Jason who invokes the gods as witnesses, and Jason who uses superlatives of vituperation. Medea is calm, remote, and secure, as he was in their first scene. The verb that Medea uses to describe her anticipated situation in Athens is the same verb that she uses as a sexual euphemism in her speech to the Corinthian women;[25] *sunoikeo* means both "to dwell in the household with" and "to share the bed with." In other words, Medea may be implying that she will be in Athens what Jason was to have been in Corinth, a royal consort. Through these and other ironic inversions, Euripides suggests that Jason has been repaid in kind, that Jason and Medea are, in their heartlessness and willingness to injure others, hardly different, and that neither passion nor cold reason is by itself sufficient to make one truly civilized. In a sense both Jason and Medea represent a distortion of the Athenian ideal of wisdom, he by shaping his arguments to expediency and self-interest, she by using her cleverness to accomplish a horrid revenge.

Our shifting sympathies, following closely those of the Chorus, are also a clue to the play's meaning. Medea's speech to the Corinthian women, combined with Creon's edict and Jason's vileness, convinces them that she is justified in seeking revenge against Creon, his daughter, and Jason. When, after Aegeus' appearance, she proclaims that she intends to murder not just the guilty but the innocent, we and the Chorus are appalled. Perhaps the meaning of the play lies in this co-opting of our sympathies and subsequent showing to us that we have acceded to murder.[26] In this view, the second half of the play is nothing more than the working out of the impulses that we have failed to condemn, and the play itself is a moral mirror.

The great scholar H.D.F. Kitto writes, "these plays must be regarded as religious drama."[27] In this context, the number of references to Zeus and to the sacredness of oaths is particularly significant, and Medea's role becomes that of divine scourge. Both Jason and the Corinthian royal house are guilty of indifference to *Zeus Horkios* (Zeus of oaths) and *Zeus Hikesios* (Zeus of suppliants). That Medea's fate, as she repeats again and again, will be one of sorrow and pain despite the refuge Athens provides her is not inconsistent with her role as divinely ordained avenger, nor is the fact that she acts out of her own pride and wrath rather than out of piety. The purposes of the gods in tragedy are complex and inscrutable: those who become their instruments do not necessarily avoid punishment themselves.

In the concluding choral formula, one that appears with almost no alternation in many of Euripides' plays, there is a unique interpolation of the word *tamias,* "guardian." It occurs once earlier in this play, and in both contexts it refers to *Zeus Horkios.* It may well be that *tamias* asserts the centrality to this play of the idea of Zeus as guardian of oaths and dispenser of justice, in which case the *Medea* illustrates the working out of that which, "though opaque to human reason, serves the divine will."[28]

ASPECTS OF STAGECRAFT

Physical Contact

Actors rarely touch in tragedy and so any physical contact between actors is significant. Twice the text indicates that Medea performs acts of supplication, first to Creon when she says, "I beg you by your knees," and then to Aegeus with the words, "I beg you by your beard and by your knees"; and both times we see Medea touch, as suppliant, the portion of the body she names and remain kneeling until her request is granted: for 25 lines to Creon, for less than half that time to Aegeus. Euripides clearly intends that these two identically-staged moments be compared to suggest the moral difference between the two kings and the better fortune for Medea that Aegeus represents.

After Medea decides to kill her sons she says, "Come, children, give me your hands, give your mother your hands to kiss ... Oh how good to hold you!" Her action of kissing and holding her sons, whom she will lose and whose physical closeness to her is stressed by the intimate recognition, "How delicate the skin, how sweet the breath of children!" is tremendously affecting and is made so in part because the act of touching is used sparingly and selectively by Euripides: this is the only other moment of physical contact for Medea in the play. When she "makes it up" with Jason, it is not she but the children who touch Jason in reconciliation. She and he never touch.

Gestures of the Right Hand

The right is the hand of oath-taking, as the Nurse at the beginning of the play reveals when she speaks of the marriage vows Medea and Jason "made to each other, the right hands clasped in eternal promise." Jason has sullied those vows, and so Euripides makes the next use of the right hand coincide with the onset of Jason's destruction. In bitter irony Medea urges her children to take their father's right hand as they walk with him to the palace, bearing the poisoned gifts. Their gesture, "stretching out their dear hands so," nonetheless moves her to tears.

Weeping, Smiling, and the Use of the Mask

In masked drama, for the audience to know that a character weeps, it must be told, either by that character or by another who "sees" the tears. When Medea weeps inside the house, both her cries and the Nurse's opening comments make clear that she is doing so. She weeps again when she speaks with Aegeus. The audience sees only her unchanging mask and learns of her tears when Aegeus asks, "But why is your face dissolved in tears?" Because the mask prevents the audience from detecting tears before being told of them, and because nothing in her lines to this point has referred to her tears, we see in Aegeus a ready compassion. In contrast, just before Medea sends her children to the palace, she bursts into tears, states that she is doing so, and receives immediate sympathy from the Chorus who reply, "From my eye too a pale tear starts." Full 20 lines elapse before Jason notices those tears and rather unhandsomely queries, "You there, why do you dampen your eyes with pale tears and turn your white cheek away, and why are you not pleased to hear these words from me?" His delayed recognition characterizes him as self-absorbed, just as Aegeus' immediate notice of Medea's distress characterized him as kindly.

The masks of the children depict smiling faces, for the Nurse says when they enter that they "are coming home after their games" and that they "have no thought of their mother's troubles." Later, as Medea laments that they will not grow to manhood, she says, "Why do you smile so sweetly that last smile of all?" The children's smiles, emblems of innocence, stand in unbearably painful contrast to the steadily worsening realities around them and demonstrate the ironic possibilities of the mask.

The Cries of the Children

Three times in the play, and for extended periods, the children are brought onstage. They remain mute, but their very presence impresses them strongly upon the audience's consciousness. Only at the moment of their death do they speak. Then, they cry out from inside the house, and the effect of hearing their voices, when we have come to expect only silence, is striking in its pathos. "What shall I do? How can I escape my mother's hands?" the first voice asks, and the second replies, with the tenderness their mother lacks, "Dear brother, I cannot tell." Then with a full consciousness that we have not ascribed to these figures, one says in his small *anagnorisis*, "We are done for."

Medea's initial cries of woe find their dreadful echo in the identically –staged cries of her children, the second instance a consequence, in a long arc of pain, of the first. That through such parallels Euripides not only arouses sensations of terror and pity in his audience, but also suggests cause and effect, is true art.

The *Mechane* and the Winged Chariot

The winged chariot ranks as one of the more stunning stage effects in all of Greek tragedy and represents the first recorded instance of the use of the *mechane* for someone other than a god. Nothing in the theatrical memory of the audience and nothing in the play itself prepares the audience for Medea's sudden appearance in a winged chariot suspended above the *skene*. (The word for "snake" in Greek is *drakon*, and thus the chariot, drawn by great snakes, is sometimes called a "dragon" chariot.) The attention of the audience is riveted on the double doors through which Medea has exited and from which she is expected to return to the stage. That Jason is onstage, battering steadily against those double doors, keeps attention at eye-level. And then, suddenly, Euripides raises the eye upward as Medea appears, resplendent, a creature operating outside the natural realm. She is visually magnificent, for a chariot sent by Helios, the Sun god, is necessarily one of gleaming gold. That inside that shining chariot are the bloodied bodies of her sons creates a visual effect of simultaneous horror and beauty. The Nurse, in the first moments of the play, had described Medea as lying flat, "neither raising her face nor taking her eyes from the ground." This final moment of the play, in its intense verticality, is therefore also strongly symbolic: Medea has gone from prone victim to triumphant warrior.

Offstage Speech and the Illusion of Reality

Medea's first words are delivered offstage. By fostering the illusion that here is a character who is speaking for no one's benefit but her own and who will not come outside and "act," Euripides produces a moment that seems free of theatrical artifice; the audience, like the Nurse and the Chorus, is made to feel that it is overhearing what is intimate and private and, therefore, "real." Medea enters and speaks calmly and rationally to the Chorus, but her offstage cries have made it clear that she is now exercising the utmost self-control, and that she is able to hide her feelings when it suits her, for she wishes to present herself to the Corinthian women as possessing the self-control that they value. In theatre, whenever the audience is made to believe that it is privy to aspects of a character's mind and thought that remain unspoken or that are only minimally alluded to, theatrical realism is created.

Additionally, through the simple expedient of keeping her hidden offstage, Euripides makes Medea a symbol of the inner life of primal emotions—rage, jealousy, love, grief, remorse, hate, pride—that we all possess but hesitate to confront. She is our inner self.

NOTES

1. Alan Elliott, "Commentary" to *Euripides: Medea* (Oxford: Oxford University Press, 1968), p. 94.

2. William Arrowsmith, "A Greek Theater of Ideas," *Ideas in the Drama, Selected Papers from the English Institute*, edited by John Gassner (New York: Columbia University Press, 1964), p. 15.

3. William Arrowsmith, *Euripides* II (Chicago: University of Chicago Press, 1956), p. 8.

4. K.J. Reckford, "Medea's First Exit," *Transactions of the American Philological Association* (TAPA) 99 (1968): 331.

5. Emily A. McDermott, *Euripides' Medea: The Incarnation of Disorder* (University Park, Pa.: Pennsylvania State University Press, 1989), p. 41.

6. Bernard M. W. Knox, *The Heroic Temper: Studies in Sophoclean Tragedy* (Berkeley: University of California Press, 1983), p. 5.

7. Moses Hadas, "Introduction," *Euripides: Ten Plays* (New York: Bantam Books, 1960).

8. Knox, pp. 5–6.

9. G.M.A. Grube, *The Drama of Euripides* (London: Methuen & Co. Ltd., 1961), p. 148.

10. D.L. Page, "Introduction" to *Euripides: Medea* (Oxford: Clarendon Press, 1938), p. xxviii.

11. Aristotle, *Poetics*, chapter 14.

12. Arrowsmith, "A Greek Theater of Ideas," pp. 3–4.

13. John Ferguson, *A Companion to Greek Tragedy* (Austin: University of Texas Press, 1973) p. 238.

14. R.B. Palmer, "An Apology for Jason," *Classical Journal*, 53 (1957): 49–55.

15. Reckford, p. 337.

16. Ann Burnett, "*Medea* and the Tragedy of Revenge," *Classical Philology* 68 (1973): 1–24.

17. Sophocles refers in the *Oedipus at Colonus* to the "ancient oath of the right hand" when Oedipus asks Theseus to clasp the hands of Antigone and Ismene and swear to protect them after Oedipus' death; that it is invoked at the holiest moment of that play attests to the great weight of such an oath.

18. David Kovacs, "Introduction," *Euripides* I (Cambridge, Mass.: Loeb Classical Library at Harvard University Press, 2001), p. 281.

19. E. R. Dodds, "The Greeks and The Irrational" *Sather Classical Lectures,* vol. 25 (Berkeley: University of California Press, 1951), p. 186.

20. Kovacs, p. 277.

21. Gilbert Murray, *Euripides and His Age* (London: Williams and Norgate, 1918), p. 85.

22. Philip Vellacott, *Ironic Drama: A Study of Euripides' Method and Meaning* (Cambridge: Cambridge University Press, 1975), p. 111.

23. Burnett, p. 22.

24. Arrowsmith, "A Greek Theater of Ideas," pp. 27–31.

25. McDermott, p. 92.

26. T. V. Buttrey, "Accident and Design in Euripides' *Medea,*" *American Journal of Philology* 79 (1958): 1–17.

27. H.D.F. Kitto, *Form and Meaning in Drama* (London: Methuen & Co Ltd, 1956), p. 231.

28. David Kovacs, "Zeus in Euripides' *Medea,*" *American Journal of Philology* 114, (1973): 58–68.

8

Euripides
The *Bacchae*

(406 B.C., performed 405 B.C.)

The *Bacchae*, written when Euripides was in his late seventies, was produced posthumously in Athens at the Great Dionysia in the spring of 405 B.C., where it won first prize. Some think it is his greatest play, and certainly, for its lyrical beauty, the spectacular nature of its Chorus of Bacchants, and the extraordinary unity and forward thrust of its plot, it is superb. There is perfect integration of each scene into the next and of each choral segment into the whole. A full understanding of the play requires familiarity with aspects of the myth and cult of Dionysus. The story of Pentheus, however, is more than the story of impiety and *hubris* punished; it is also a profound study of psychological repression and its consequences.

SUMMARY OF THE BACCHAE

The *Bacchae* is the story of the death of Pentheus, king of Thebes, at the hands of his mother, Agave, whom the god Dionysus has made mad.

EURIPIDES' USE OF MYTH IN THE BACCHAE

The Myth of Semele

Semele is one of the daughters of Cadmus, King of Thebes. Zeus impregnates her and is then tricked into revealing himself to her in his full glory as thunder and lightning. Zeus' epiphany kills her, but the unborn child, Dionysus, is rescued and sewn into the thigh of Zeus, from which he is born.

According to legend, Dionysus later returns to Thebes, his mother's city, where he establishes his cult and punishes the sisters of Semele for doubting his divinity. Pentheus, King of Thebes and cousin to Dionysus, opposes the introduction of the cult and is torn apart by Maenads, the female followers of Dionysus.

Vase paintings that antedate 406 B.C., the approximate time of composition of the *Bacchae,* show Agave, Pentheus' mother, infected with Bacchic madness, in the act of killing Pentheus. There are, however, contemporaneous versions of the story in which Agave has no part. Euripides has chosen the mythic elements that best serve his dramatic purposes.

The Myth of Actaeon

Actaeon is a hunter who angers the goddess Artemis, in one version of the myth by boasting that he is as great a hunter as she, in another version by happening accidentally on her grotto as she bathes. Euripides may or may not have known the second version, but the version he has Cadmus tell is the first, which involves *hubris.* In both, the sin is the dishonoring of a deity. As punishment for his transgression, Actaeon is torn apart and devoured by his own hounds. The parallels to Pentheus' fate are sharp.

Mythological and Geographical Terms

Dionysus is a god of many names: "Dionysus," "Bacchus," "Bromius," "Iacchus," "Evius" (the vocative form of which is "*evohe,*" the cry often associated with worship of Dionysus) and "Dithyrambus." The Bacchic cult is associated particularly with Lydia, the place from which "the Stranger" in the play says he comes; "Bacchus" is the Lydian name for Dionysus.

The Curetes to whom Dionysus refers at the play's beginning are semi-divine beings who protected the infant Zeus by dancing around him and clashing their weapons so that his cries were not heard. The Corybantes are attendants on Rhea or Cybele. The name is sometimes used synonymously with "Curetes." Rhea is the wife of Cronos and the mother of Zeus. Cybele is the great mother goddess of Anatolia and is associated with ecstatic states, prophetic rapture and insensibility to pain, and with the use of the tympanum in her worship. Pieria is the area in Macedonia surrounding Mount Olympus; it is holy to Apollo and the Graces who dance there. Paphos (or Cyprus) is the island sacred to Aphrodite (who is also called "Cypris"). Cithairon is the mountain outside the city of Thebes. Tmolus is the mountain in Lydia, holy to Bacchus. Dirce and Ismenus are the rivers of Thebes. The *thyrsus* is the wand wreathed in ivy and vine leaves with a pinecone at the top. It is also described as a giant fennel (narthex) stalk.

THE HISTORICAL CONTEXT: THE CULT
OF DIONYSUS[1]

The religious cult of Dionysus is Asiatic in origin (the term "Asiatic" here, as in the play, refers to "Asia Minor"). It is a form of ecstatic worship; its followers reach the state of ecstasy through dance that involves intense rhythmic movement and the tossing of the head in ecstasy; the place of worship is in wild nature—in woods and on mountaintops. The ecstasy culminates in a ritual tearing apart (*sparagmos*) and eating (*omophagia*) of the god, represented by a god-substitute, so that the essence of the god may enter the bodies of the followers. One such god-substitute for Dionysus is wine; another is an animal that the followers hunt; in its earliest and most primitive form, the god-substitute is human, a sacrificial victim who is ritually dressed in special garments for the sacrifice. While in the ecstatic state, followers are imbued with paranormal physical capacities: strength, speed, and imperviousness to pain. They are called "Bacchae" (or "Bacchants" or "Bacchantes") from one of the alternate names of the god Dionysus, "Bacchus." They are also called "Maenads" from the Greek word for "frenzy" or "mania/madness." Union with the god offers freedom and ecstatic union with the natural world and with impulses that civilization restrains or represses. Because the union with the god represents freedom, the cult appealed most strongly to women, who were the least free.

The cult followers wear fawn-skins, which signify a rejection of the loom and spindle, an expression of unity with their animal nature, and a manifestation of the god, who is sometimes hunted in the form of a fawn. The god's more fearsome manifestations, as Euripides indicates, are the snake, lion, and bull. The cult followers carry two things: the *tympanon* (drum), which they strike as they dance and that may be thought to replicate the thunder of the god, and the *thyrsus*. There are many references to Dionysus and to his Bacchants as hunters in the play, and these references to the hunt are directly tied to the climactic ritual of the cult. Pentheus is also frequently described as a hunter, for in his death he is the god-substitute, both hunter and the hunted. Through brilliant compression, references to hunting that surround Pentheus also suggest Pentheus' psychic need to capture and repress the animal urges in his own nature.

The line between religious ecstasy and sexual ecstasy was easily crossed, and Maenads were widely believed to engage in sexual union during their revels. Euripides, however, indicates repeatedly that the Asian Bacchae, who form the Chorus, and the Theban Bacchae, who—maddened by the god—now worship him in the wilds of Cithairon, are absolutely chaste.

THE PLOT OF THE *BACCHAE*

General Comments

The construction of the *Bacchae* is ironic in that the first character who appears on stage announces an identity that he will withhold from all others. What Dionysus knows is who he is, the self-knowledge that mortals, and Pentheus in particular, lack. Thus, not only is the play structurally ironic, but the very source of its irony, identity, is thematically central to an *agon* between god and humans. Irony is also central to the plot. Dionysus punishes those who oppose his rites by making them part of those rites. When his vengeance comes, it is terrible, and it is ironic in form: it makes overt in Pentheus the very urges Pentheus is at pains to suppress in others, and it accomplishes the fall of Pentheus through his own acquiescence. In addition, Dionysus is "rejected by those very ones *who ought least to* have done so"—his mother Semele's sisters, Agave, Autonoe, and Ino,—and in return, Dionysus has Pentheus destroyed "by those *who ought least to* attack him, his mother and his aunts."[2]

In its second half, the *Bacchae* is a revenge plot. The absoluteness and rapidity of the protagonist's fall stun us: once the hero agrees to view the Bacchants, his destruction is assured. There is probably no *peripeteia* so instantaneous in all of Greek tragedy. The protagonist's "fall from good fortune to bad" is occasioned by his literal "fall" from the treetop that has been his vantage point. The moment of *anagnorisis*, "I have sinned," is brief, coincides with the literal fall, and immediately precedes death. The fuller *anagnorisis* belongs to Agave, a figure who appears only at the play's conclusion. Where Pentheus' suffering ends, Agave's begins, also without her immediate apprehension, and thus the sense of suffering is given particular force by its being made continuous.[3] The scene between Cadmus and Agave has been called one of the finest recognition scenes in tragedy.[4]

The foundling myth that is central to the plot of the *Oedipus Rex* is also central to the plot of the *Bacchae*, although in a different way: the child is divine and "recognition amounts to acknowledgment of the divinity." The further component of the foundling myth, the return home of the foundling, represents "establishment of cult in its proper place."[5]

The Setting

The setting is in front of the royal palace of Pentheus at Thebes. The time is several generations before Troy.

Dramatis Personae

Dionysus	the god
Chorus of Asian Bacchae	worshippers of Dionysus
Teiresias	blind Theban prophet
Cadmus	former King of Thebes, Pentheus' grandfather
Pentheus	king of Thebes
The "Stranger"	Dionysus, disguised as a Lydian prophet of the god
Guard	
Herdsman	
Second Messenger	
Agave	mother to Pentheus, daughter to Cadmus

Scene Divisions

Prologue:	1–63	[Dionysus]
Parodos:	64–166	[Chorus]
Episode One:	170*–369	[Chorus, Teiresias, Cadmus, Pentheus]
First Choral Ode:	370–431	[Chorus, Pentheus *onstage*]
Episode Two:	434*–519	[Chorus, Pentheus, Servant, Dionysus]
Second Choral Ode:	519–603	[Chorus]
Episode Three:	604–861	[Chorus, Dionysus, Pentheus, Herdsman]
Third Choral Ode:	862–912	[Chorus]
Episode Four:	913–976	[Chorus, Dionysus, Pentheus]
Fourth Choral Ode:	977–1023	[Chorus]
Exodos:	1024–1392	[Chorus, Messenger, Agave, Cadmus, Dionysus]

*Numbering of the text is not consecutive.

Synopsis

Prologue: 1–63   [Dionysus]

The god Dionysus enters and points to the miracle of the still-smoking tomb of his mother Semele. He has driven her sisters into Bacchic frenzy as a punishment for denying his descent from Zeus. They now roam the precincts of Mt. Cithairon, wearing dappled fawn-skins and worshipping him. He intends to introduce his rites to Thebes, and to that end has taken on human form as a "Stranger."

Parodos: 64–166   [Chorus]

The Chorus of Asian Bacchae enter to the sound of the flute, accompanying themselves on drums and cymbals and dancing in ecstasy. They sing of Dionysus and call others to his worship.

Episode One: 170–369   [Chorus, Teiresias, Cadmus,
                                                 Pentheus]

Teiresias summons Cadmus to join him in the mountain rites of the god. Like the Chorus, both are outfitted with fawn-skin, ivy crown, and *thyrsus*. Pentheus enters, complains of the licentiousness of the women of Thebes who have become Bacchants, and threatens to capture the Stranger who is promoting these rites. Pentheus scolds the two men, who argue that it is folly to oppose these new practices.

First Choral Ode: 370–431   [Chorus, Pentheus *onstage*]

The Chorus sing of the joy of worshipping the god and of the importance of pleasure, condemn impiety, and predict misery for the proud and impetuous.

Episode Two: 434–519   [Chorus, Pentheus, Servant,
                                                 Dionysus]

The Stranger is led on in chains. The Servant describes the miraculous escape of the women from prison. Pentheus notes the sensuality of the Stranger's appearance, threatens to cut off his hair and take his *thyrsus*, questions him about the secret rites of the god, and orders that he be shut up in the stables. They exit into the palace.

Second Choral Ode: 519–603   [Chorus]

The Chorus in agitated rhythm respond to the arrest of the Stranger. They pray that Dionysus will once again lead them in dance. The god's cry, apparently from within the palace, interrupts their song. They call out to him as an earthquake is felt. The palace roof seems to split apart and lightning strikes Semele's tomb.

Episode Three: 604–861   [Chorus, Dionysus, Pentheus, Herdsman]

The Stranger enters from the palace and tells the Chorus that Pentheus, instead of tying him up, is struggling to tie up a bull sent by Dionysus. A Herdsman reports the strange deeds of the women on Cithairon who were gentle until their rituals were interrupted, after which they tore apart cattle and ravaged local villages. The Chorus, the Herdsman, and the Stranger urge Pentheus to acknowledge the divinity of Dionysus, and the Stranger offers to bring the women back peacefully from the mountain. Pentheus rejects the offer and instead calls out his army. The Stranger asks if Pentheus would like to see the rituals. Pentheus immediately agrees and goes off to costume himself like a woman in order to watch unobserved. The Stranger tells the Chorus that Pentheus will be butchered on the mountain by his own mother and follows him off to help him dress.

Third Choral Ode: 862–912   [Chorus]

The Chorus liken their release from Pentheus' threat of imprisonment to the joy of a fawn in green fields and then sing of the pleasure that comes from destroying one's enemies.

Episode Four: 913–976   [Dionysus, Pentheus]

Pentheus, drunken and dressed as a Bacchant, primps and fusses. He sees two suns, two Thebes, and the Stranger in the form of a bull. The Stranger tells Pentheus that Pentheus' own mother will carry him back from Cithairon. Pentheus delights in that anticipation, and they exit.

Fourth Choral Ode: 977–1023   [Chorus]

The Chorus envision events on the mountain as they unfold and sing of their eagerness for Pentheus' destruction.

Exodos: 1024–1392   [Messenger, Chorus, Agave,
                                                Cadmus, Dionysus]

A Messenger reports the death of Pentheus. Agave enters bearing the head of Pentheus, which she thinks is that of a lion cub. The Chorus urge her to summon her father Cadmus and her son Pentheus to show them her trophy. Cadmus enters with servants who carry the body parts of Pentheus on a stretcher. Cadmus' questions bring her back to sanity, and she slowly realizes what she holds in her hands and what she has done. After a lament, parts of which have been lost, Dionysus appears aloft in the *mechane* wearing the same smiling mask that he has worn though the play, but dressed now in the garments of the god. He decrees punishment for Cadmus, as father and daughter bid each other farewell and go into separate exiles. The Chorus depart.

ANALYSIS OF SECONDARY CHARACTERS' SPEECHES

Teiresias' Speech to Pentheus: 265–327

Teiresias, like Cadmus, is a "company man" who, in a long lifetime, has learned that avoiding trouble is the easiest course. Although he is a priest of Apollo, Teiresias' nonreligious sensibility and dry rationalism have the ironic effect of demonstrating to the audience precisely what is most appealing about the Bacchic cult.

The scene begins when Pentheus, finding the two elders of Thebes "dressed in dappled fawnskin" and "playing the Bacchant with a wand," says (1) they look absurd; (2) the Bacchic rites, and particularly the drinking of wine, provide the women of Thebes with an excuse for lust; (3) Dionysus "was burnt up together with his mother" and is not a god; (4) Teiresias "wants still another god revealed to men" in order to "pocket the profits from burnt offerings and from reading bird signs;" and (5) were it not for Teiresias' "gray hair," Teiresias would be in jail.

Teiresias' weapon is indirection. He pretends to offer benign, worldly advice to the king he calls a "young man" but his real message is that Pentheus is hardly different from what he would suppress: "You are mad ... some drug [*pharmakois*] has caused it, and no drug can cure it," applying to Pentheus the same word (*pharmakos*) he applies to the wine of Dionysus, and noting that Pentheus desires public acclaim, which is hardly different from Dionysus' desiring the spread of his cult. A subtle rhetorician, Teiresias distorts Pentheus' words and says Pentheus urges them to "fight against a god," begs the key question of Dionysus' divinity, turns Pentheus' criticism of their complicity with the cult into disrespect for his grandfather, argues that Dionysus is essentially an Olympian, and concludes with an argument of pure expediency, saying that the worship of Dionysus will be "very big in Hellas."

The most important aspect of Teiresias' speech is not the illumination of his character, but the illumination of Pentheus'. Teiresias' subtleties stand in sharp contrast to Pentheus' bluntness and perhaps make that bluntness a little more appealing than it initially is. Pentheus is a very young man, as Agave's lines later tell us, still beardless. Thus, he is inclined to speak with directness when he thinks he is saying something true, and he has difficulty imagining that others may not wish to hear the truth he speaks. And in the manner of the very young and idealistic and intelligent, he not only prides himself on seeing beneath the surface but also believes that beneath the surface is where all truth resides. Thus, he looks first and foremost for hidden motives. That the women appear entirely chaste, as the Herdsman later attests, is for Pentheus, who discounts appearances, no proof at all. Mistrust of motive is his young way of knowing the world.

In addition, Pentheus dislikes uncertainties and dualities: either the women are chaste, in which case they do not roam mountains at night, or they are voluptuaries who do. The complexities articulated by Teiresias and Dionysus, which indicate that place and time are no guarantors of conduct and which require one to know each person individually, are unbearable to a young man who craves clarity. Their insistence that women are free, as are all human beings, in any place and at any time, to choose either chastity or licentiousness, represents for him the potential fluidity of all things, a frightening thought for the rule of the city and for the boundaries of the self. And in the same way, it is easier for him to call Teiresias a seeker after "dirty pennies" than to envision him as the complicated trimmer that he is.

The Herdsman's Report to Pentheus: 664–774

The Herdsman's report follows the Stranger's description of the palace miracles, and together they present seemingly irrefutable proof of the power and reality of the god. When Dionysus arrives at Thebes, he declares that he will "prove," using a verb often associated with evidentiary proof in court, to Pentheus and every man in Thebes "that I am god indeed." The testimony of the Herdsman is the last benevolent "proof" that Dionysus will offer; if it is rejected, the next proof of his divinity will be the seduction, agony, and death of Pentheus, a proof of the god's power that Pentheus finally acknowledges when he cries out to his mother, "I have sinned."

At the conclusion of his speech, the Herdsman, although deferential, urges his master to "receive this god into the city, whoever he is." The Herdsman's speech represents a conundrum for Pentheus and leads directly to the crisis of the plot. The miracles are evidence of the god and are linked to behavior that is barbaric. Logic demands the acceptance of evidence, but, in this case, to be rational is to welcome the irrational. Pentheus rejects the proofs in order to wage war against what he considers the infinitely more dangerous sort of irrationality the Bacchae represent.

The immediate effect of the Herdsman's report is to redirect Pentheus' rage from Dionysus to the women.[6] This, in turn, leads Pentheus to do the very thing that Dionysus, in his entry into Thebes, had identified as that which would make him counter-attack: "If the men of Thebes attempt to force my Bacchae from the mountainside by threat of arms, I will meet them in battle." Dionysus offers to bring them back without bloodshed; Pentheus rejects the compromise and calls for his armor. In the next line, Dionysus asks the fatal question: "Do you want to see them sitting together on the mountain?" The Herdsman's speech is, thus, critical to the plot.

It is also a speech of extraordinary vividness, as it must be if it is to place the setting that is the counterpart of Thebes, with its gates and walls and prisons, directly before the audience. The Herdsman speaks of fir boughs and oak leaves; of crowns of ivy and flowering briony; of the green wood; of uplands, cliffs, and mountain dells; of plains, springs, and streams. The wild world of Cithairon, vast and various, is made an emblem of freedom by the Herdsman's words.

His speech is descriptive rather than argumentative, and, as he is a simple man, he tells his tale chronologically. Thus the initial effect on the audience of the exquisite opening descriptions is particularly strong because it is undiluted by the anticipation of something dreadful to follow. Nor is that initial impression of loveliness cancelled even by the horror of *sparagmos* (the "tearing apart" of a live creature); instead, it remains vivid to the audience and thereby forces the audience to confront the duality that is at the heart of Dionysiac experience.

The Herdsman's speech contains three points of special relevance to Pentheus, none of which Pentheus heeds. First, the Herdsman states categorically that the women are chaste. His own modesty, expressed through his use of euphemism, lends credibility to his affirmation. He does not say what Pentheus himself has said, that "they sneak off, one here, one there, to serve the lusts of men." Instead, he says that they were "not going off separately in the green wood to find Cypris," the goddess. Even his description of "new mothers, their babies left behind and their breasts overfull with milk" who "cradled gazelles or wolf cubs in their arms and gave them to drink of their white milk," is filled not with prurience but with tender respect for the maternal scene that he observes. Second is the Herdsman's description of the women as impervious to men's weapons hurled against them. Third, when the women attack the cattle and the men of the village, their aggression is provoked by an action that interrupts a trancelike state, either of ecstatic dancing or of racing and swooping up whatever is in their path. They are mad but, if not provoked, not dangerous. The Herdsman's report also serves as a warning or foreshadowing of what may happen again. Indeed, when later the second Messenger reports the horrendous *sparagmos*, not of heifers and bulls but of the live body of Pentheus, that report contains within it, albeit in different proportions, the same components found in the Herdsman's description: initially self-contained activity on the part of the women, an interruption, and a consequence.

In style the Herdsman's speech relies heavily on the use of lists and on items joined by one and sometimes by two "ands." These coordinate series are especially apparent in the first half of the Herdsman's speech and replicate grammatically the sense of abundant nature with which the women are associated. The Herdsman uses simile and metaphor to substitute, in his explanations to Pentheus of what he has seen, for the generalizations that he cannot provide. These devices appear primarily in the second half of his speech, with one exception: in the first half of his report, the Herdsman calls the three groups of sleeping women "three choruses." Choruses dance in choreographed movement that, however dynamic, is also orderly. And his metaphor immediately links the Theban Bacchae with the Chorus of Asiatic Bacchae standing before him on the stage. The fifth-century audience is reminded that their festival is called the Great "Dionysia" and that the stage, with its origins in choral song, is sacred to Dionysus. For a moment, the audience, the stage Chorus, and imagined women merge; and before the drama moves to its terrible resolution, we are one with the Bacchants on Cithairon. The action of the women rising up is echoed in the natural world by the cattle that "were climbing to the uplands." Out of the earth, to each as they desire, flows water or wine or milk, from all of their wands drip "streams of honey," and from the young mothers flows milk to the infant animals they suckle. In every way the women are attuned to nature. All proceeds with order and regularity: they begin their worship of Dionysus "at the appointed time of day" and call on the god with "one voice."

Three similes appear in the second portion of the Herdsman's report when he describes miracles of a different sort: reactions in the women that he has never before witnessed in any human being, reactions whose parallel exists, if anywhere, in the animal kingdom. Thus, trying to describe the transformative nature of the sudden shared motion that overtakes them, he says they rose "like birds" and "carried up by their own speed, they flew across the spreading fields." Euripides again produces an extraordinary sense of motion in the passage when Agave summons to her the women by calling them "my coursing hounds." The final simile of the passage remarks in a different way on the changed nature of the women: the Herdsman says "like an invading army they fell" on the surrounding villages.

Only once does the Herdsman remark on a particular action that he calls "terrible, dreadful" in the sense of miraculous. This is not the *sparagmos* or the gushing fountains that the god sends or the serpents licking the women's cheeks or their speed or ability to carry fire in their hair or untied plunder on their backs. What is "terrible" is that they are not bloodied by weapons that strike them: the physiological processes of the body in a state of trance appear to the Herdsman as the greatest miracle of the god. It is the women's invulnerability that stops him in his catalogue of events; it is, therefore, something to which Pentheus should pay heed: the god bestows glory in battle on his adherents.

Whether the running women have intended to ravage the villages, or whether their running is simply the instinct of a flock responding to agitation, with pure chance bringing them to the villages, is not made clear in the text. In the next ode, the Chorus sing of a fawn who has escaped a hunter (just as Agave, fawn-dressed, has escaped the Herdsman) and who then keeps on running. Lattimore reads into that running "a love for the loneliness of the forest, for its own sake, because it is lonely, or unspoiled, or meaningless, or for all these reasons." It is this feeling that the Herdsman can present in only its outward manifestation but which the Chorus of Asian Bacchae can know and express "directly."[7] It is the disturbance of this joy that the Herdsman has witnessed. In their ecstatic state they are as amoral as animals, capable of fawnlike and bird-flock motion and of lionlike *sparagmos*. The double perspective created by the juxtaposition of the Herdsman's speech with the Choral ode deepens the audience's understanding of what the Herdsman observes; at the same time, the testimony of a common fellow like the Herdsman lends credibility to the extraordinary responses the Chorus sing of.

THE *BACCHAE* AND THE SUBCONSCIOUS

Virtually all commentary remarks, in one way or another, on the contrast between Dionysus and Pentheus. In their scenes together, Pentheus is associated with rejection of pleasure, rigidity, and confinement, and Dionysus is associated with hedonism and freedom. Pentheus is seen as a divided self and Dionysus is seen as representing half of that divide.

The choral odes, and especially the *parodos*, express the joy that comes from the release of natural, and thus Dionysian, impulses and desires. Pentheus' adamant opposition to Dionysus, his insistence that Dionysus is a fraudulent god despite repeated proof to the contrary, is regarded as a measure of Pentheus' own terror at the prospect of the unimpeded release of the Dionysian urges within himself.

Dionysus is nature in all its elemental power. The opening lines of his prologue end with words for three of the four elements: earth, fire, and water.[8] Dionysus is freedom, emotional and physical, and that freedom finds its geographic counterpart when he describes himself as ranging throughout "the gold-rich lands of the Lydians and Phrygians ... the sun-drenched plains of the Persians, the fortifications of Bactria, the harsh country of the Medes, Arabia the blessed, and all that part of Asia that lies along the salt sea." Through his sweeping catalogue of countries, he is associated with all that is distant, forbidden, and free. Dionysus is also fertility and abundance. He has made the "clustering growth of grapevines" cover the still-smoking tomb of his mother Semele. His *thyrsus* is itself a phallic symbol and represents generative power. Where he travels "the ground runs with milk, runs with wine, runs with the nectar of bees." Even the locks of his hair are "luxuriant." He is the bull, the symbol of potency, and the lion, the symbol of ferocity. Like all nature and all animals, he is amoral, pitiless, pure "necessity." He is what he makes happen to his followers: the ecstatic release of self, and thus he is worshipped through the body in motion, through the dance.

Dionysus' world is nonarchitectural; in his opening monologue he describes the Theban Bacchae as sitting "beneath the silver firs on the *roofless* rocks"; Pentheus, on the other hand, is associated with the architecture of repression, with the locked gates of Thebes, with the prison within the palace. Pentheus' palace represents his and everyman's psychic landscape: the hidden self, dank horse stables "as dark," he tells the Stranger, "as the night sky under which you prefer to perform your rites." Such spaces are emblems of the secrets of the self. It is not altogether Dionysius' anger that makes him send earthquake and fire to destroy Pentheus' palace: if Pentheus is to survive, his palace, his place of retreat, must be destroyed.

In psychological terms, the action of the play can be regarded as a struggle within the self, with the repressed self finally exposed. The many references Pentheus makes to prisons, nets, manacles, and other means of constraint, and the enactment of capture within the play at his order, may be said to dramatize in theatrical terms his wish to control and repress what he fears exists within him. Pentheus' addiction to violent punishment may be a projection onto others of punishment that subconsciously he thinks he deserves.[9] The proliferation of hunting terms in Pentheus' speech is another form of projection unto others of the animality he fears within himself and an expression of his desire to "hunt" down and restrain that animality. He uses such language so frequently that his own Guard jokes, in words designed to please the king, that Dionysus, "the prey," has been "captured." The "quarry" was "tame."

As Euripides recognized, what is repressed finds an outlet in some inadvertent form. Pentheus begins his interrogation of the captured Stranger with comments that suggest a fascination with the Stranger's effeminate appearance and thus with sexuality itself: the god's long hair, soft skin, perfumed body, and languid posture each draw from Pentheus a comment immediately qualified with criticism. This see-sawing occurs four times in six lines and then resolves itself in a business-like *non sequitur*.[10] The second direct expression of Pentheus' voyeurism is more elaborate than the first. Because it occurs just before he goes off to engage in actual voyeurism on Cithairon, it suggests the nature of what arouses and motivates him. Pentheus' words, "I imagine that like birds caught in bushes they are held fast in sweet enclosures of their beds," join images of physical restraint and animal impulse to erotic action. Sale argues that Pentheus' voyeurism is a "compromise mechanism" that allows Pentheus to relieve his inner desires without actually participating in the acts that would make those desires undeniable. That Pentheus expresses unalloyed pleasure at the thought that he will be "carried home in his mother's arms" is, Sale suggests, a form of infantile regression that, like voyeurism, is a mechanism that protects the conscious self from engagement with what the self fears, this time not through restriction of access but through return to a period of life before restraint was necessary.

The climactic moments of the play occur when Pentheus appears onstage dressed as a Maenad and enacts, with Dionysus playing his maid, a scene of transvestitism that, to everyone but himself, seems to reveal his secret desires. Pentheus' costume in no way performs the function Dionysus and he assign to it, of allowing him to blend into the company of women unnoticed. That Pentheus puts it on only to forget its ostensible purpose, points, one can argue, to something other than practical necessity. Three times earlier in the play, when talking to Dionysus, Pentheus refers to "wrestling," the sport of condoned physical contact between men, once when he comments on Dionysus' long curls as an impediment to wrestling and twice as a metaphor for debate between them. That he threatens to cut off those same long curls, combined with his later willingness to wear long curls, suggests to a modern audience an inner conflict.[11]

Pentheus' death occurs when, aloft on the "tip of a fir tree that rose toward heaven," he is seen by the women, who, in Bacchic frenzy, rip the great fir out of the ground. He falls and they tear him apart. In dramatic terms the tree is important because it makes Pentheus visible. What Euripides shows us literally in this scene is, then, an emblem of self-exposure. It is a nightmare image. Inadvertent self-exposure, however it occurs, is a source of psychological disruption and terror, for we all either consciously or subconsciously believe ourselves to harbor secrets that, even if we cannot name them, we would wish to remain hidden. The terrible irony of Pentheus in this scene is that he has covered himself with a costume that exposes something deep within, and the location that he thinks of as covert and private is a place of maximum exposure. In this, and in his subsequent suffering, he is emblematic of us all. Secrets are central to Bacchic worship. They are not revealed to the uninitiated, as Dionysus' replies to Pentheus demonstrate, but only to the initiates. In fact, in the ecstatic release that is a component of such worship, the communal secret replaces individual secrets, for anyone engaged in an act of ecstasy escapes the confines of the superego and allows others intimate revelations of the self.

"How did you see him? In a dream or face to face?" Pentheus asks the Stranger when they speak of the god. Pentheus' question associates Dionysus with the idea of dreams early in the play. Each of the three miracles of Dionysus that Pentheus experiences personally is oneiric or "dreamlike" in form and, like a dream, is revealing of Pentheus' inner conflict. It is almost as if Euripides has imagined and transcribed a dream.

In the first "miracle," Pentheus "found a bull." Yet, the perception that what is before him is a bull does not stop him from trying to tie it up as he has intended to tie up the Stranger. In dreams, things suddenly and inexplicably appear, and a person, whom we know, may look like someone or something quite different, yet the dreamer somehow understands the representation as identical to the expected thing. Pentheus' inability to tie up the Stranger/bull represents Pentheus' message to himself that he cannot restrain this Stranger, just as he cannot restrain the bull. Because a bull manifestation is claimed by the Chorus for Dionysus, and because that claim is apparently current in Thebes, Pentheus also subconsciously acknowledges the god.

Dionysus' second miracle involving Pentheus occurs onstage and is described by Pentheus as it happens. It is also oneiric. The delusion Pentheus experiences is preparatory to his being led off to Cithairon to die as sacrificial victim. Pentheus' vision of the "two suns" and the "two" seven-gated cities suggests that the cosmos is disordered and dual, a projection outward of inner duality. Also psychologically revealing perhaps is the perception that the bull "goes before him": he is led by a beast, by impulse. The dream vision of Pentheus suggests that he is in possession of knowledge that his conscious mind represses. If he is led off by the bull who "goes before him"—and the scene concludes by clearly indicating the opposite, for he precedes Dionysus offstage—then perhaps he is himself the beast, since he leads himself. The chipper tone of his speech is hardly consonant with the confusion it reports, and by that very inappropriateness suggests the deterioration of Pentheus' reason.

The third dreamlike miracle that Pentheus witnesses involves Pentheus' bending of the fir tree. Pentheus is silent, even frozen. The god takes hold "of the tip of a fir tree" and bends it with superhuman strength and control so that Pentheus can set himself on it from the ground. How can the Stranger reach the tip if Pentheus cannot? The miracle is unremarked by Pentheus, who sees, in an almost trancelike state and for the first time, direct evidence of the divine powers of the Stranger.

The "dream-work" of the play is perhaps not accidental. Euripides has presented, in the portrait of Pentheus, and in his *agon* with Dionysus, a dramatic reenactment of conflict within the subconscious mind. It is a tribute to Euripides' great genius that this is only one way to read the play, and that it in no way impedes a simultaneous reading of a story of the return of the god Dionysus to Thebes, of the establishment there of his cultic ritual, and of the enactment of a fierce revenge for impiety.

THEME IN THE BACCHAE

Dionysus tells Pentheus, "You do not know ... what you are doing or who you are." It is this, in a sense, that the play illustrates: that we do not know these things, as Pentheus does not know himself, as Agave does not know what she has done. Might one be exactly the opposite of what one thinks one is? Euripides seems to say yes. Are there unexpected correspondences between things? Euripides suggests there are.

The suffering of the play is very great: for Agave, madness is a preferable state, and for both mother and son, understanding comes slowly and at unbearable cost. At the moment his mother, "like a priestess with her victim, fell upon him," Pentheus cries, "I have done a wrong, but do not kill your own son for my offense." After Cadmus helps her to understand what she has done, Agave says, "Now, now I see: Dionysus has destroyed us all." Understanding does not bring with it compensatory relief. Lattimore makes the point that the end is joyless and that even the god lacks the energy and beauty associated with his prior manifestation.[12]

It is clear that the *Bacchae* asserts the power of god and the wisdom of recognizing and accepting one's need for joy. It also asserts our capacity for brutality. Grube draws a moral from the play, and, defining Dionysus as god of wine, says:[13]

> Wine lays bare Eros in its deepest and wildest sense, and in a sense therefore may be taken as a symbol of those passions. Recognise them as a necessary and welcome element in human life ... they will give you loveliness and joy.... Deny them altogether, fight them, proclaim they do not exist, and they will tear you limb from limb like Pentheus.

ASPECTS OF STAGECRAFT

The Flexibility of Stichomythia

Euripides uses stichomythia for many of the Dionysus/Pentheus scenes to emphasize the conflict between them. In the climactic moments that seal Pentheus' doom, single-line exchanges intensity into half-line exchanges, with Pentheus always assigned the less powerful end-line position of response. An equally brilliant and flexible use of stichomythia occurs when Cadmus, in exquisitely graduated steps, restores Agave to sanity.[14] As the Bacchic frenzy leaves her and she grows quieter, a necessary prelude to the dreadful recognitions that will follow, that change is indicated by the only two-line response in a series of one-line exchanges: Cadmus asks, "Does your mind still feel the same flurry?" and Agave answers, "No, I feel— somehow—calmer. I feel as though my mind were somehow changing," the pace of the stichomythia replicating the mental processes returning to the maddened mother.

The Chorus of Asian Bacchae

Euripides' making the Chorus votaries of the god, Asian Bacchae, is masterly. It allows him to keep steadily before the audience the tremendous energy that Dionysus represents. The rhythms of the whirling dancers, the sound of tympanum, cymbal, and flute, the repetitions, and the exclamatory cries convey Bacchic ecstasy and make us voyeurs of their rites, even as Pentheus would wish to see them in "frenzy."

In some of the subsequent odes, the same Chorus assert the value of moderation, humility, and wisdom, and seem almost to be sensible citizens of the *polis*. Thus, when they later rejoice in the torture and death of Pentheus, as they do, and when they mock the pathetic Agave, we see them both as morally deficient human beings and as god-surrogates in touch with a necessity beyond right and wrong. The Chorus unite us with the god and his purposes, only to divorce us from the god so that our sympathies may finally be fully engaged by Pentheus and Agave, who represent the terrible blindness of mortals who know neither themselves nor anyone around them.

Dionysus' Mask

Dionysus wears the smiling, white mask of the god, as Pentheus' strangely interested comment, "And you deliberately keep your skin so pale," makes clear. Dionysus appears in the same mask throughout, whether god or Lydian Stranger. His smile reflects his assurance and his imperturbability, his calm when he is manacled, and his bemusement as he toys with Pentheus in ambiguous phrases. His smile also represents the joy and pleasure that the Chorus claim inhere in Bacchic worship. At the play's end, his smile is terrifying in its impersonality: the mask indicates that, because he can smile at his barbarity, there is no recourse and no refuge from it.

Bacchic Costume

Costume has ironic force in the *Bacchae*. The dress of the Chorus, their long swirling robes, fawn-skins, wreaths of ivy or—if the splendid painted cup in the collection of the Staatliche Antikensammlungen at Munich is to be taken as definitive—writhing snakes, must have been stunning as they whirled onto the orchestra ground. Immediately after the visual and auditory splendor of the *parodos*, two old men, Teiresias and Cadmus, hobble onstage in dress that absurdly imitates that of the Bacchic dancers. Their costumes also foreshadow a terrifyingly grotesque sequel: the robing scene in which Pentheus appears in Bacchic dress; but Pentheus intends not to imitate but to become indistinguishable from the Bacchae. Dionysus has "made his hair to grow long" or given him a wig, and when Pentheus reappears from the palace, his mask has long curls attached to it. In all but smiling expression, he is a double of Dionysus, the god whose sacrificial "double" he will soon unknowingly become.[15] By the end of the play everyone on stage wears the costume of the god. Dionysus has triumphed, and Euripides has shown us so, not simply through his text, but through his stagecraft as well.

NOTES

1. The discussion is derived from the magisterial work of E. R. Dodds, "Maenadism," *The Greeks and The Irrational* (Berkeley: University of California Press, 1951), pp. 270–282, and "Introduction" and "Commentary" to the *Bacchae* (Oxford: Oxford University Press, 1960).

2. Richmond Lattimore, *The Poetry of Greek Tragedy* (New York: Harper & Row, 1966), p. 133.

3. William Arrowsmith, "Introduction" to the *Bacchae*, *Euripides V* (Chicago: University of Chicago Press, 1959).

4. Arrowsmith, p. 150.

5. Lattimore, p. 128.

6. Dodds, "Commentary" to the *Bacchae*, p. 159.

7. Lattimore, p. 142.

8. John Ferguson, *A Companion to Greek Tragedy* (Austin: University of Texas Press, 1973), p. 467.

9. William Sale, "The Psychoanalysis of Pentheus," *Studies in Fifth-Century Thought and Literature*, Yale Classical Studies 22, (1972): 63–82.

10. Shirley Barlow, *The Imagery of Euripides* (London: Methuen, 1971), pp. 90–91.

11. Scholars debate whether he actually does so or is stopped by Dionysus' statement that his curls "belong to the god."

12. Lattimore, p. 134.

13. G.M.A. Grube, "Dionysus in the Bacchae," *Transactions of the American Philological Society* (TAPA) 66 (1935): 53–54.

14. These graduated steps are discussed in detail in George Devereux, "The Psychotherapy Scene in Euripides' Bacchae," *Journal of Hellenic Studies* 90 (1970): 35–48.

15. Helen Foley, "The Masque of Dionysus," *Transactions of the American Philological Society* (TAPA) 110 (1980): 129.

9

Aristophanes
The *Birds*
(414 B.C.)

ARISTOPHANES' LIFE AND REPUTATION

Aristophanes is the supremely funny comic playwright of Attic Greece and the sole surviving representative of Old Comedy. Only names of other comic playwrights—Cratinus, Eupolis—have come down to us. Aristophanes' plays blend the bawdy with the satiric and the lyrical. He is of the generation just after that of the great tragic playwrights, having been born around 450 B.C. and having died in 385 B.C. That Aristophanes was outspokenly political in his comedies is clear from an unsuccessful indictment brought against him by Cleon in 426 B.C. for libeling the state. A demagogue who replaced the great statesman Pericles and led Athens from 429 B.C. to 422 B.C., Cleon refused the Spartan peace proposals, demanded that higher tribute be paid to Athens by her allies, and recommended razing the city of Scione and executing all its citizens. He and his policies are frequent targets of attack in the comedies of Aristophanes. Another favorite target of Aristophanes was Cleonymus, one of Cleon's adherents, to whose ignominious act of dropping his shield on the field of battle at Delium Aristophanes frequently refers, most brilliantly in the choral verses of the *Birds* that describe the yellow "Cleonymus tree" that in winter "drops its shields like leaves." Little is known of Aristophanes' family except that his father's name was Philippos and that his sons were also comic dramatists.

In Plato's *Symposium*, composed about a year after Aristophanes' death, Aristophanes is one of the diners who assemble at the house of Agathon to drink and talk, and he is credited with telling the following story in answer to the question of the evening, what is Love? In the beginning, there were three sorts of persons, of three sexes, and every person was spherical, with four legs and four arms, and a head with two faces, pointing in opposite directions. Since the form of each creature was spherical, "whenever it started running very fast, it went over like our acrobats, whirling over and over with legs stuck out straight." It was very strong, and somewhat rebellious, and frightened Zeus, who said, "if they continue turbulent, I will slice every person in two, and then they must go their ways on one leg, hopping." When they continued obstreperous, Zeus divided the spheres "as they slice sorb-apples," drew each portion together "just like the purses which you draw close with a string and smoothed away most of the puckers, though he left just a few which we have just about the belly and navel, to remind us of our early fall."

From this very funny proem Aristophanes goes on, still in a comic vein but with lyricism as well, to describe love as the seeking by the now-divided selves of their once-connected other halves. "When one of them happens upon his own particular half, the two of them are wondrously thrilled with affection and intimacy and love." Among the halves that were originally man-man or woman-woman, there is "no great fancy" for the other sex; from those that were originally man-woman, "our adulterers mostly descend." Aristophanes' jokes continue, but he concludes the discourse by saying, wisely and beautifully, that "our original form was as I have described, and we were entire and the craving and pursuit of that entirety is called Love."[1]

Whether Plato records or imagines such a discourse, it nonetheless tells us that Aristophanes the man was sociable and endlessly inventive, and that as a fantasist he was able seamlessly to join the rollickingly funny to the wise and lyrical. His works were read and studied after his death, even as tastes changed and Menander's realistic New Comedy became the vogue.

To such later generations, until the taste for Aristophanic comedy revived in the twentieth century, Aristophanes was often read as a model of fifth- and fourth-century Attic dialect, as a guide to how ordinary citizens spoke and reacted. From his plays one gets "the *feel* of ancient Athens, the sense of having actually been there oneself, of knowing exactly how they talked and what they talked about and what they liked to eat and what they thought about sex and clothes and money and democracy and what it felt like to be a woman or a slave and how much anchovies cost and how fed up they got with a war that went on for years and years."[2] He was, in other words, a playwright who delighted in the common things of everyday life and presented them vividly in his plays.

CHARACTERISTICS OF ARISTOPHANES' "OLD COMEDY"

The type of comedy that Aristophanes writes is called "Old Comedy" because its characteristics differ significantly from the comedy of about a century later, called "New Comedy." Aristophanes is the only representative of the form. "Middle Comedy" is a term coined to refer to plays that blend characteristics of both. The subject matter of Old Comedy, unlike the subject matter of tragedy, consists not of myths retold but of inventions by the comic poet. Insofar as gods and heroes appear, they are treated with "extreme irreverence." For example, a fragment that has survived of a comedy by Aristophanes titled *The Heroes* has a Chorus of dead heroes who threaten evil-doers with diseases, ranging from itching to madness.

Plots in Old Comedy are usually fantastic in that, while the context of the plot is a contemporary situation, the protagonist takes some action that may violate laws of nature or may show a complete disregard for normal laws of cause and effect. Aristophanes' situations turn on the "crazy logic with which he works them out."[3]

Full of scatological and sexual jokes and *double entendres*, the plays are bawdy, and male characters are costumed with extended phalluses, although that is not true of the *Birds*, which, as Henderson notes, has "the least obscenity in all Aristophanes' plays." The comic Chorus is significantly larger than the tragic Chorus and is thought to have numbered 24. The Chorus leader, in what is called the *parabasis*, addresses the audience directly, and jokes often break the "fourth wall" between actor and audience, constantly reminding the viewers that they are participating in the artifice of theatre. In structure, the tradition that Aristophanes inherited and expanded on seems to have consisted of a prologue, a battle, a *parabasis*, and a conclusion.

Men prominent in contemporary society are ridiculed and parodied broadly and by name. Dover argues that the "devaluation of gods, politicians, generals and intellectuals" represents a means of self-assertion against the restrictions that Athenian society generally imposed on its members, and cites, as an example of such restrictions, the fact that for one citizen to strike another could result in a claim that the one was treating the other as a slave, a charge of "*hubris*" that could carry with it the death penalty.[4] In contrast, in the New Comedy of Menander characters are fictitious, plots are naturalistic and turn on coincidence, and, at the conclusion, everything feels neatly wrapped up. We don't ask, as we might at the end of the *Lysistrata* or the *Birds*, "what happened then?"[5]

Comedy burlesqued tragedy, and protagonists such as Lysistrata and Peisetairos, with the single-mindedness and confidence of Sophoclean tragic heroes, pursue self-serving or idealistic schemes that they have concocted and firmly believe in. The absolutely improbable success of these ordinary people allows average members of the audience to imagine, for a moment, an absurdly successful transformation for themselves as well.

Old Comedy represents a unique mix of elements that does not reappear until, perhaps, the twentieth-century skits of Laurel and Hardy or the madcap films of the Marx Brothers, whose "mélange of parody, satire and sight gags interwoven with direct addresses to the audience recaptures the spirit of Aristophanes."[6] In the comic plays of Aristophanes, we find every aspect of comedy, every comic turn, every comic method that we know.

A LIST OF ARISTOPHANES' PLAYS

Comedy officially became part of the great drama festivals several decades after tragedy. In 486 B.C., the Athenians first made financial and administrative provision for the regular inclusion of comedy in the City Dionysia and in 445 B.C., similar arrangements were made for the Lenaia. Tragic playwrights selected for the competitions were expected to present four plays, but the comic playwrights entered only one. As the end of the first *parabasis* in the *Birds* suggests, the comedy was performed at the end of each day of the competition, after the tragic performances and the satyr-play.

Aristophanes wrote perhaps 40 comedies, of which 11 survive. He won many prizes and clearly enjoyed winning. In the second *parabasis*, the Chorus of Birds say to the audience and to the judges in the audience that they will attack the judges with bird droppings if the play isn't awarded first prize. It came in second and is perhaps Aristophanes' masterpiece. Performance information about the *Lysistrata* is scanty; it is not known at which festival it was presented, nor whether it won a prize. The 11 extant plays are:

The *Acharnians*	425 B.C.	1st Prize: Lenaia
The *Knights*	424 B.C.	1st Prize: Lenaia
The *Wasps*	422 B.C.	2nd Prize: Lenaia
Peace	421 B.C.	2nd Prize: Dionysia
The *Clouds*	ca. 417 B.C.	(revised from version of 423 B.C.)
The *Birds*	414 B.C.	2nd Prize: Dionysia

The *Lysistrata*	411 B.C.	
The *Poet and the Women*	411 B.C.	
The *Frogs*	405 B.C.	1st Prize: Lenaia
The *Assemblywomen*	392 B.C.	
Wealth	388 B.C.	

SUMMARY OF THE *BIRDS*

The *Birds* is the story of Peisetairos and his friend Euelpides' leaving Athens to seek a pastoral existence, and of Peisetairos' creating, in mid-air, an imperialistic walled city of birds, called "Cloudcuckooland," which he, replacing the Olympian gods, then rules as master of the universe.

THE USE OF MYTH IN THE *BIRDS*

Aristophanes uses myth in the *Birds*, in parodic fashion. For example, Euelpides and Peisetairos seek out Tereus, the mythic king who married Procne, daughter of Pandion and, after raping her sister Philomela, was turned into a hoopoe bird and she into a nightingale. The prologue of the *Birds* refers to the fact that Sophocles wrote a tragedy about Tereus; it has not survived but it seems certain that Aristophanes' audience knew it well and found Tereus' complaint of "shabby treatment" in the tragedy particularly funny. Possibly Sophocles included the story of Philomela and the death of Itys, Tereus and Procne's child, but here Tereus and Procne seem an amiable married couple.

There appears in the *parabasis* a comically distorted version of the cosmogony of Hesiod in which birds are the first created beings—in fact, the first gods.

Iris, Prometheus, Poseidon, and Herakles appear in the play and, like the myth of Tereus and Hesiod's *Theogony*, are broadly parodied. Iris, Zeus' messenger, is presented as a dumb tart; Prometheus, the heroic fire-bringer, comes on stage crouching beneath an umbrella, so that he may not be seen by the Olympians; and the three gods of the delegation, Poseidon, Herakles, and Triballos, are depicted, respectively, as a "pompous aristocrat," a "bully and glutton," and a "gibbering foreigner."[7] Herakles, about whose paternity a joke is made, is the son of Zeus and Alcmene, Zeus having disguised himself as her husband Amphitryon. A new goddess is conjured up by Aristophanes for the occasion, whom he names "Basileia" and makes the keeper of Zeus' thunderbolts and occasional girlfriend; the "myth" of Peisetairos ends with his marriage to Basileia ("Sovereignty"), a dramatized pun, Peisetairos having wrested "Sovereignty" from Zeus.

THE HISTORICAL CONTEXT OF THE *BIRDS*

Athenian Ambition and the Peloponnesian War (431–404 B.C.)

By 431 B.C., Athens was enforcing regular tribute payments from her allies and requiring that allied cases involving the penalties of death, exile, loss of rights, and property confiscation be heard in Athens. When, in 421 B.C., the Peace of Nicias was concluded, Athens had the opportunity to emerge from the war intact and powerful; however, Alcibiades urged his fellow citizens to attack and subjugate the island of Melos, with which Athens was not at war. The Melian Campaign, involving an Athenian naval blockade of the small neutral island of Melos and the subsequent starvation and enslavement of its population, became a byword for Athenian imperialism in its most raw form. "It is, of course, a deliberate part of Aristophanes' general ironic design that the tactics used by Peisetairos against the gods are, in fact, the brutal military tactics of Athenian imperialism. However fantastic the play may seem, its purpose is the relentless satirical equation of Athens and Cloudcuckooland."[8] About a year after the Melian Campaign, Alcibiades convinced the citizens of Athens to undertake another expedition, and, in 415 B.C., Athens launched against Sicily the finest armada that Athens had ever assembled: 134 triremes, 30 cargo ships, and 150 smaller vessels. By the fall of 413 B.C., the fleet was utterly destroyed, a blow from which Athens never recovered. At the time of the production of the *Birds* in 414 B.C., however foolish the expedition might have seemed, its success was still a possibility in the minds of Athenians. The ambition of Peisetairos to displace the gods and rule the universe, and the particular method he uses, the interdiction of all air traffic, both in the form of incense rising to the heavens and in the form of lustful gods descending to earth to cohabit with attractive mortals, is a comic version of the unbridled political and economic ambition of Athens to control and tax all movement across the seas.

Athens and the Spirit of *Polupragmosune*

Thucydides reports the Corinthians describing the Athenians as "given to innovation and quick to form plans and to put their decisions into execution." They are "bold beyond their strength, venturesome beyond their better judgment, and sanguine in the face of dangers."[9] It is a description echoed by the great Pericles himself, who, in his Funeral Oration says, "we have compelled every sea and every land to grant access to our daring." The spirit of Athens embodied in the comic heroes of the *Birds* may be summed up in the word *polupragmosune*, which appears throughout the play. Literally, it means "doing many deeds," and, when applied to Athens, suggests the endless energy, for both good and ill, of the Athenian character—busyness, enterprise, daring, and love of whatever is new and experimental.[10] Peisetairos and Euelpides think they desire a bucolic existence; they no sooner arrive in a pastoral setting than they busy themselves, in true Athenian fashion, with schemes and activities designed to mold that setting to their wills and to replicate the city activity they have abjured. Additionally, the arrogance and grandeur of Peisetairos' vision are typically "Athenian." Ordinary citizens expressed their *polupragmosune* in mindless activity, like that pursued by the Poet and Geometrician, or in litigiousness. *Polupragmosune* is the spirit of military expansion and of the acquisition of power for its own sake, and those motives are precisely what animate Peisetairos, Euelpides, and, ultimately, the Birds themselves.

Aristophanes "gives a comic representation of the high schemes and ambitions which were in the air; not as *encouraging* them, for his caricature is fantastic and ludicrous in the extreme; yet not as *discouraging* them, since Peisetairos' fantastic adventure is crowned with brilliant success."[11]

The only truly unpleasant figures in the *Birds* are the legal hangers-on: the Legal Inspector, the Decree Seller, and the Informer. Athens was a place of a tremendous litigiousness, as indicated by both the number of legal parasites who appear in the play and by the frequent jokes about jurors. When Peisetairos says that they are Athenians, Tereus replies with mock horror, "Not jurymen, I hope!" During the time of the Peloponnesian War, Athens was a place of rapidly multiplying laws, statutes, and decrees; and parasitic Decree Sellers appeared, like the one in the play who has a bunch of new laws that the new city has certainly not yet heard of and who wishes to be paid for delivering them. Informers were those who, without the legal standing that derives from personal injury, made it a career to inform on other citizens whom the state then indicted, and from the recovery in such lawsuits the Informers received a bounty. Among the laws promulgated in Athens at this time, to which Aristophanes jokingly alludes, were laws about inheritance; a bastard could not inherit, as Peisetairos informs Herakles when trying to lure him from his purposes as Zeus' emissary.

Athenian Bird Jokes

The Athenians appear to have had as many jokes and proverbial sayings about birds as we do. In addition to the following, Aristophanes makes up scores more.

- "Go to the ravens": go to the devil.
- "Kick the rock with your foot and the birds will fall down": a child's jingle that here becomes the literal truth.

- "A Slavebird": Greeks called the loser in a cockfight the "slave" of the winner. (The Slavebird here is literally the former "slave" of Tereus.)
- "Bringing an owl to Athens": bringing something to a place already full of, and renowned for, such things.
- "By Goose": *ksain* ("by goose") is a euphemistic form of *Zain* ("by Zeus"), the rhyme in English replicating the rhyme in Greek. It is equivalent to saying "darn" for "Damn."
- "None but some little bird knows where my treasure lies": a way of saying "no one knows."
- "Play the partridge": evade one's pursuers, as the partridge does by weaving movement.
- "Birds' milk": a nonexistent thing.
- "Twitter like the swallows": talk nonsense.

THE PLOT OF THE *BIRDS*

General Comments

Nobody denies, Arrowsmith says, that the *Birds* is "a masterpiece, one of the greatest comedies ever written and probably Aristophanes' finest."[12] At 1,765 lines, it is a long play with many episodes but with tremendous comic energy and speed.

The *Birds* modifies the traditional pattern of Old Comedy in that the *parodos* merges immediately into an *agon* between the Chorus of Birds and the men, and the *parabasis* is not an interruption but a continuation of the themes of the play. Thus, the "demands of dramaturgy have triumphed in the *Birds* over the need for certain traditional components, and the result is a play of singularly sustained dramatic force."[13]

The conflict between the Birds and the men is resolved mid-way through the play when they decide to construct "Cloudcuckooland." At that point a second *agon* replaces the first, and the Birds and Peisetairos together oppose the gods and the human interlopers. What follows after the first resolution are a series of episodes in which the consequences of that decision are presented: a flood of hangers-on, a treaty with the gods, an apotheosis of the protagonist.

Setting

The setting is the wood surrounding the rock where the Hoopoe makes his nest. The time is the present (414 B.C.). After the first *parabasis* "the scene is presumably in the air."[14]

Dramatis Personae

Euelpides	citizen of Athens
Peisetairos	citizen of Athens
Slavebird	servant to the Hoopoe
Hoopoe	formerly King Tereus
Chorus of Birds	(24 types are specified)
Nightingale	formerly Procne, wife of Tereus; flute player
Priest	
Poet	
Soothsayer	
Meton	a geometrician and astronomer
Legal Inspector	
Decree Seller	
First Messenger	
Sentry	
Iris	goddess of the rainbow, daughter of Zeus
Second Messenger	
Father-Beater	
Kinesias	a dithyrambic poet
Professional Informer	
Prometheus	
Poseidon	
Herakles	
Triballos	primitive god of Thrace
Herald	
Basileia	Sovereignty, a beautiful maiden (*non-speaking role*)
Xanthias	slave of Euelpides and Peisetairos (*non-speaking role*)
Manodoros/Manthes	slave of Euelpides and Peisetairos (*non-speaking role*)

Scene Divisions

Prologue:	1–297	[Peisetairos, Euelpides, Slavebird, Tereus, Xanthias, Manodoros]
Parodos:	298–675	[Chorus, Peisetairos, Euelpides, Tereus]
First *Parabasis*:	676–800	[Chorus, Procne]
Episode One:	801–1057	[Chorus, Peisetairos, Euelpides, Priest, Poet, Soothsayer, Meton, Inspector, Decree Seller]
Second *Parabasis*:	1058–1117	[Chorus]
Episode Two:	1118–1469	[Chorus, Peisetairos, First Messenger, Sentry, Iris, First Herald, Father-Beater, Kinesias, Professional Informer]
Choral Stanzas:	1470–1493	[Chorus]
Episode Three:	1494–1552	[Chorus, Prometheus, Peisetairos]
Choral Stanza:	1553–1564	[Chorus]
Episode Four:	1565–1693	[Chorus, Poseidon, Herakles, Triballos, Peisetairos, Manodoros]
Choral Stanza:	1694–1705	[Chorus]
Exodos:	1706–1765	[Chorus, Herald, Peisetairos, Basileia]

SYNOPSIS AND COMIC ANALYSIS

Prologue: 1–297

Action in the Prologue

Euelpides and Peisetairos have left Athens, have been retracing ground, and are now talking with some irritation to the birds perched on their wrists. They seek Tereus, the king who was transformed into a bird, in the hope that he, having an aerial view, can direct them to a city where life is debt-free and pleasure-laden. Because there is an Athenian saying, "Kick a rock and find a bird," and because nothing else is working, they kick the rock in front of them. A hitherto-unseen door opens and a terrifyingly long-beaked bird emerges. They convince the bird to summon Tereus; meanwhile each castigates the other for being frightened. Tereus appears from the door in the rock, and Peisetairos, staring upward at Tereus and the sky beyond, suddenly thinks of an Athenian kind of scheme: they can build a tribute city in the sky, populated solely by birds. Tereus, with the help of his wife, the Nightingale fluteplayer, summons the Birds to hear Peisetairos' plan. The original intention of Peisetairos and Euelpides to achieve a bucolic existence is utterly forgotten.

Sources of Humor in the Prologue

It is farcical to see two men talking earnestly to two birds and translating the caws of the crow and jackdaw for each other. The same pretense about nonsense language returns at the end of the play when Herakles "interprets" Triballos' gibberish for Poseidon. The fantasy of being able to buy talking birds in any old pet shop immediately merges into mundane complaints about their suspicion that the bird-seller cheated them.

The appearance of a door and a man-sized bird, summoned up by a verbal joke, begins the comic emphasis of the play on the dizzying power of words to create realities.

As Aristotle says, "the laughable is one category of the shameful. For the laughable comprises any fault or mark of shame which involves no pain or destruction."[15] In comedies, fear is laughable, and mutual fear is even more laughable. When the Slavebird suddenly appears, the men and the Slavebird both shriek at the sight of the other. Because the Slavebird regards human beings as mortal enemies, Euelpides and Peisetairos deny that they are human. Peisetairos claims to be a rare species called a "Fearbird"; Euelpides offers a variant on the same theme, claiming to be a "Puddle Duck" and proving that he is by pointing to the puddle being produced below his legs by his fear.

The Slavebird explains that he was formerly the butler to King Tereus and has been transformed into a Butler Bird. If Tereus craves fish, the Slavebird fetches some, not from the fishmonger as he was wont to do, but directly from the river in his beak. The comically collapsing boundaries between bird and human continue: the Slavebird explains that it is hard to fetch Tereus right now, as he is taking a nap, having just finished a lunch of ants and berries. Euelpides and Peisetairos simultaneously realize that their pet birds have flown off, and each man accuses the other of having released the string in terror. Duplicative action is funny, especially when it exposes our tendency to absolve ourselves of responsibility while reproaching another for the very fault we have. In addition, this initial picture of a timid Peisetairos makes his apotheosis later into a god and ruler of the universe comic in contrast and comic in what it asserts about rulers, both human and divine.

Tereus appears and Peisetairos and Euelpides tell him that he looks rather inadequately feathered; he explains that birds molt in winter and that he's sort of stuck with this look because this is how Sophocles depicted him in the tragedy *Tereus*. Aristophanes takes pleasure in such double realities, presenting a fictional character who is conscious of his fictionality and who also has a few complaints about one of his authors. When Tereus asks what sort of city they were hoping to find, both describe an inverted reality: a city where a neighbor begs you to come to a wedding feast and says that if you don't, he will refuse to share his woes with you the next time he's in trouble, or a city where a neighbor scolds you for not molesting his lovely young son at the baths. In their utopia, pleasure is morally compulsory, and to fail to pursue it is a sign of general unfriendliness. Tereus speaks of the pleasures of living among the birds—no money is exchanged, an advantage that particularly appeals to the two deadbeats, and there is a plentiful supply of sesame seed and mint—arguably less appealing to the two men. Suddenly, looking upward at Tereus in the rock cliff and seeing the sky beyond, Peisetairos conflates the word *polos* with the word *polis* and declares that, just as in sound they are one and the same, so shall they be in reality: the *polos* ("sky") shall become a *polis* ("city"). In Aristophanes' comic world, words are realities, not simply signifiers of reality.[16] On such "airy nothings," Aristophanes may be suggesting, the imperialistic schemes of human beings are based. Peisetairos explains that a city in the sky can interdict all air traffic and demand that tribute be paid to the birds. How, Peisetairos wonders, suddenly overcome by practicality, can he communicate his dream to the birds? Tereus says that, as he's "lived with them a long time," these birds speak Greek, which, of course, they do, being the Chorus of the play. The constant back and forth between fantasy and quotidian concern is part of what makes this comedy of Aristophanes so splendid.

Tereus summons the Birds. The arrival of four different species—a Flamingo, a Medos, a second Hoopoe, and a Gobbler—is an occasion for a joke at the expense of the ambitious, cowardly, and gluttonous "gobbler" Cleonymus, from whom the stage Gobbler can be distinguished by its not having dropped his "crest" (helmet) in hasty retreat on the battlefield.

Parodos: 298–675

The *parodos* is divided into two parts, a mock battle between the Birds and the men, and a rhetorical contest in which Peisetairos presents his plan and responds to challenges from the Birds.

Action in the Mock Battle of the Parodos

A Chorus of 24 different species of birds enter rapidly and react with horror to the presence of the two men. They immediately prepare for battle. Tereus calms the Birds and they agree to hear what the men have to say.

Sources of Humor in the Mock Battle of the Parodos

The battle preparations are farcical and anticlimactic. Responding to the military command of the *Koryphaios* of "beaks leveled!", the Birds close ranks and form themselves into an attack squadron. The two men, meanwhile, grab the only weapons they can find, a few cooking pots and skewers to fend off the Birds, and saucers and bowls to cover their heads and eyes. The Birds utter the heroic battle cry of "*Eleleleu*," as the *Koryphaios* urges them onward with a series of increasingly violent commands, "drag, pluck, hit, flay," culminating in the wonderfully anticlimactic order, "attack the cooking pots first."

Fear is again a source of humor. Euelpides, terrified, but not so terrified as to fail to blame his friend for getting them into this spot, asks where they will be buried if they die in battle. The Cemetery of the Potters, replies Peisetairos, referring not only to the pots they are using but to the famous cemetery of Cerameikos ("the Potters") in Athens where the war dead are buried. Peisetairos adds that to be permitted burial there, they'll have to tell the general they died at Orneae, a real city that means "place of the birds" and whose citizens decamped rather than face Athenian soldiers. Thus, no one died at Orneae. And, of course, it is not possible, once dead, to tell your general where you died.

Tereus calms the Chorus and the Chorus swear an oath of temporary non-aggression, the *exoleia* of which is "if I break my oath, may I win First Prize for Comedy in this Dionysia by only one vote" rather than by an unanimous verdict of the jurors.

Action in the Argument of the Parodos

Peisetairos explains his scheme of building a city to extract tribute from the gods and restore the birds to what he claims was their initial supremacy over gods and men. Tereus invites Peisetairos and Euelpides inside for lunch and a set of wings, while his wife, the curvaceous flute-player Procne, enters to accompany the Chorus in their song.

Sources of Humor in the Argument of the Parodos

The Chorus sing a parody of tragic choral song, full of awkward and repetitive phrases such as "a quality overlooked by my witless mind" and "whatever

advantage you may provide me will be an advantage." Their unwieldy language is followed immediately by the Chorus leader's breezy directness: "Now
then, about this idea of yours that you've come to see us: explain what kind
of business it is, and never fear, we won't break the truce before you've had
your say."

Peisetairos first presents a series of silly proofs of the ancient greatness of
birds and then arouses a sense of self-pity and outrage in the Birds for what
has been "stolen" from them and for what has been done to them. Humans
are "not content" to roast and broil them, but insult them further by grating
cheese all over them and pouring "oil, silphium, vinegar" on them. Combining
farce with satire, these silly complaints remind us of the "birdness" of his
auditors and mimic the lists of imagined grievances the Athenians compiled
to stir up sentiment for military action. Peisetairos' catalogue of culinary
wrongs reaches its climax when he exclaims that in cooking you, they treat
you "as if you were dead meat!" The lament of the Chorus that follows is in
the grand style: it begins with the traditional formula of repetition followed
by the superlative form of the adjective, *chalepotatous*, used by Thucydides
to describe desperate, grievous situations of poverty, loss and massacre. Their
lament reveals the rapidity with which we are thrown into despair by the
absence of what, a moment earlier, we were blissfully happy without.

Having finished the proem of his speech in which he states the problem
and wins the sympathy of his auditors, Peisetairos moves to his remedy and its
implementation. The Chorus leader raises questions and objections, each of
which Peisetairos disposes of with great aplomb. He concludes his argument
by mentioning that men will find it additionally advantageous to worship
birds because, as birds already have nests, there will be no need to construct
elaborate and costly temples. The argument ends as it has begun, with the
Chorus singing in stiffly tragic mode and the *Koryphaios* restating, colloqui-
ally, their adoption of Peisetairos' scheme. The *Koryphaios'* description of
the division of labor, in which humans will provide the "brain" (*gnomei*) and
the Birds will provide the "brawn" (*rhomei*) is also funny in summoning up a
vision of muscle-bound birds.

First *Parabasis*: 676–800

Action in the First Parabasis

The *parabasis* begins with "what might be called an Avine Cosmogony"
and then passes into "an overtly humorous bid for support, as though the
Birds were campaigning for the votes which will make them gods."[17]

Sources of Humor in the First Parabasis

The *parabasis* proper begins with the Chorus leader's lament for all mortals and all mortal achievement. It addresses the audience in words both sorrowful and condescending, and concludes with self-praise by the Chorus of Birds:

> ye men ... faintly alive ... race of leaves ... artifacts of clay ... shadowy and feeble ... wingless ephemera ... suffering ... dreamlike ... pay attention to us, the immortals, the everlasting, the ethereal, the ageless, whose counsels are imperishable.

The words of the Muses to the shepherd Hesiod in the *Theogony* follow the same pattern, albeit shortened, of blunt statement of mortal insufficiency followed by an expression of the contrasting nature of the Muses: "'Shepherds of the wilderness, wretched things of shame, mere bellies, we know how to speak many false things as though they were true, but we know, when we will, to utter true things.'"[18] The *parabasis* goes on to rewrite Hesiod's account of the birth of the gods. This new version assigns wings to nearly everyone and describes being born as being "hatched." What the *parabasis* illustrates is the burgeoning of a tremendous vanity on the part of the formerly undistinguished. The *Koryphaios* notes the meteorological usefulness of birds: when Orestes, a well-known Athenian thief, sees the crane's autumn flight to Libya, he is reminded to "weave a cloak" so that when he goes out to mug people he won't catch cold. The leader's speech ends in a burst of electioneering as, again and again, Aristophanes weaves political satire into pure burlesque.

The final lines of the *parabasis* belong to the *Koryphaios* who moves now from topical satire to farce as he asserts that "there's nothing better" than wings. The three examples that follow are deliciously, coarsely funny, and all address the audience as audience: if you're at the theatre and get hungry and bored by the tragedies, with wings you can fly home, grab a bite, and be back here "to see us" (that is, "to see the comedy") later in the day. If you're sitting in the audience and, like Patrocleides (according to the Scholiast, an Athenian whose nickname was "the shitter"), have to go, you can fly out, "blow a fart" and come right back. If you're an adulterer and see the lady's husband in one of the specially reserved Councillor seats in the theatre, you can fly right to her house, "have a fuck" and be back before the play is over.[19]

Episode One: 801–1057

Action in Episode One: The Parasites Arrive

The plot moves into its second stage when Euelpides and Peisetairos enter costumed as birds. Each notes the scrawny look of the other but not of himself. They seek a name for the city to be built in the clouds, something "grand" and "notable," and they come up with the seven-syllable *Nephelokokkygia*, "Cloudcuckooland." In rapid succession six different self-promoters arrive, two of them twice, to offer their services to the city. Each is rejected in turn.

Sources of Humor in Episode One: The Parasites Arrive

The chief form of comedy in this scene is social satire, but there is a good deal of physical comedy as well. That the action begins with a comic list is a splendid prelude to the serial action that follows. Peisetairos issues 13 commands to Euelpides and assigns himself one task. A priest enters with a small goat. Things seem to be going fairly well until the priest, in listing the dwellers within the city to be granted wealth and safety, suddenly throws in the Chians, residents of an island in the eastern Mediterranean who, "in recognition of their faithful help at the beginning of the Peloponnesian War ... had a regular place in the public prayers of Athens."[20] Peisetairos interrupts him, says the goat is too little to feed all those birds, and resumes the rites himself. Immediately thereafter a would-be Poet appears, reading dreadful dedicatory verses and reciting bits of Pindar about "one who possesses no shuttle-actuated raiment." Peisetairos, fed up, tosses him a cloak as he exits, still reciting. A third imposter appears, followed, in rapid succession, by a host of other frauds: Meton, the geometrician, who pulls out a number of bizarre surveying implements and explains that he plans to parcel the air into acres, a corrupt Inspector sent by the Athenian Assembly to enforce Athenian policy and collect fees for doing so, and a Decree Seller with a list of the latest decrees of the Assembly for sale. The real fun of the scene comes chiefly from the comic predictability of the pattern, once established. At its conclusion, the Inspector and the Decree Seller come back yet again and are roundly beaten. The humor lies in seeing something like an irrepressible jack-in-the-box on stage. The scene is not only great farce, but also fine satire in its attack on the Athenian legal system, imperialism, and *polypragmosune*.

Second *Parabasis*: 1058–1117

Action in the Second Parabasis

In this second *parabasis*, the Birds tout themselves and the blessings they bring. It allows dramatic time for Euelpides and the birds to build the city.

Sources of Humor in the Second Parabasis

After the comic boasting of the first strophe, in which the Chorus of Birds speak of themselves in heroic terms as protectors of crops, slayers of the enemies of fragrant gardens, and wreakers of murderous destruction upon insects, the Chorus leader, in the manner of formal Athenian public denunciation meetings, denounces not a tyrant but a local bird-seller. To the Judges in the audience, the leader promises birds in the form of silver coins called "owls" that will "nest" in their wallets and "hatch" small change. On the other hand, if the Judges fail to vote for the *Birds*, whenever they are wearing clean white cloaks, they would be wise to cover their heads with "copper lids."

Episode Two: 1118–1469

Action in Episode Two: Messengers and Additional Visitors

Comic digressions now give way to action that focuses on the building of the city and the problem of policing air traffic. Peisetairos enters to announce the conclusion of the sacrifice and is followed by a breathless Messenger, informing him that the wall has been built. No sooner does the Messenger deliver his message and depart than a Sentry appears with the alarming news that the wall has been breached by "some god" who turns out to be Iris on a mission to earth. She is intercepted and sent back to Olympus. A second Messenger arrives, this time from earth, to proclaim humanity's esteem for Peisetairos and to relay the fact that wings and Cloudcuckooland are now all the rage, and that hoards of Athenians are on their way. Peisetairos finds the first three visitors so distasteful that he stops selling wings.

Sources of Humor in Episode Two: Messengers and Additional Visitors

When Peisetairos sights the first Messenger, he says "Here comes someone on the run, panting like an Olympic sprinter." The Messenger is in fact so out of breath that, pantingly, what he says is *pou pou'sti, pou pou pou'sti, pou pou pou'sti, pou pou Peisetairos*, the Greek interrogative *pou* ("where?") forming the nonsense syllables of a bird call, as the Messenger tries to articulate, "Where's Peisetairos the ruler?" This adaptation of the traditional joke of the out-of-breath-messenger is particularly funny, as the Messenger has not been running at all: he is a bird and flapping his wings on stage.

In the dialogue between Iris and Peisetairos, each registers irritation in a different key. Peisetairos excoriates her for not having a visa and threatens her with death. She replies that she is deathless. He says that she'll be put to death anyway. She threatens that "her father will fix them" and then suddenly launches into the diction of high tragedy: "O, fool, fool! Provoke not the terrible spleen of the gods, lest Justice wielding the Spade of Zeus utterly eradicate all your race; lest fiery fumes inflame your body and the enfolding embrace of your palace with thunderbolts Licymnian!" She becomes the subject of a lecherous comment and departs on the *mechane* by which she has come.

The arrival of the Messenger from earth is marked by a theatre joke also dependent on repetition that makes his entry as funny as the entry of the first Messenger. What the second Messenger says is "O Peisetairos, O blessed, O most wise, O most renowned, O most wise, O most slick, O thrice-blessed," and just as we wonder at such endless effusiveness, the voice of the actor is heard in a final phrase also beginning "O"—"O, just give me my cue!" Of course, his cue is the request for "my cue." Peisetairos accepts a golden crown from the Messenger, who tells him that, a moment before, Sparta was all the rage among sophisticated Athenians who therefore "wore their hair long, went hungry, and never bathed." Now birds are the fashion and everyone wants wings and woodland pasture. That both Sparta and the Birds, one actually and one fictively, intend to dominate Athens means nothing to the fashionable Athenian, for it has always been a feature of "broadmindedness" to appropriate the emblems of the enemy.

Peisetairos' response to the Messenger's report that people are "crazy for wings" and on their way to Cloudcuckooland is a satire of Athenian commercialism: he immediately orders his slave Manodoros to haul baskets of wings onstage at a pace impossible to maintain, and a satire on the irresistible pull of trade and money-making is joined to slapstick when Peisetairos keeps smacking Manodoros for being slow while Manodoros exhausts himself racing back and forth. Three applicants for citizenship arrive. The third is an Informer who wishes to acquire a pair of wings to fly all over the Aegean, dropping off indictments and flying back to Athens ahead of the defendants so as to make a fortune through default judgments. Peisetairos advises the Informer to try making an honest living; the Informer counters that his father and grandfather before him have been Informers: for him to do otherwise would be to act in derogation of family honor.

Choral Stanzas: 1470–1493

The next three choral interludes comprise a related, three-part satire, each of which satirizes particular, odious Athenians. In the strophe the Chorus describe the Cleonymus tree, which in springtime sprouts denunciations and in wintertime drops its shields like leaves; in the antistrophe the Chorus mock the thief Orestes.

Episode Three: 1494–1552

Action in Episode Three: Prometheus

Prometheus sneaks down from Olympus to tell Peisetairos that "Zeus is finished" and to advise Peisetairos about the terms of surrender. Ambassadors will be coming to Cloudcuckooland from Zeus; refuse, Prometheus says, to make peace unless Zeus "returns his scepter to the birds and gives you *Basileia* for your bride."

Sources of Humor in Episode Three: Prometheus

A figure skulks onstage, unrecognizable, hooded, swathed in blankets, and carrying a ladies' parasol. He is so covered up and cowering that he does not know whether it is night or day, or whether Zeus is gathering or parting the clouds, and keeps asking about the time and weather. The parasol is not, as it turns out, for protection from the elements, but a means of stopping Zeus from seeing who is under it, for Prometheus, "friend to man" here transformed into "friend to bird," has come to reveal the desperate situation of the now-sacrifice-starved gods. The high comedy of an heroic figure, quivering and outfitted with a ladies' parasol, reaches its peak when, ready to leave, he grabs his parasol back from Peisetairos and explains that if Zeus should see him, Zeus will take him for the virgin who carries the parasol that shades the basket bearer in the great Panathenaia. The message he brings is not only that the Olympians are ravenous from lack of sacrifices, but also that they are being pressured by "the barbarian gods" whose sacrifices are also being interdicted. Both ideas are comically reductive of the Olympians. Since the barbarian gods are "swearing to invade Zeus from the North unless at once he throws the markets open, lowers all obstacles to trade, and lets them freely import their meat," the passage is yet another comic political analogue. The scene ends with praise for Prometheus, the great fire-bringer, for without him there would be no "barbecues."

Choral Stanza: 1553–1564

In this strophe the Chorus lampoon Socrates' hygiene, the cowardice and superstition of the politician Pisander, and the clothing of the politician and general Chaerephon.

Episode Four: 1565–1693

Action in Episode Four: The Delegation

A delegation of three gods arrives to sue for peace. Negotiations are carried on while the smell of Peisetairos' onstage cooking wafts to Herakles who is immediately willing to concede anything in exchange for lunch. Poseidon holds out, but Herakles controls the vote of the incoherent Triballos, and ultimately gets his way. The Olympians concede full power to Peisetairos and agree to his marriage to Basileia.

Sources of Humor in Episode Four: The Delegation

The comedy of this culminating moment in the plot is both broad and ironic. As the delegation enters, Poseidon is fussing over the appearance of Triballos, the barbarian god who cannot seem to drape his cloak properly. Poseidon, with the distaste of the aristocrat, sees in the rancid appearance of Triballos the effect of democracy, and apostrophizes, "O democracy, what will you bring us to in the end, if the gods can elect this person ambassador?" He no sooner finishes dressing Triballos than he has to restrain Herakles whose idea of conducting negotiations is to "strangle the guy." The byplay between the three members of the delegation continues throughout the scene and moves toward comic chaos when it is discovered that Triballos neither speaks nor understands Greek—he is, after all, a "barbarian." Because Poseidon and Herakles disagree about which concessions are acceptable, the deciding vote goes, absurdly, to Triballos. Herakles appoints himself Triballos' interpreter, and since full concession means a taste of the meat Peisetairos is elaborately seasoning and cooking onstage, Herakles simply interprets Triballos' gibberish as acquiescence to Peisetairos' terms and overrides Poseidon by a vote of two to one, a cynical example of Athenian democracy in action.

Peisetairos not only plays to Herakles' gluttony by ostentatiously roasting meat right under Herakles' nose and by loudly conferring with his slave about the proper seasonings to be applied, but is verbally manipulative as well. He avoids mentioning the critical concession of the transfer of Basileia from Zeus to himself until agreement is reached on all other points, and then presents it as an afterthought, while saying that he is willing to concede Hera, whom neither he, nor, probably, Zeus, wants. When his terms are rejected, Peisetairos feigns indifference and gets back to his cooking, which, of course, excites Herakles to a near-frenzy.

The final round of negotiations satirizes Athenian domestic legislation. Poseidon tells Herakles that however much of Zeus' power they grant to Peisetairos is that much less for Herakles to inherit when Zeus "dies," itself a comic proposition. Peisetairos counters that Herakles, a bastard by decree because his mother is an "alien"—by which Aristophanes, in an Olympian context, means a "mortal,"—cannot inherit anything anyway, as Athenian law forbade the conveyance of property to bastards, so that such property thereby escheats to the state.

The barbecue provides the moment of culminating comic irony of the play. As Peisetairos enters, he orders, "Hand me the cheese grater. Pass the silphium. Someone get the cheese. Poke up these coals," and we realize that we have heard identical culinary language before—in fact, from Peisetairos himself when, in the *parodos*, he describes in compassionating tones how men roast and season birds. This dish he is preparing turns out to be none other than "some birds" whose demise he rationalizes politically as anti-democratic insurgents. When, a moment later, Peisetairos says, "There is no oil in the bottle," and Herakles replies, "And bird meat should be glistening with it," and when Peisetairos orders his Cook to be "sure you make the sauce sweet," the political satire is complete. Not only does Peisetairos' scheme unfold itself as self-aggrandizement masquerading as benevolence, but the tendency of people to be duped by politicians and to find that they have simply exchanged one taskmaster for another is presented to us in bold and brilliant comic strokes.

Choral Stanza: 1694–1705

The Chorus conclude their satiric "travelogue" in an antistrophe that mocks Gorgias and Philippus, popular teachers of rhetoric.

Exodos: 1706–1765

Action in the Exodos

A Herald enters, announcing in grandiloquent terms the imminent arrival of Peisetairos and his bride Basileia. The royal couple enter and the Chorus respond in praise and joy, with a traditional, if exaggerated, marriage song, likening the couple to Zeus and his consort Hera. The couple lead the Chorus of Birds in dance, as the play ends.

Sources of Humor in the Exodos

That the Chorus note how "beautiful" the bride Basileia is, is witty, for power is beautiful to those who desire it. The traditional marriage song, invoking the model of Zeus and Hera, is funny because Peisetairos has just dethroned Zeus and stolen his other bride, Basileia. The play ends with a wedding dance in which the lady Basileia cannot take her beloved by his hands, as he now has none, but must, as he enjoins her, take his "wings." The couple dance themselves onto the *mechane* and are lifted to the high heavens in complete comic apotheosis. Peisetairos has undergone two metamorphoses in the course of the play, from human to beast and then from beast to god. Aristophanes leaves us to contemplate that particular progression.

THEME IN THE *BIRDS*

Self-Love

In tragedy, as Aristophanes' audience knew, having that very day sat through three tragedies, *hubris* may lead to suffering and death, but in the *Birds* the blatant *hubris* of Peisetairos is crowned with success. Heroic self-assertion is celebrated rather than punished and, within the confines of comedy, is an entirely safe expression of overweening pride and self-love. Aristophanes seems to be suggesting that even within the least of us may be found a will to power and a thirst for glory, and in that sense, Peisetairos is "everyman." There is, as Aristotle noted of comedy, a turn from bad fortune to good, and, in this play such a *peripeteia* occurs twice. Not only is neither coincident with *anagnorisis*, but there is no troublesome *anagorisis* at all: self-knowledge is out of the question. The play laughs at and celebrates such pride and such schemes as an expression of our endless, foolish, and yet divine capacity for invention: to be "doing" and "seeking" in these ways is to be alive and Aristophanes' comedy celebrates life.

Nothingness

As a fantasy, the *Birds* is about "nothing," and the stage is the ideal medium to represent "nothing," as everything on it must be imagined. If a character says that he sees a certain thing in the distance, or that he has come from such-and-such a place, we know, of course, that these are imaginary things—"nothings"—and yet, within the convention of performance, we accept them as "real." And, in a way not possible in the plastic arts, action on stage can be "nothing"—a pause, a freeze, a moment of silent waiting that suddenly makes us conscious of "nothingness." Aristophanes exploits the idea of nothingness in the *Birds* in little and big ways, his purpose being to show, ever so gently, that we and all our important schemes and plans and expectations have no reality, but are, in a sense, "nothing."

The play begins with two travelers, Euelpides and Peisetairos, utterly lost—"nowhere"—who kick a cliff, which suddenly opens and reveals something where before there was "nothing"—just sheer rock. When Peisetairos is suddenly inspired, "nothing" is his inspiration and his focus: the empty sky. The Birds are summoned, but at first do not appear; Peisetairos asks Euelpides if he "sees any birds?" Euelpides' answer is that he sees "nothing." The Athenians explain to the Birds that they, reduced to "nothing," once had everything. The Olympians can easily be routed: their power is fictive, a "nothing." The endless puns of the text are concocted of words that momentarily are made to come together and that, immediately thereafter, dissolve into nothingness—they are not even running gags but are utterly and deliciously momentary. Herakles gives away everything, not for a roast bird, because Poseidon hustles him along before he can taste it, but for the odor of the roasting meat: for "nothing."

ASPECTS OF STAGECRAFT

Comic Use of Stage Machinery

The *ekkyklema*, used by the tragic dramatists to reveal bloody tableaux, is in the *Birds* used to wheel out a giant bird, half-feathered, sitting imperiously in his nest. His appearance from the rock face is comic because it is entirely unexpected and because the *ekkyklema* is associated with tragic disclosure.

The *mechane*, or stage crane, the two-story piece of machinery that lifts and lowers actors, is put to its traditional use in the *Birds* as the vehicle of descent and ascent of the gods, but it is put to that use with astounding frequency. The nature of the deities who travel on it and the fact that it is in continuous use are funny: Iris arrives on it and departs on it a moment later in ignominious haste; the delegation of the gods (Poseidon, Herakles, and Triballos) enters and exits by means of the *mechane*, Herakles longingly reaching out for some of the missed barbecue, and Basileia and Peisetairos dance their way onto it and are raised to the heavens in glorious apotheosis. The repeated use of the device associated with divinity on the tragic stage diminishes the audience's sense of religious awe, a process entirely in keeping with the initial intention of Peisetairos and the scheme of the *Birds*. When Peisetairos rises in the *mechane* with his bride Basileia at his side, it is the visual analogue of the status he has sought. If Prometheus makes no use of the *mechane*, but skulks on from the wings hiding under his umbrella, then the comic indignity of his entrance is heightened by contrast to the traveling gods.

Bird Costumes

The reference by Tereus to his having "molted in winter" and the remarks by Peisetairos and Euelpides, each to the other, about how scruffy their feathers look once they acquire wings, are necessary in that the principals must be marked as having metamorphosed and as still retaining remnants of their human form, in order to be identifiable among the full-fledged birds.

Procne, to whose figure lustful reference is made by Peisetairos, Euelpides, and the Chorus, is also an amalgam of human and bird, her body being costumed to represent a naked or perhaps partially draped woman, her mask being beaked and necessitating the beak's being "peeled off, like the shell of an egg" by Euelpides for a kiss and for the flute-playing.

Euelpides and Peisetairos' "catalogue" of the species of birds means that each of the 24 Chorus members is costumed differently. The effect, in terms of color alone, must have been spectacular.

NOTES

1. Plato, *Symposium*, 189c–193d.

2. David Barrett, "Aristophanes, Comedian and Poet" in *Aristophanes: The Knights, Peace, Wealth, The Birds,The Assemblywomen* (New York: Penguin Books, 1985), p. 26.

3. Barrett, p. 25.

4. K.J. Dover, *Aristophanic Comedy* (Berkeley: University of California Press, 1972), pp. 37–38 and 41.

5. Dover, p. 23.

6. Peter D. Arnott, *Public and Performance in the Greek Theatre* (New York, London: Routledge, 1991), p. 163.

7. Dover, p. 31.

8. William Arrowsmith, "Notes" to *The Birds* in *Aristophanes: Three Comedies* (Ann Arbor: Ann Arbor Paperbacks, 1969), p. 112.

9. Thucydides, *History of the Peloponnesian War*, Book I. 70–71.

10. Arrowsmith, pp. 1–6.

11. Benjamin Bickley Rogers, *Aristophanes II* (London: Wm. Heinemann Ltd., 1930), p. 127.

12. Arrowsmith, p. 1.

13. Cedric Whitman, *The Heroic Paradox: Essays on Homer, Sophocles and Aristophanes* (Ithaca, N.Y.: Cornell University Press, 1964), p. 169.

14. Whitman, p. 187.

15. Aristotle, *Poetics*, 1449a. 33–35.

16. See Whitman, pp. 167–199 for an extended discussion of this topic.

17. Arrowsmith, p. 115.

18. Hesiod, *Theogony*, 26–28, trans. Hugh G. Evelyn-White, *Hesiod, Homeric Hymns, Homerica* (Cambridge: Loeb Classical Library, Harvard University Press, 1998).

19. From the translation by Jeffrey Henderson, *Aristophanes III*, Loeb Classical Library 179 (Cambridge: Harvard University Press, 2000).

20. Gilbert Murray, *Aristophanes: The Birds* (London: George Allen & Unwin Ltd., 1950), p. 165.

10

Aristophanes
The *Lysistrata*
(411 B.C.)

SUMMARY OF THE *LYSISTRATA*

The *Lysistrata* is the story of the successful scheme of Lysistrata, a young woman of Athens, to bring peace and reconciliation to the warring cities of Greece by enlisting the young women of all its cities to withhold sex from their soldier-husbands until a truce is concluded.

SEXUAL HUMOR IN THE *LYSISTRATA*

Whereas the *Birds* is richly satiric, the *Lysistrata* depends for its fun on bawdy humor. Lysistrata, determined, intelligent, and well-spoken, a serious heroine in a funny play, is funny "because of the nature of her plan,"[1] a scheme that turns on its head the expected role of women in society and makes public and explicit the sexual intimacies that are part of the private sphere of life.

The *Lysistrata* is not prurient, in part because of its very directness. Jokes about sexual desire force a relaxation of inhibition, reduce difficult political issues to simple, earthy terms, and suggest that diplomacy and government overcomplicate and overlook those values in life that should be clear and elementary. Husbands seek both immediate sexual relief and the restoration of the marriage relationship between them and their wives; the wives have similar wishes and at the same time seek "the marriage of Athens and Sparta."[2] It is a mark of Aristophanes' comic genius that he has the capacity to weave together the two threads, the sexual and the political, so that, like Lysistrata's wool, they become a single dramatic garment.

Double entendres are everywhere—in the language of shoemaking, in maps, in cooking pots. While objects and occupations are thoroughly and ingeniously invested with innuendo, poised against and absolutely integrated into the sexual imagery of the play is domestic imagery of babies being changed and fed, of water drawn from the local well, of spinning and carding wool and flax, of Persian slippers, cambric gowns and saffron-dyed robes, of little girls dressed up for civic processions, of mattresses and pillows, of picnics and feasts, of sulky old men being kissed by old women, of unmarried maidens growing old and unattractive as young men go off to war. Sexuality is grounded in a framework of domesticity and becomes that which enables the continuation of that domestic world, the internal life of the city, even as that world is the sphere in which sexuality cheerfully operates. There is in this play no shame, no jealousy, no voyeurism, none of the emotions that make sexuality painful or tragic. In the bawdy disposition of "territory," both sides get something they want and relinquish something to the other side. Thus, through broadly comic and tender imagery, a case is made again and again for peace, internal and external, among the factions of the city, between states, and between the sexes.

All actors were male: when, for example, Lampito's breasts are admired by her co-conspirators, what the audience sees is a male actor in female costume and mask, with a full bosom: no person's own body is ever on display. The extended phalluses of the male characters are just that, comically exaggerated props, and when Kinesias draws attention to himself, he draws attention to a prop. And if the illusions of nudity on stage and some of the wordplay are initially shocking as well as funny to us, we need only remember that Aristophanes wrote for an audience who "invested sex with little transcendental significance";[3] the *Lysistrata* would presumably have struck them as hilarious but not obscene.

THE HISTORICAL CONTEXT OF THE *LYSISTRATA*

The Political Context

The *Lysistrata* was performed in 411 B.C., although there are no records to indicate whether at the Great Dionysia or the Lenaia. In the autumn of 413 B.C., the news of the overwhelming naval catastrophe in Sicily had reached Athens. During the war, there was factionalism, corruption, a fifth column, and the replacement of Periclean democracy with oligarchy within the city of Athens. The Athenians built a new fleet in place of the one they lost. It was reported that, when the fleet stood off the coast of Ionia, the cry in Athens was "Let the war begin," precisely the words Aristophanes attributes to the women after they hear Lysistrata's proposal.[4]

Athens and Sparta, combatants in the Peloponnesian War, were allies in 480 B.C. during the Persian invasion. It is to that comity that Lysistrata would have them return.

Six years after the performance of the *Lysistrata*, the remnants of the once-great Athenian navy were destroyed at Aegospotami in the Hellespont. Athens capitulated to Sparta in the spring of 404 B.C.

The Religious Context

Athene and the Acropolis

In Athene, guardian of the city, masculine and feminine aspects join: she is both goddess of weaving and of war, of military strategy and of domestic arts. Further, she is the virgin goddess, *Athene Parthenos*, who, like Lysistrata but unlike the wives Lysistrata must monitor, feels no temptation. She appears with shield, spear, and war helmet. The Acropolis and its environs, the setting for much of the play, are sacred to her.

The Acropolis, all of which was holy ground, is a rock outcropping about 500 feet above sea level. On its leveled top was the Erectheum, the most ancient temple in Athens, in which rested the ancient wooden statue of Athene. In the Parthenon was the great gold-ivory statue of Athene by Phidias and the Athenian treasury. The *Promachus*, a huge bronze image of Athene with helmet and spear, stood in the open air. "The Acropolis was approached by a sloping road, which led to the Propylaea, or entry, of five gates. Near this, outside the wall, ... [were a] spring ... and the grotto of Pan."[5]

Young girls of noble Athenian families participated in four ceremonies that combined religious with civic allegiance. The Chorus of Old Women recall their girlhood and assert their civic loyalty as they name these four ritual moments: (1) "I bore, at seven, the mystic casket"; (2) "was, at ten, our Lady's miller"; (3) "then the yellow Brauron bear"—the Brauronia was a ceremony honoring Artemis, the virgin goddess and protectress of wild animals: little girls dressed up in saffron-colored robes and walked in procession, representing little bears, and were symbolically dedicated to Artemis; and (4) "next a maiden tall and stately with a string of figs to wear bore in pomp the Holy Basket." The littlest girls "were called *appephoroi* because they carried certain mysterious objects in caskets. The *aletrides* were of ten years and upwards, also of noble birth, selected to grind on the holy mills (*hieroi mulones*) grain for the sacred cakes. The crowning honour was to carry a basket in the great Panathenaic procession.... Each Athenian girl, before marriage, had to 'play the bear' at the festival of Brauronian Artemis, wearing a yellow robe in place of the ancient bearskin."[6]

Cultic Practice

Athenian women participated in the *Adonia*, a cult of yearly mourning for the beautiful youth Adonis, beloved of Aphrodite. The Proboulos complains that when the Sicilian expedition of 413 B.C. was being readied, the ritual laments of the women disturbed the Assembly and were deemed an ill omen. Sabazios is a Dionysus-like god whose worship was briefly popular in Athens. Eileithyia was the goddess invoked for successful labor and childbirth. The wife on the Acropolis who hopes to return home by pretending she is having labor pains loudly invokes Eileithyia as she tries to get past Lysistrata.

The Geographical Context

The play contains many geographical references. Lacedaemon, or Laconia, is the district that surrounds Sparta. Mt. Taygetus rises above it. Corinth is a city on the isthmus that separates the Peloponnese from Attica. Boeotia is a district north of Athens. Imports that the women need for their scheme of seduction, or desire for their pleasure, and that the war interdicts, are flax from Amorgos, of which were made "the very thinnest gowns"; wine from Thasos; and eels from Boeotia. Areas referred to during the *diallage*, or "reconciliation," scene, and chosen because of their potential as *double entendres* include Pylos, Echinous, the gulf of Melis, and the corridor connecting Megara with its port city of Nisaia.

THE PLOT OF THE *LYSISTRATA*

General Comments

The plot of the *Lysistrata*, which is, quite literally, a "plot," requires a double set of antagonists and a double action. Lysistrata's plan is to create keen sexual arousal in the husbands of all the cities that are fighting each other, not to satisfy those husbands until peace is declared, and to capture the Acropolis and its treasury to prevent further allocation of funds for war.

Opposition comes from four sources, the first three of which are broadly comic: from the wives themselves who do not wish to be continent; from their husbands, represented by Kinesias, who develop permanent erections; from the old men who are outraged at the audacity of the old women; and from the Proboulos, the government official who wants control of the Treasury restored to him. The attempt to end political conflict is itself built on successive scenes of conflict. The pacifist tendencies of the play are thereby spoofed, even as they are advocated.

The double Chorus, unique to this play, is a brilliant device. The idea of gender conflict is placed directly before us, but without the sexual urgency of the principals. When the two Choruses become one, they express the play's basic metaphor. In addition, these Old Women represent, in the non-romantic but maternal tenderness of their reconciliation with the Old Men, a stage in life perhaps even more suited to political reconciliation than that of youth. These women are, after all, in negotiation with the Old Men at all times, whereas the younger couples necessarily remain sexually separated. The *Lysistrata* insists on the wisdom, civic responsibility, and cooperative spirit of women, but is not militantly feminist in that the sphere that the women fervently desire and to which they happily return is the domestic one.

Setting

The setting is in front of the Acropolis in Athens. The time is the present (411 B.C.). The Peloponnesian War between Athens and Sparta, begun in 431 B.C., has been raging for 20 years. The terrible defeat of the Athenians in Sicily occurred about a year and a half before.

Dramatis Personae

Lysistrata	a young woman of Athens
Kalonike	a young woman of Athens
Myrrhine	a young woman of Athens
Lampito	a young woman of Sparta
A Boeotian Woman	
A Corinthian Woman	
Chorus of Old Men	
Chorus of Old Women	
Proboulos	one of the council of 10 oligarchs that ruled Athens after 413 B.C.

Scythian Archers   the police accompanying the
                                       Proboulos

Kinesias   husband to Myrrhine
Child   of Kinesias and Myrrhine
Spartan Herald
Spartan Ambassador
Athenian Ambassador
Diallage   ("Reconciliation" or "Peace Treaty")
                                       a naked woman

Spartan Men
Athenian Men
Idlers
Flute Player

Scene Divisions

Prologue:	1–253	[Lysistrata, Kalonike, Myrrhine, Lampito, Wives]
Parodos:	242–386	[Chorus of Old Men, Chorus of Old Women]
Episode One:	387–613	[Choruses, Proboulos, Lysistrata, Wives]
Parabasis:	614–705	[Choruses]
Episode Two:	706–780	[Chorus of Old Women, Lysistrata, Wives]
Second Choral Song:	781–828	[Choruses]
Episode Three:	829–953	[Lysistrata, Kinesias, Myrrhine]
Choral Interlude:	954–979	[Chorus of Old Men, Kinesias]
Episode Four:	980–1013	[Kinesias, Spartan Herald]
Third Choral Song:	1014–1071	[Choruses]
Episode Five:	1072–1188	[Ambassadors from Sparta and Athens, Lysistrata]

| Fourth Choral Song: | 1189–1215 | [Chorus of Old Men and Old Women] |
| Exodos: | 1216–1321 | [Chorus, Ambassadors, Idlers, Flute Player] |

SYNOPSIS AND COMIC ANALYSIS

Prologue: 1–253

Action in the Prologue

It is early morning. Lysistrata enters in the middle of a conversation with herself—her first word is "but"—lamenting that the women have not yet appeared and indicating that, had they been called to some shrine of Bacchus, "there would have been no room to stir, so thick the crowd of timbrels." Her neighbor, Kalonike, arrives and reassures Lysistrata that the women will be along soon. Gradually, more and more appear, having had to tend to their husbands, rouse their servants, put their children to sleep, wash them, or give them pap. Lysistrata asks if they miss the husbands and especially the lovers who go off to war. They do. She proposes a way to end the war. They declare their willingness to do anything, and their declarations continue to gather force until she states her plan: they must give up *peous* (which Liddell and Scott defines as "the membrum virile"). The women immediately recant. Finally, Lampito of Sparta says she will join Lysistrata in this endeavor and the others reluctantly agree. A formal oath-taking follows in which, hilariously, Lysistrata describes every conceivable posture and action that the women must abjure. The *exoleia* ("punishment for breaking the oath") is "may I be given water instead of wine." The demure Lysistrata takes so lengthy a turn at the wine cup that Kalonike has to remind her that others need to drink also. Lysistrata tells the women to return home and don their most sheer and seductive gowns, the better to tantalize their husbands who, before their wives are to accommodate them, must promise to cease fighting. She explains that she has already sent the Old Women of the city to commandeer the Acropolis. The wives exit.

Sources of Humor in the Prologue

Comic methods in the prologue include the use of cosmetic and delicate items (rouge, perfume, silks, and sheer linen) as weapons, the shift from vociferous commitment to sudden retraction, the incremental horror each provision of the oath creates, and the contrast between the enthusiasm of Lysistrata and the reluctance of the young women.

The women's solution to the need for a sacrificial animal to seal the oath is reflective of the comic method of the play as a whole. With no animal available, the women agree to "sacrifice" a Thasian wine jar and to call it an animal sacrifice. Ritual slaughter consists of cracking the clay vessel open and pouring "the blood of the victim" into a very large wine cup. In addition to the jokes that attend drunkenness, humor is created by the women's having made one thing represent another thing so perfectly that the literal and the metaphoric become fused, as occurs in the perfect merging within the play of images of sex and war: a helmet hidden beneath a robe is presented as a sign of pregnancy, an erect phallus beneath a cloak is perceived as a spear, the action at the Acropolis represents frustrated coitus, and the desire of the Athenian and Spartan males to "make peace"[7] when Diallage appears on stage is understood in two ways. The prologue is, in addition, full of puns. When Kalonike asks Lysistrata, "Why have you, dear, convoked the women? What is the matter? How large is it?" Lysistrata replies, "Big." Kalonike continues her inquiry with *pacho?* ("thick," "massive"?). Lysistrata says, "by god, yes." Kalonike then, referring simultaneously to two things, says, "Why don't we come, then?" When the women reply to Lysistrata's question of whether the war has disrupted their sex lives, they say they've "had no joy, no solace, not a bit," and use for "a bit" the graphic word *dactylon* ("a finger's worth"). The prologue ends with a cry from the older women indicating that they have taken the Acropolis and with Lysistrata's assertion that the men will "not make us open these *gates* again," preparing the spectators for the visual *double entendres* of the next scene.

Parodos: 242–386

Action in the Parodos

A Chorus of Old Men, so aged and decrepit that it takes them 60 lines to cross the orchestra and reach the raised stage, enter, bearing logs on their backs, unlit torches in one hand, smoking firepots in the other. Their goal, as they shuffle toward the platform, is to light a fire underneath the Acropolis and force from it the Chorus of Old Women who have commandeered it. The Chorus of Old Women appear, probably at the second-story level of the stage, vilify the men, who respond in kind, and then douse the men and their fires with buckets of water.

Sources of Humor in the Parodos

Comedy comes from the exaggerated decrepitude and exaggerated rage of the Old Men, and from the broadly phallic visual symbolism both of the logs they bear and of their attempt to storm the gated citadel of the Virgin goddess. That they express the wish to burn the whole gaggle of Old Women, and then are bested by them is comically satisfying. Furthermore, the choice of weapons is unlikely: fire is a standard element of siege warfare; however, water, poured from women's water jugs, is not and the fact that it repels a siege further ridicules the Old Men. That they are in disarray literally and figuratively after the dousing, and complain to the Proboulos when he arrives that they have been made to look like they have peed in their pants (400–402), is a further source of merriment.

Comic discrepancies of tone are created when the mundane and the mock heroic are joined. The invocation of the Old Men, "O pot," which they beg not to go out before they light their torches, is immediately followed by a second invocation in exaggeratedly high style, the archaic and redundant address, "Goddess, Victory, God-descended."

Violent excoriation and physically explicit comments make the choral exchanges funny. The women and men refer to each other's musty odors and the women, preparing to douse the men, inquire whether the men would like some soap to go with the water. The women's sexual mockery of the men reaches its peak when they say they are dousing them "to make them grow."

Episode One: 387–613

Action in Episode One: Lysistrata and the Proboulos

The Proboulos enters, accompanied by a group of Scythian archers who served, historically, as members of the Athenian police force. He has heard that the women have taken the citadel and is outraged, as are the Old Men. The Proboulos wishes immediate access to the Treasury to outfit the fleet with oars. Lystrata appears and the Proboulos orders her arrest, but his archers are no more effective against the women than the Old Men have been. The Old Men and Old Women exchange insults. A long debate follows between the Proboulos and Lysistrata, at the conclusion of which the Proboulos, outraged and no closer to a solution, withdraws. The women reenter the Propylaea and close the gates behind them.

Sources of Humor in Episode One: Lysistrata and the Proboulos

The Proboulos' tirade inadvertently includes a number of *double entendres* that are all the funnier for being inadvertent and for coming from an official insisting on propriety. Explaining that rebellions of this sort come about because husbands are too indulgent, he says, "You'll see a husband go into a jeweler's. 'Look,' he'll say, 'you remember that gold choker you made for my wife? Well, she ... broke the clasp. I have to sail to Salamis: if you have leisure, do not fail to visit her this evening and fit in the peg.' Another one goes to a cobbler—young, but with a man's equipment—and says, 'My wife's new sandals are tight. Drop in at noon with something to stretch her cinch and give it a little play.'" Aristophanes' genius makes the vocabulary of a craft obscene.

The scene relies on the stock comic situation of a leader, the Proboulos, urging others to take aggressive action that he hesitates to take, and finding his fierce henchmen easily cowed. A domino effect is created: as soon as Lysistrata is threatened, Kalonike comes forward to protect her; as soon as Kalonike is threatened, Myrrhine comes forward to protect her, then Stratyllis, and so on, in endless procession. In the hand-to-hand combat that ensues, the women win and, in parodic inversion of the Homeric practice of stripping armor off the fallen enemy, Lysistrata tells her women to "forbear to strip the slain."

Aristophanes invests Lysistrata with humor of a milder sort than that of other characters, but every way as rich. It establishes her quick intelligence and draws its inspiration from the realities of domestic life. In her debate with the Proboulos, she twice proffers items of clothing to the Proboulos to underscore her points and to make him look as ridiculous as he sounds. Using a derisive metonymy, the Proboulos says that he will not listen to a "wimple," and Lysistrata replies quick wittedly, "Do not suffer my wimple to stand in the way. Here, take it and wear it and gracefully tie it, enfolding it over your head and be quiet." Kalonike and Myrrhine immediately present him with comparable markers of femininity, a spindle and a basket for carding wool. And when the Proboulos responds with indifference to her exquisite metaphor of wool-working and her direct statement of what war steals from women—for mothers, their sons who die on the battlefield; for maidens, the opportunity for marriage—Lysistrata and her women comically deck him in a funeral wreath, hand him coins for Charon, and promise to bake him a funeral cake, for he is emotionally and intellectually dead.

Lysistrata's humor is based on similes. She points out how ridiculous fully armed Athenian soldiers look in the marketplace, where no enemy lurks among the vegetables. The soldiers, she says, are "like Corybantes jangling in their armour" as they "fiercely stalk about in the midst of the crockery." Through the discrepancy between attire and locale, she suggests the absurdities of militarism. Lysistrata compares the skills needed for housework to the skills appropriate for governing. The unlikelihood of such a linkage and the detailed manner in which she extends that simile make the audience smile, if not laugh outright. We women, she says, "will ourselves be the Treasurers now." "Are we not skilled in domestic economy, and do we not manage the household finances?" Her great metaphor of wool and weaving is simultaneously lyrical and witty, a comic conception that seems initially unsustainable but turns out to be complexly envisioned and thoroughly relevant:

> Just as a woman, with nimble dexterity, thus with her hands disentangles a skein ...
> So would this weary Hellenic entanglement soon be resolved by our womanly care,
> So would our embassies neatly unravel it, drawing it here and pulling it there....
> Ah, if you only could manage your politics just in the way that we deal with a fleece.
> First, in the washing-tub plunge it and scour it, and cleanse it from grease,
> Purging away all the filth and the nastiness; then on the table expand it and lay,
> Beating out all that is worthless and mischievous, picking the burrs and the thistles away ...
> Then you should card it, and comb it, and mingle it, all in one basket of love and of unity,
> Citizens, visitors, strangers and sojourners, all the entire, divided community ...
> Also remember the cities, our colonies, outlying states in the east and the west,
> Scattered about to a distance surrounding us, these are our shreds and our fragments of wool;
> These to one mighty political aggregate, tenderly, carefully, gather and pull,
> Twining them all in one thread of good fellowship; thence a magnificent bobbin to spin,
> Weaving a garment of comfort and dignity, worthily wrapping the people therein.[8]

Parabasis: 614–705

Action in the Parabasis

The Chorus of Old Men complain that the Old Women have seized their pension funds and are planning a coup d'état within the city. The Old Women assert their patriotism by alluding to their participation, as girls, in all the religious and civic processions of the city. They accuse the men of bringing nothing to the city, not even sons. The Chorus of Old Men strip for battle. The Old Women remove their outer mantles and complain that the men and their stupid decrees have interfered with dinner parties and prevented a favored "guest," a Boeotian eel, from crossing the border to join the feast.

Sources of Humor in the Parabasis

In their mistaken attribution of militaristic ambition to the Old Women, the Old Men introduce two *double entendres*. In the first, they warn, "O these women! Give them once a handle howsoever small," where, by "handle," they mean "opportunity." A moment later, they suggest that the women may intend to fight as cavalry, and, if so, they, the Old Men, had better watch out, since " a woman is an easy rider with a natural seat. Take her over the jumps bareback, and she'll never slip her mount." Both jokes are obscene, but the first, because it is entirely inadvertent and because it makes the speakers the butt of their own insult, is funnier than the second. The "eel" joke, in its conflation of a female eel with a female party guest, is unexpected and funny, but also goes to the heart of the fact that war interrupts domestic life in all sorts of ways and prevents feasts, which themselves are symbols of communal life.

Episode Two: 706–780

Action in Episode Two: Women on the Acropolis

Lysistrata bemoans the fact that the young wives are sneaking off to their husbands. As she complains to the Chorus of Old Women of what has already happened, four more wives come past her, each proffering a different reason to go home immediately: one must prevent "moths" from eating her "wool"; another must "unhackle" her "flax"; a third, having stowed a helmet beneath her dress, claims she is about to give birth; a fourth is afraid of the holy snake; a fifth is kept awake by the owls on the Acropolis. Lysistrata hustles them all back inside and then, adopting their method, produces a fake oracle to keep them there.

Sources of Humor in Episode Two: Women on the Acropolis

The chief sources of humor in this scene are the women who have committed themselves to Lysistrata's scheme finding such sexual deprivation unendurable and the ingenuity of the various escape plots. The type of *double entendre* that invests the technical vocabulary of a craft with secondary sexual meaning, as in the Proboulos' references to the goldsmith and the cobbler, reappears here in the references to the processing of wool and flax, and is particularly funny given the dignity with which Lysistrata has invested such imagery in her extended metaphor. Her dialogue with the young wife who is pretending to be pregnant is funny because, when her ruse is discovered, the wife attempts to justify the presence of the helmet with a further fabrication, because in her desperation the young wife has not scrupled to steal the great bronze war helmet of the statue consecrated to the goddess, and because war, represented metonymically, has indeed usurped the "place" of husband and child.

Second Choral Song: 781–828

Action in the Second Choral Song

The Men sing of Melanion, who hated women; the Women sing of Timon, who hated men. At the end of the Men's song, the Men move to kiss the Women on their cheeks and then to kick them; at the end of the Women's song, the Women move to slap the Men on their cheeks and then to kick them. Both comment about the unattractive views produced when the opposite Chorus raises its legs to kick.

Sources of Humor in the Second Choral Song

That the two Choruses so precisely mirror each other is comic because of this almost mechanical reductiveness; their mirroring also suggests, even as they both sing of their mutual loathing, the possibility, as yet unperceived by them, of a reconciliation.

Episode Three: 829–953

Action in Episode Three: Kinesias and Myrrhine

This scene dramatizes Lysistrata's plan. Kinesias, the husband of Myrrhine, represents the general condition of men in Athens on this, the sixth, day of the sex strike. Lysistrata, as lookout, spies a man approaching the Acropolis. He is in a state of permanent erection and Myrrhine identifies him as her husband. Lysistrata reminds Myrrhine of her oath, which Myrrhine has not forgotten. Kinesias, meanwhile, begs Myrrhine to leave the Acropolis and come home with him. She refuses until he points to their child, whom he has thought to bring with him, and whom he urges to call out, "Mommy, mommy, mommy." Myrrhine descends and pretends to accede to Kinesias' importuning but interrupts their preparations, first to get a cot, then a mattress, then a pillow, then a blanket, then one type of perfumed ointment, then another. Finally, when all is supposedly ready, she runs off, leaving Kinesias in a far worse state than he was in at the beginning of the scene. The Chorus of Old Men offer him their sympathy.

Sources of Humor in Episode Three: Kinesias and Myrrhine

From this point on in the play, verbal humor is combined with visibly phallic humor. In subsequent scenes, every male on stage—the Spartan Herald, the Spartan Ambassador, the Athenian Ambassador, and the Chorus of Spartan and Athenian men—will, like Kinesias, sport extended artificial phalluses and walk doubled-over. Kinesias does not try to hide his erection, but the others, embarrassed and with little hope of a solution, do try to disguise theirs, which are mistaken for spears and other weaponry hidden under their cloaks, an appropriate misunderstanding given the natural suspicion existing between enemy combatants.

It is Lysistrata, not Myrrhine, who begins teasing Kinesias. As Acropolis sentry, she asks, "Who's this?" He replies, "I"; she feigns surprise, "A man?"; and he responds, "A man, undoubtedly," referring to the obvious signs. Lysistrata, who has already instructed Myrrhine how to behave, draws out her welcome and renders it slightly bawdy by miming, at its conclusion, the action described, opening her mouth wide as if to eat an egg or apple: "O welcome, welcome, dearest man; your name is not unknown nor yet unhonoured here. Your wife forever has it on her lips. She eats no egg, no apple, but she says, *This to Kinesias!*" He responds, in comic agony, "O, good heaven! Good heaven!" He begs Lysistrata to call Myrrhine to him immediately, she asks what he will give her for doing so, and he replies, "I'll give you anything I've got" or "a standing promise" or "I'll raise whatever I can," depending on the translation. And, as they prepare for bed and Myrrhine offers Kinesias the second perfume flask, he replies, "I've all the flask I want." Thus, at all times, the verbal byplay returns to the physical image of erection.

Aristophanes' use of the child of Kinesias and Myrrhine is extremely funny. Kinesias has brought with him the child and an attending slave. To draw Myrrhine down to him from the upper stage, he expresses fatherly concern for the child's lack of a mother. Myrrhine descends from the Acropolis to coddle their child and tease Kinesias with a display of affection for the baby. She then uses the presence of the baby as an excuse not to make love right there beneath the Acropolis. Kinesias, his fatherly concern entirely gone, immediately transfers the child to the arms of the slave whom he instructs to "take this home," using, hilariously, the demonstrative pronoun, *touto* ("this"), rather than a personal pronoun.

The chief comic devices of the scene are, first, the costuming of Kinesias, and second, the scene's pattern of coitus interruptus : anticipation, near fulfillment, disappointment, and new anticipation, a pattern repeated at least six times as Myrrhine, on six separate trips, brings cot, mattress, pillow, blanket, first bottle of performed ointment, and second bottle of perfumed ointment, and then runs off until Kinesias is left to be consoled by the Chorus of Old Men. Myrrhine's seemingly endless excuses and Kinesias' beginning the scene in a state of acute agony that is constantly intensified are both standard comic devices that play off against each other.

Many times in this scene, Kinesias speaks with genuine affection of his wife and of his home. These sentiments are entirely believable in that they are offered in soliloquy before she appears or to the Chorus of Old Men after she has gone. His contradicting the Chorus in its criticism of Myrrhine is funny because the Chorus think they are simply echoing his own attitude; thus, the comic inconsistency of his immediate defense of her is a sign of his besotted affection. His comments to himself before she appears on the platform are reflective of genuine love. Aristophanes avoids sentimentality by resolving these expressions of emotion in an abrupt shift to Kinesias' plaint about his physical condition (*estuka gar*, "for I am standing up"). Kinesias' statements nonetheless temper the crude tone that pure phallic reference, however comic, necessarily produces, and make the scene and the picture of marriage simultaneously erotic and loving.

Choral Interlude: 954–979

This interlude, consisting of the lamentations of Kinesias and the choral response, mimics the tragic convention of a hero in despair and a Chorus sympathetic to him. The language is both metaphoric and exaggerated: Kinesias, for example, refers to his erection as a "motherless child."

Episode Four: 980–1013

Action in Episode Four: Kinesias and the Spartan Herald

In this brief scene are the men's *anagnorisis* and the *peripeteia* of the action. A Herald, seeming to have a concealed spear inside his cloak, arrives from Sparta. As Herald describes the general situation in Sparta and Lampito's role in that situation, Kinesias realizes what the women's plan is. The Herald is directed back to Sparta to summon the Ambassadors so that peace negotiations can get under way, while Kinesias goes off in search of the Ambassadors' Athenian counterparts.

Source of Humor in Episode Four: Kinesias and the Spartan Herald

Mirror images are always funny and the two male figures in this scene not only are images of each other but also set off on identical errands, the summoning of another set of mirror images, the Ambassadors.

Third Choral Song: 1014–1071

Action in the Third Choral Song

The two Choruses, like the Herald and Kinesias, and like the two cities of Athens and Sparta, discover that they wish to reconcile. That reconciliation is not the result of rational discussion, but of kind gesture and physical contact. After they have made their "treaty," they discover that they find the same things funny, which is evidence of a shared sensibility long forgotten. Thus, in comic form and in a variety of ways, the two Choruses replicate the political reconciliation that will end the play.

The Old Men liken angry women to savage beasts and to fire, but the Women of the Chorus are not angry and thus the Men's words have no immediate applicability. The Women shrug off the anger and insist on helping the Men put their clothes back on so that the Men will not look so silly. The Women then offer to remove the gnats, tokens of anger, from the eyes of the men. This involves coming closer still, for the Women say "if you weren't so spiteful that no one can come near you, I'd have pulled out the insect that's sticking in your eye." The gnat removal occupies 10 lines, as is perhaps appropriate, given the difficulty of uprooting anger. The Women wipe the tearing eyes of the Men and, over the Men's objections, kiss them. The Men conclude that you can't live with women or without them and make a peace with the Women. The two Choruses join together to sing a strophe and antistrophe. The strophe is an elaborate offer to loan money to the audience, the antistrophe an invitation to a scrumptious dinner. In the final line of each, the offer is, with some jollity, retracted. Apparently the Old Men and the Old Women find this joke hilarious, as they repeat it in strophes of identical length in their next Choral Interlude. Such a joke casts into harmless form the reversal of expectation, the betrayal of trust, the breaking of one's word—perhaps a small analogy to the breaking of a Thirty-Years' Truce that led to the Peloponnesian War.

Sources of Humor in the Third Choral Song

Particularly funny here are the motherly attention the Chorus of Old Women shower on the Old Men, and the gradual, predictable, crotchety erosion of the Old Men's resistance to being helped and to being kissed. The retracted-offer joke of the strophe and antistrophe is of a sort that appeals to 5-year-olds, and it is truly funny that these mature men and women find it a hoot. It is possible that Aristophanes is suggesting, given the advanced age of the Old Men, that such jokes are their way of replicating and returning to the time of their youth, that older world of Hellenic harmony.

Episode Five: 1072–1188

Action in Episode Five: The Diallage Scene

The Spartan embassy arrives, followed by the Athenian embassy, all in a similar physical state. Lysistrata comes onstage accompanied by the naked and remarkably well-endowed lady, Diallage ("Reconciliation" or "Peace Treaty"), whom Lysistrata instructs to conduct the Ambassadors of both cities to a spot just in front of her. Lysistrata then delivers a formal speech in the manner prescribed by leading rhetoricians: an initial presentation of her credentials as speaker; a summation of the topic; a chastisement, cast in the form of rhetorical questions, of the Spartans for ingratitude to the Athenians, their former allies; a similar chastisement of the Athenians; and a brief peroration urging them to come to terms. The Spartans and the Athenians negotiate briefly while contemplating Diallage with barely containable lust. The negotiations are quickly concluded as the men, in states of extreme erection, follow Diallage offstage. Lysistrata invites everyone to a feast, after which, she promises, all husbands will be reunited with their wives. When the Athenian ambassador refers to "Lysistrata," it is the first time in the play that her name, which means "dissolver of armies" or "deliverer from fighting," is heard. Aristophanes' use of it at the climax of the action is deliberate and dramatic.

Sources of Humor in Episode Five: The Diallage Scene

Lysistrata's formal speech is repeatedly interrupted by the men in uncontrollable outbursts of appreciation of and desire for Diallage; Lysistrata is oblivious to this comic counterpoint to her serious presentation.

The Spartan Ambassador begins what become truly obscene and entirely hilarious "territorial" negotiations. Aristophanes' comic genius is clear in the complex intersection of metaphor and *double entendre*. The proper names of actual territories of some geopolitical relevance comprise the first level of meaning; each place name is also a pun on a metaphor for a part of the body, as, for example, "gates" (*pyloi*), or "hedgehog" (*echinus*), or "fold" (*kolpon*). These punning metaphors, because they require visualization to be understood, are actually not euphemistic but far more salacious than the literal term for that part of the body. The metaphors are understood to refer, simultaneously, to parts of the nude female Diallage standing before the hard-pressed Ambassadors and to the geography that a peace treaty between Athens and Sparta necessarily involves. Diallage is both a woman and a war map. Thus, territorial negotiations comically reflect both political realities and the sexual preferences not simply of individuals, but of city-states. Looking longingly at Diallage's rump, the Spartan expresses a desire for what he calls the "spherical area," which he then specifies as *Pylos* (the "gate"), and, indeed, the capture and fortification of Pylos in the Peloponnese in 425 B.C. "had been a major victory for Athens."[9] The Athenian reluctantly concedes the port of Pylos in exchange for three areas that are closer to Attica in geopolitical terms, and presumably more sexually to the taste of Athenians: *Echinounta*, *Melia kolpon*, and *Megarika skele*. Echinounta was a village in Thessaly, Melos, an island in the Aegean just south of the Cyclades, and Megara, a town on the isthmus of Corinth with a walled corridor, known as "the legs of Megara," linking it to its eastern port of Nisaia on the Saronic Gulf. Indeed, in contemporaneous negotiations the "Athenians insisted upon keeping Nisaia because the Thebans refused to give up Plataia: this was one of the unresolved issues."[10] The speed with which the negotiations are concluded, a speed prompted by the immediate needs of the participants, is also funny. Lysistrata invites all the company to a feast that the women prepare on the Acropolis, and when everyone goes offstage through the great Propylean gates, Aristophanes' sexual metaphor is complete.

Fourth Choral Song: 1189–1215

Action in the Fourth Choral Song

The Chorus sing a strophe and antistrophe that mimic in content their first strophe and antistrophe, this time offering and retracting rich robes and endless supplies of wheat.

Exodos: 1216–1321

Action in the Exodos[11]

As the scene begins, a group of people is assembled onstage in front of the Acropolis gate, obstructing egress. The festive meal inside has concluded, and the celebrants are gradually emerging. A tipsy Athenian, seeing how drunkenness promotes good fellowship, suggests that in the future all envoys should negotiate while drunk. When sober, no one, he says, listens to anyone else and everyone draws the wrong inferences. The Spartans, to the accompaniment of a flute, dance and sing of the unified command of Athenians and Spartans during the Persian Wars and praise Artemis. Another song, sung perhaps by the Athenians, calls on the gods to "witness the peace and the harmony which divine Aphrodite has made." The Spartans conclude the festivities by singing a hymn to Athene of "the House of Brass," the temple to Athene on the Spartan acropolis, thereby joining the resident deities of the two cities, just as the cities are now joined in peace. Husbands and wives are reunited, and the play ends.

Sources of Humor in the Exodos

The humor of the *exodos* is not bawdy but ritually celebrative: it represents the pleasure taken, not in double meanings and human foibles, but in restoration and community. The feast is a sign of peacetime, for earlier Kalonike had bemoaned her inability to serve Boeotian eels "at a little party" for the ladies. The slightly drunken good fellowship that obtains is reminiscent of the ladies' eagerness to drink the "sacrificial" wine at the conclusion of their oath-taking in the prologue. The little byplay at the gates, urging the crowd away so that the celebrants can leave the Acropolis, "works a comic reversal of the preceding action, where men had attempted to enter, not escape from, the Akropolis."[12] Thus, action has come full circle in what is said and seen onstage: the gates, literally and symbolically, have been opened and what follows is pure song. That the Spartan singers recall the cooperation between Athens and Sparta in the Persian Wars of almost a century earlier, the Athenian naval victory at Artemisium and the heroic stand and sacrifice of Leonidas, King of Sparta, at Thermopylae, again points backward as a model for the present. The play concludes, not in hilarity, but in lyricism. The world, as Whitman so beautifully says, has been "somehow rewrought."[13]

THEME IN THE *LYSISTRATA*

Since by 411 B.C. the possibility of a negotiated peace between Athens and Sparta was truly remote, it may be that what Aristophanes is advocating is expressed in Lysistrata's metaphor of wool-working: a cleansing of the corruption and factionalism in the city, a drawing together of Athens and its allies under equitable terms, and the establishment of internal peace to strengthen the city for whatever follows. Additional support for such an argument appears in the domesticity and forgiveness that mark the unification of the two Choruses. The Old Men and the Old Women, unlike the sex-starved husbands and wives, have been angry at each other, and clearly represent not people of different states, but Athenian men and Athenian women. Internal dissension and bellicosity are presented as injurious when the men, approaching the Acropolis to smoke out the women, find their own eyes smarting from the smoke, and when the gnats, who have made inroads into their eyes, are removed.

That visual polarities in the play temporarily merge, as is the case with spear and phallus when the Spartan Herald appears, or with the helmet that represents imperial Athens and that is briefly used as a token of pregnancy and domesticity, may, in comic form, suggest the need for transformations of mind and spirit.

NOTES

1. Cedric Whitman, *The Heroic Paradox: Essays on Homer, Sophocles and Aristophanes* (Ithaca, N.Y.: Cornell University Press, 1964), p. 211.

2. Whitman, p. 143.

3. Douglass Parker, "Introduction to *Lysistrata*," *Four Comedies by Aristophanes*, edited by William Arrowsmith (Ann Arbor: University of Michigan Press, 1969), pp. 1–3.

4. Hans-Joachim Newiger, "War and Peace in the Comedy of Aristophanes," translated by Catherine Radford, in *Aristophanes: Essays in Interpretation* Yale Classical Studies, 26 (Cambridge, Mass.: Cambridge University Press) 1980: 228–229. He comments about the significance of gnats in the eyes of the Old Men.

5. Benjamin Bickley Rogers, Aristophanes, Vol. III (London: William Heinemann Ltd., 1931), pp. 2–3.

6. Rogers, pp. 66–67.

7. Douglass Parker's ingenious translation.

8. Rogers, pp. 58–59.

9. Jeffrey Henderson, "Commentary" to *Aristophanes: Lysistrata* (Oxford: Clarendon Press, 1987), p. 204.

10. Henderson, p. 205.

11. Scholars have had to reconstruct portions of the *exodos*, and there is not a clear consensus about who the speakers are at the beginning of the scene.

12. Henderson, p. 208.

13. Whitman, pp. 132–159.

Selected Bibliography

BOOKS AND PERIODICALS

Arnott, Peter D. *Public and Performance in the Greek Theatre*. London, New York: Routledge, 1991.

Barlow, Shirley A. *The Imagery of Euripides*. London: Methuen & Co, Ltd, 1971.

Bloom, Harold, ed. *Greek Drama*. New York, Philadelphia: Chelsea House Publishers, 2004.

———, ed. *Modern Critical Interpretations: Sophocles' Oedipus Rex*. New York, Philadelphia: Chelsea House Publishers, 1988.

Burian, Peter, ed. *Directions in Euripidean Criticism*. Durham: Duke University Press, 1985.

Burkert, Walter. *Greek Religion*. trans. John Raffan. Oxford: Basil Blackwell Publisher; Cambridge, Mass.: Harvard University Press, 1985.

Burnett, Anne Pippin. *Revenge in Attic and Later Tragedy*. (Sather Classical Lectures, Vol. 62),Berkeley: University of California Press, 1998.

Dodds, E. R. *The Greeks and the Irrational*. Berkeley: University of California Press, 1951.

———. "On Misunderstanding the *Oedipus Rex*" (reprinted in *Modern Critical Interpretations*).

Dover, K. J. *Aristophanic Comedy*. Berkeley: University of California Press, 1972.

Easterling, P. E., ed. *The Cambridge Companion to Greek Tragedy*. Cambridge: Cambridge University Press, 1997.

Ferguson, John. *A Companion to Greek Tragedy*. Austin: University of Texas Press, 1973.

Gardiner, Cynthia P. *The Sophoclean Chorus: A Study of Character and Function*. Iowa City: University of Iowa Press, 1987.

Goheen, Robert F. *The Imagery of Sophocles' Antigone*. Princeton, N.J.: Princeton University Press, 1951.

Grube, G.M.A. *The Drama of Euripides*. London: Methuen & Co., Ltd., 1961.

Kitto, H.D.F. *Form and Meaning in Drama*. London: Methuen & Co., Ltd., 1956.

———. *Greek Tragedy*. Garden City, N.Y.: Doubleday & Co., 1954.

Knox, Bernard M.W. *The Heroic Temper: Studies in Sophoclean Tragedy*. Berkeley: University of California Press, 1983.

———. *Oedipus at Thebes*. New Haven, Conn.: Yale University Press, 1966.

Lattimore, Richmond. *The Poetry of Greek Tragedy*. New York: Harper & Row, Publishers, 1966.

———. *Story Patterns in Greek Tragedy*. Ann Arbor: University of Michigan Press, 1965.

Lebeck, Anne. *The Oresteia: A Study in Language and Structure*. Published by The Center for Hellenic Studies, distributed by Cambridge, Mass.: Harvard University Press, 1971.

Macleod, Colin. *Collected Essays*. Oxford: Clarendon Press, 1983.

Nardo, Don, ed. *Greek Drama*. San Diego: Greenhaven Press, 2000.

Nussbaum, Martha C. *The Fragility of Goodness*. Cambridge: Cambridge University Press, 1986.

Reinhardt, Karl. *Sophocles*, trans. Hazel Harvey and David Harvey. Oxford: Basil Blackwell Publishers, 1979.

Segal, Charles. *Sophocles' Tragic World: Divinity, Nature, Society*. Cambridge, Mass.: Harvard University Press, 1998.

Storey, Ian C., and Arlene Allan, *A Guide to Ancient Greek Drama*. Oxford: Blackwell Publishing, 2005.

Taplin, Oliver. *The Stagecraft of Aeschylus: The Dramatic Use of Exits and Entrances in Greek Tragedy*. Oxford: Clarendon Press, 1977.

———. *Greek Tragedy in Action*. London: Routledge, 2003.

Whitman, Cedric. *Aristophanes and the Comic Hero*. Cambridge, Mass.: Harvard University Press, 1964.

———. *The Heroic Paradox: Essays on Homer, Sophocles and Aristophanes*. Ithaca, N.Y.: Cornell University Press, 1964.

———. *Sophocles: A Study in Heroic Humanism*. Cambridge, Mass.: Harvard University Press, 1951.

Zeitlin, Froma I. "The Dynamics of Misogyny: Myth and Mythmaking in the *Oresteia*." Buffalo, N.Y.: *Arethusa* 2 (1978).

VIDEOS

The Gospel at Colonus, 1983 adaptation of the *Oedipus at Colonus*, as a gospel service. Morgan Freeman as Messenger/Preacher, Clarence Fountain and the Five Blind Boys of Alabama as Oedipus. Taped in 1983 by WNET/Thirteen.

Medea, 1959 television production. Judith Anderson as Medea. Ivy Video. DVD. Also available for viewing at the Museum of TV and Radio in New York City.

Medea, 1983 Kennedy Center stage production. Zoe Caldwell as Medea, Judith Anderson as the Nurse. VHS

Oedipus the King, 1968 film. Christopher Plummer as Oedipus. Universal Studios. VHS.

Oedipus Rex, an oratorio by Igor Stravinsky, with Latin libretto. Jessye Norman as Iocaste, Bryn Terfel as Creon, musical direction by Seiji Ozawa, staging by Julie Taymor. Cami Video and NHK.

Oedipus Rex, 1957 stage adaptation by William Butler Yeats. Directed by Sir Tyrone Guthrie, and performed in masks. Corinth Films. DVD.

Index